THE OTTOMAN SCRAMBLE FOR AFRICA

THE OTTOMAN SCRAMBLE FOR AFRICA

Empire and Diplomacy in the Sahara and the Hijaz

MOSTAFA MINAWI

STANFORD UNIVERSITY PRESS
STANFORD, CALIFORNIA

Stanford University Press
Stanford, California

© 2016 by the Board of Trustees of the Leland Stanford Junior University.
All rights reserved.

Printed in the United States of America on acid-free, archival-quality paper

Library of Congress Cataloging-in-Publication Data

Names: Minawi, Mostafa, 1974– author.
Title: The Ottoman scramble for Africa : empire and diplomacy in the Sahara and the Hijaz / Mostafa Minawi.
Description: Stanford, California : Stanford University Press, 2016. | Includes bibliographical references and index.
Identifiers: LCCN 2016004871 (print) | LCCN 2016013794 (ebook) | ISBN 9780804795142 (cloth : alk. paper) | ISBN 9780804799270 (pbk. : alk. paper) | ISBN 9780804799294 (electronic)
Subjects: LCSH: Turkey—Foreign relations—1878–1909. | Turkey—Foreign relations—Europe. | Europe—Foreign relations—Turkey. | Imperialism—History—19th century. | Africa—Colonization—History—19th century. | Hejaz (Saudi Arabia)—Colonization—History—19th century. | Berlin West Africa Conference (1884–1885 : Berlin, Germany)
Classification: LCC DR571 .M56 2016 (print) | LCC DR571 (ebook) | DDC 327.56009/034—dc23
LC record available at http://lccn.loc.gov/2016004871

Typeset by Newgen in 10/14 Minion

To the refugee,
the migrant,
and the stateless.

CONTENTS

FIGURES

PREFACE

This project began as an investigation into the life and work of an itinerant Ottoman officer from Damascus, Sadik al-Mouayad Azmzade (Figure 1),[1] who left behind a handful of travelogues and book manuscripts about topics as varied as photography, European literature, and Islamic history, and whose life spanned a number of turbulent periods in the history of the Ottoman Empire. Azmzade was a member of one of the most influential families in Syria that maintained its dominance well into the 1960s, having gained prominence in the late seventeenth century as the Istanbul's representatives in Damascus. The Azmzades—or al-ʿAzms as they are better known today—grew in size, power, and wealth until their influence spilled over into other cities in the Levant.

A branch of the family by the name of al-Muʾayyad al-ʿAzm (al-Mouayad/ el-Müeyyed Azmzade) appeared at the end of the eighteenth century. They survived the political crisis following the 1860 massacre of Christians in Damascus, which led to a large, albeit temporary, upheaval in the local power structure.[2] As one of the ruling families in Damascus, the Azmzades were held particularly responsible for failing to prevent the massacre and were harshly punished. The six most prominent family members were sentenced to ten-year terms in the Famagusta (Mağusa) Fortress in Cyprus, where the two eldest died. Despite the expulsion of the patriarchs and the Azmzades' apparent fall from grace, however, within a decade they had bounced back and reestablished their ties with Istanbul.

Managing to infiltrate the increasingly centralized administrative system as well as the ballooning bureaucracy and military under the rule of Sultan Abdülhamid II (r. 1876–1909), the Azmzades soon spread their influence beyond the province of Syria, particularly in the provinces of Aleppo and Beirut and the imperial capital. The generations coming after the turbulent 1860s managed to continually adapt to the region's quickly changing political and social structures, which was, in part, why they were able to hold on to some of the

قائمقام صادق بك مؤید

FIGURE 1. Sadik al-Mouayad Azmzade (Nadir Eserler Library, Istanbul University, 91052/8).

highest municipal and provincial positions in Syria, even after the 1908 con-
stitutional revolution and continuing through the rule of the Hashemite king
Faisal (1918–1920), the French Mandate (1920–1946), and the early years of Syrian independence.[3]

Sadik Pasha, along with several brothers and cousins, was a member of the
Hamidian-era[4] generation of Azmzades who further spread the family's influence. His career took off in Istanbul under the autocratic rule of Sultan Abdülhamid II, who appointed him to a number of highly sensitive diplomatic posts
from the Hijaz to Addis Ababa. He survived the 1908–1909 Young Turk purge
of officials deemed too close to the deposed sultan, only to pass away in 1911
during a term as governor (*kaymakam*) of Jeddah.[5]

Azmzade typified a new generation of Ottoman elites who defied the singular ethnic, linguistic, and regional categories of national identitarian politics
of the time. Fluent in both Arabic and Turkish and conversant in French and
German, he wrote extensively in Ottoman-Turkish (*Osmanlıca*) and traveled
throughout the empire, Europe, and Africa, living in Damascus, Beirut, Berlin,
Istanbul, Sofia, and Jeddah. Establishing his household in the Teşvikiye neigh-
borhood of Istanbul, he quickly rose through the ranks of the Ottoman military
and eventually occupied the critical post of Ottoman special commissioner to
Bulgaria from 1904 to 1907, which was a very delicate time in the life of the
newly established principality. As a man who strongly identified with the ideals
of Ottomanism under the rule of Abdülhamid II, this proud Ottoman officer
witnessed and reflected on the rapid demise of the imperial world he embodied
during the span of his lifetime.

Azmzade's surviving children, brothers, and cousins would have to choose
where they belonged when the empire expired. It was perhaps a blessing that he
did not live long enough to see his family, the proud Azmzades, with historical
roots in both western Anatolia and the Levant, scattered among the Republic
of Turkey, the Syrian Arab Republic, and the Lebanese Republic and eventually
forced to choose between an "Arab"- and a "Turk"-sounding family name. With
the end of the empire came the crashing halt of the cosmopolitan life of Istanbul's Ottoman elites, whose life stories now had to be reimagined along newly
established national boundaries and whose "authentic" national identities had
to be vigorously and repeatedly defended.

As fascinating as Azmzade and his family were, I decided that a biography would have to wait because of what I stumbled on after several months in
the Başbakanlık Osmanlı Arşivi (Ottoman Archives). As I followed Azmzade's

career and travels across the world—a near impossible task given that no family names were used in official documents and that a multitude of Ottoman officials were named "Sadık"—I started to piece together the unknown story of late nineteenth-century Ottoman imperial expansionism in which Azmzade and his generation of imperial loyalists were deeply invested.

To bring into focus a global project of Ottoman imperial self-reinvention, I triangulated the rank and/or honorary title of a document's author, his locations, and the document date, and devised a simple computer program to cross-reference the thousands of pieces of paper I had collected from a number of archives. Academic curiosity, which had started with an Ottoman officer's life, was leading me to a Pandora's box of late Ottoman competitive interimperial strategies that used diplomacy, local alliances, and international law to claim the empire's "right" to colonies (*müstemlekat*) in Africa. Along the way, I was forced to question all of my assumptions about Hamidian-era Ottoman imperialism on the empire's southern frontiers. When I started investigating the life of Azmzade more than a decade ago, I never imagined that this book would become a study of Ottoman participation in the so-called scramble for Africa and its impact on Istanbul's practices of imperialism along the empire's southern frontiers-cum-borderlands in Africa and Arabia.

Taking the reader from Istanbul to Berlin, the eastern Sahara, the Lake Chad basin, the Hijaz, and back to Istanbul over a period of two decades, this book sheds light on the Ottoman Empire's experiment in a *new* kind of competitive imperialism and its transcontinental implications for Istanbul's strategy along the empire's vulnerable African and Arabian frontiers. Privileging Ottoman archival sources, it examines the empire's participation in the Conference of Berlin (1884–1885) and its subsequent engagement in aggressive interimperial competition for territorial expansion as an attempt at self-reinvention of this once powerful global empire. The book stretches the parameters of agency in late nineteenth-century colonial expansion in Africa to include the Ottoman Empire, challenging the perception of the European powers as the sole agents of change on the global stage and the only states concerned with finding a solution to the so-called Eastern Question.[6]

ACKNOWLEDGMENTS

I want to express my deepest gratitude to my friends, colleagues, and mentors, inside and outside of academia, who have fed me; housed me; discussed history, politics, and philosophy with me; listened to me while I shared my research, doubts, and hopes; and provided me with the emotional support and mental stimulation necessary to survive the often solitary roller-coaster ride of research and writing. In particular, I would like to acknowledge my dear friend Spence Halperin, who has been my unfailing compass, my reality checker, and my reminder of what truly mattered throughout the ups and downs of the past decade. My parents Firyal Shourafa and Adel Minawi and my sisters Rima and Nahed Minawi continue to be an infinite well of love, support, and encouragement.

I am indebted to the disciplinary training, guidance, and support of many mentors and advisors including Khaled Fahmy, Leslie Peirce, Zachary Lockman, Christine Philliou, and Frederick Cooper. I am also forever grateful to Virginia Aksan for planting a seed of curiosity about the history of the Ottoman Empire in a lost civil engineering and management undergraduate student twenty years ago. I owe a debt of gratitude to Jens Hanssen for introducing me to the writing of Sadik Pasha, for his support and mentorship throughout the years, and for exploding the world of a business consultant thirteen years ago with his contagious passion for the humanities.

The Social Science and Humanities Research Council of Canada, the Society for the Humanities at Cornell University, the Council for European Studies, Koç University, and New York University have all been generous supporters of this research. I would like to express my appreciation to the Schoff Fund at the University Seminars at Columbia University for their help in publication. Ideas presented here have benefited from discussions in the University Seminar on Ottoman and Turkish Studies. I would like to send a special thank you to Georges Khalil, the academic coordinator of EUME (Europe in the Middle East, The Middle East in

Europe) at the Wissenschaftskolleg zu Berlin, and Ulrike Freitag, the director of the Zentrum Moderner Orient in Berlin, for providing me with the ideal intellectual environment for reflecting on my research and taking my first steps toward writing this book during an otherwise very difficult period in my life.

For generously facilitating my research with their knowledge and expertise, I thank the staff of Istanbul University's Nadir Eserler Kütüphanesi, İslam Arıştermaları Merkezi, Beyazıt Kütüphanesi, Atatürk Kütüphanesi, and Süleymaniye Kütüphanesi in Istanbul; the Archives and Special Collections Department at the American University of Beirut and the German Oriental Institute in Beirut; the Syrian National Library, the al-Zahiriyya Library, the Syrian National Archives, and the Institut Français du Proche-Orient in Damascus; the Bulgarian Historical Archives in Sofia; the National Archives and the British Library in London. I also thank my friend Margarita Debrova of the Institute of Balkan Studies, and I am grateful to the multinational branches of the Azmzade/al-ʿAzm family for their openness in sharing their family history and records. Last but not least, I would like to extend a special thank you to the tireless staff of the Başbakanlık Osmanlı Arşivi for their help, patience, and invaluable expertise.

I am truly lucky to be part of the rich intellectual environment of Cornell University and for having the encouragement of my colleagues in the Department of History and the unwavering support of its chair, Barry Strauss. I am especially grateful to my colleague Durba Ghosh for being such an inspiring scholar and a truly generous and supportive mentor. Durba, along with my colleagues Robert Travers, Eric Tagliacozzo, and Ernesto Bassi, read drafts of research proposals, articles, and chapters from this book and provided me with invaluable feedback and advice. I am also grateful for the wisdom and support of Isabell Hull, Derek Chang, Jullily Kohler-Hausmann, Judi Byfield, and Fred Logevall throughout the past three years.

I have no doubt that this book is infinitely better because of the rich feedback that I received from various anonymous reviewers as well as the time and effort generously given by Kent Schull, Thomas Kühn, and Holly Case, who read and commented on early drafts. Nevertheless, I can say with complete confidence that any shortcomings are entirely of my own doing.

Finally I would like to express my thanks to Kate Wahl, the publishing director and editor-in-chief at Stanford University Press, for her encouragement, invaluable advice, and patience as I progressed through the many writing and revision phases of this book's creation.

NOTE ON TRANSLATION AND TRANSLITERATION

The Ottoman Empire was multilingual, and many of its officials, bureaucrats, and diplomats working on both the imperial and the provincial levels spoke several languages. For official correspondence, Ottoman-Turkish was the rule, although there were many exceptions. In my transliteration choices, I have tried to reflect as accurately as possible the multilingual nature of everyday life and the multitude of ethnocultural realities of nineteenth-century Ottoman society in both the capital and the provinces.

I have also tried to make Ottoman-Turkish and Arabic words as accessible as possible for non-Turkish and non-Arabic readers without losing the accuracy of pronunciation or the nuances of the rich vocabulary of these languages. For this reason, where Turkish or Arabic words have been adopted in English, I used the English equivalent—for example, *pasha*, not *paşa*; *amir*, not *amīr* or *emir*. Also, I found literal translation of Ottoman-Turkish sentences into English prose difficult because the syntax and logic of the two languages are very different. Thus, I took certain liberties in translation if they did not change the overall meaning of the text and if they made it easier for an English reader to follow.

For the transliteration of Ottoman-Turkish or Arabic text, I followed the *International Journal of Middle East Studies* transliteration method. Therefore, Ottoman-Turkish is rendered in modern Turkish with minor exceptions to reduce the problematic distortion of Ottoman-era pronunciation—for example, Mehmed Ali Pasha, not Mehmet Ali Pasha or Muhammad ʿAli Basha.

For well-known place-names, I used English and the transliteration from Turkish or Arabic depending on the common language of each place: Istanbul, not İstanbul; Jeddah, not Cidde; but Yanbuʿ; not Yanbu.

Proper names and titles are much more complicated than place-names. In the multilingual Ottoman Empire, ethnicity or place of birth did not necessarily determine the language spoken by the individual or the people in this immediate circles. Thus, if no records reflected how the individual wrote his or her name in the Latin alphabet, I relied on context, locality, and social milieu, not "ethnic" origin, arriving at the local *sheikh al-mashāyikh* in Mecca and the imperial *şeyhülislam* in Istanbul. Similarly, it is İzzet Pasha of the imperial government, not ʿIzzet Pasha of Damascus; but ʿAwn al-Rafiq Pasha of Mecca, not Awn el-Refik Pasha of the imperial government. If certain transliterations look unusual, I advise the reader to consider the context in which they are being used. Finally, all translations from Arabic, Turkish, Ottoman-Turkish, and French are mine.

What follows is a pronunciation guide to certain Turkish letters that are not found in the English alphabet or are pronounced differently in Turkish than they are in English. The rest of the alphabet reflects straightforward phonetic pronunciation as in English.

\a\ as in **father**

\e\ as in **gay**

\ı\ as in **oven**

\i\ as in **bee**

\o\ as in **bowtie**

\ö\ as in German sch**ö**n

\u\ as in **blue**

\ü\ as in German **ü**ber

\c\ as in **j**acket

\ç\ as in **ch**icory

\g\ as in **g**lobal

\ğ\ very soft *g* mostly extending the vowel it follows

\j\ as in mea**s**ure

\ş\ as in **sh**y

THE OTTOMAN SCRAMBLE
FOR AFRICA

INTRODUCTION

Old Empire, New Empire

On Tuesday evening, the 19th of September of the Julian year 1311, I received orders to leave the Abode of Felicity [Istanbul] in two to three days, and to travel to southern Benghazi and from there to take an approximately one month long journey to Kufra, which is in the middle of the Sahara. I spent the whole night thinking of all that had to be done in order to prepare for such a long trip. No sleep ever entered my eyes.

Sadik al-Mouayad Azmzade, Aide-de-Camp to His Imperial Majesty, Istanbul, October 1, 1895

IN THE SUMMER OF 1876, the newspaper cafés (*kıraathaneler*) of Üsküdar and the taverns of Beyoğlu must have been abuzz with rumors of impending disaster for the empire. Christian Bosnian Serbs and Bulgarians were in revolt; representatives of the European powers were in Istanbul to discuss the fate of Greek Orthodox Ottoman subjects; and the first Ottoman constitution and parliament were declared amid rumors of the empire's bankruptcy and a sultan struggling with alcoholism.[1] It was in the middle of all of this chaos that Abdülhamid II (Abdülhamid-i Sani) ascended the throne to inherit the problems of an empire in crisis. Soon after his ascension, the Russian Empire, determined to take advantage of this chaotic period, attacked the empire from the east and the west. In 1878, following a number of humiliating defeats to the Russian Empire and a series of negotiations sponsored by several European powers, the Ottoman Empire agreed to the terms of the Treaty of Berlin.

The war with Russia was disastrous to Ottoman pride and served as indisputable evidence of a poorly trained and ill-equipped military. Following defeat, Istanbul was forced to concede vast Ottoman territories in the Balkans and eastern Anatolia to the Russians, the Austro-Hungarian Empire, and other Balkan states, and hand over the rule of Cyprus to the British.[2] In the same year, Sultan Abdülhamid II prorogued the parliament and suspended the constitution as emergency measures supposedly taken to put the empire on the road to recovery.[3]

The events of 1876–1878 made the Ottoman Empire's admission to the Concert of Europe seem a purely symbolic "gesture," effectively null and void.[4] That and the signing of the Paris Peace Treaty in 1856 should have protected it from late nineteenth-century European competition for territorial expansion, but a mere two decades after the European powers pledged to protect its territorial integrity, the empire found itself caught in the crossfire of European competitive geopolitics—"utterly demoralized" and in "financial ruin."[5] A quick rundown of its key territorial losses during the long nineteenth century offers a clear image of this once powerful global empire under unrelenting attack.

Years of Russian-supported rebellions in the Danubian principalities and the subsequent Greek Revolt (1820–1829), and then the establishment of the Kingdom of Greece under British tutelage threw the sultan into a state of panic and led to a set of reactionary measures that struck at the very fabric of Ottoman society by decimating the Greek Orthodox community of Istanbul.[6] Soon after, in 1830, the French invaded and annexed the Ottoman province of Algeria.[7] The 1880s and 1890s witnessed further territorial losses in the Mediterranean and the Persian Gulf through direct foreign occupation or French- or British-brokered secessions of Ottoman provinces.[8]

These events, listed one after the other in a narrative that collapses time and reduces political viability to the exercise of territorial sovereignty, might make it seem logical that historians assume that the Ottoman Empire played no appreciable role in the interimperial competitions of the late nineteenth century and often dismiss its representatives as nothing more than "minor actors"[9] on the diplomatic stage. In fact, some historians go so far as to question whether an empire that seemed defenseless against Russian expansionist whims and dependent on the Great Powers for its very survival can even be studied as "an empire" alongside the other European empires. To justify the Ottoman Empire's exclusion from the study of imperialism, some weigh its position as an "object" against its position as an "agent" of the politics of international relations.[10] Others assess European interference in Ottoman internal affairs to determine whether Istanbul was independent enough not to be counted as an "informal" colony. The verdicts range from an outright exclusion of the empire from the study of imperialism[11] to a qualified exclusion that treats it as an exceptional case, using newly minted categories such as "borderline imperial."[12] The result, with a few exceptions, is that, explicitly or implicitly, the Ottoman

Empire has been left out of the study of the interimperial competition of the late nineteenth century, and by extension its role has been underestimated—as a subject of history—in the events leading up to the Great War that drastically altered the global world order.

At the heart of the study of Ottoman participation in late nineteenth-century interimperial competition are fundamental theoretical questions that I grappled with. Considering generally accepted notions about the late empire's weakness, can scholars of imperialism in the nineteenth century safely discount it in investigations of "new imperialism" and the role it played in the history of the twentieth century? What do we lose by ignoring the Ottomans as imperial competitors in what Eric Hobsbawm famously calls the "Age of Empire?"[13] Indeed, can we include British, French, and Ottoman imperialism in the late nineteenth century in the same category of inquiry?

Labels such as "nonimperial," "borderline imperial," "informal colonialism," and the like are informative in certain respects. However, I contend that they have had a chilling effect on the range of historical inquiry possible through an automatic exclusion of the Ottoman Empire from the study of late nineteenth-century interimperial competition and its long-term consequences. To avoid the trap of binary questions that lead to mutually exclusive categorical distinctions—Was it or was it not an empire? Was it an object or a subject of imperialism? Did it belong to an old and dying form of imperialism, or can we talk of it as we do "new empires?"—I follow an open-ended inquiry that assumes imperialism to be essentially adaptive, a process, not a category. Thus, I believe that the productive question is not whether but how the Ottoman Empire adapted to the new demands of imperialism in the late nineteenth century. This book demonstrates some of the important dimensions of world history that we miss when we assume that the Ottoman Empire can be dismissed or ignored in the study of imperialism in the Age of Empire.

The Ottoman Scramble for Africa challenges the narrative of an exclusively defensive and inward-looking empire following the Russo-Ottoman War of 1877–1878 and the loss of much of the Balkan provinces. Contrary to the commonly accepted understanding of the post-1878 Ottoman Empire, it argues that the Ottoman government's efforts after the Congress of Berlin were not simply survival strategies requiring a necessary withdrawal from the world of late nineteenth-century competitive imperialism.[14] In fact, the 1880s and 1890s witnessed a reinvigorated Istanbul that followed competitive strategies that cannot simply be attributed to an ideological aversion to the West, the paranoia of a besieged sultan, or the Hamidian government's rhetoric of pan-Islamism coming from the mythologized seat of power in Istanbul, the Palace of the Stars (Yıldız Sarayı). The palace of Sultan Abdülhamid II was much more than his residence. In many ways, it resembled the White House in Washington, a place where much of the state's business was discussed under the watchful eye of its head.[15]

If we focus on Yıldız Palace–driven negotiations, disputes, and rivalries with its European counterparts on the one hand and its strategic partnership with the leaders of the Sanusi Order and its followers in the eastern Sahara on the other, the outlines of a multileveled expansionist Ottoman strategy become clear. Following the methods of the so-called new imperialism, the empire reinvented itself as one clamoring for its "rightful" colonial possessions beyond its southern frontiers in the Libyan Desert. This Ottoman strategy in Africa between 1885 and 1900 had a direct impact on Istanbul's policies along its southern frontiers-cum-borderlands in the Sahara and the Hijaz.

In spatial and temporal terms, this book focuses on the eastern Sahara, the Lake Chad basin, and western Arabia, roughly between 1880 and 1902. In present-day geography terms, the Lake Chad basin includes portions of Nigeria, Niger, Chad, Cameroon, Sudan, and Libya, while western Arabia corresponds roughly to the Saudi Arabian Red Sea coast. Sadik Pasha al-Mouayad Azmzade, who described his trepidation about what was to be his second journey deep into the Sahara, would play a leading role in negotiations with locals in both the Sahara and the Hijaz, between 1886 and 1902.

Can an Old Empire Learn New Tricks?

New imperialism assumed that territorial expansion was the only way to guarantee global power in what increasingly resembled a zero-sum game played by Europeans on African lands in the last twenty years of the nineteenth century.[16] What brought on the shift to new imperialism? Historians have mostly focused on the British and French models for answers.

Some of the most common explanations for the acceleration of colonial competition are economic: the turn to new imperialism is thought to have come about because of the failure of so-called gentlemanly colonialism, the exploitation of local resources through a network of negotiated partnerships with local intermediaries. By the 1870s, failure to transfer resources and solidify local institutions as means of entrenching long-term colonial interests in Africa and Asia had proven detrimental to the colonial project.[17] By 1880, having local intermediaries do the "dirty work" of the colonial masters had lost its purchase and a new, expensive, and dangerous method of protecting the metropole's commercial interests had to be implemented. This meant direct or near direct occupation of the territories.[18] The colonization project could no longer be justified economically; it needed a "moral" argument to bolster calls for increasingly dangerous and expensive endeavors.[19] The new focus on a moral justification for colonialism becomes more explicit in the French case.

Some historians have investigated the motivations behind this late nineteenth-century brand of expansionist imperialism by probing the logic of French colonialists. Their main refrain was that the Maghreb—namely, Morocco, Algeria, and Tunisia—formed the core of the North African French Empire while sub-Saharan Africa was assigned the role of the empire's "hinterland." Ideological and material motivations seemed to work hand in hand as the mission to "civilize" the colonial subject, the colonies' economic viability, and the economic prosperity of the metropole became one and the same.[20] The involvement of the Ottoman Empire is especially relevant for understanding French colonial ambitions in Africa. The French dream of connecting Senegal and western Sudan with French possessions in North Africa came up against the Ottoman expansionist dream, whose epicenter was the Lake Chad basin.[21]

As late as 1880, about 80 percent of the African continent remained free of foreign rule.[22] However, new imperialism resulted in accelerated colonial expansion in the 1890s to such an extent that by World War I only Liberia and Ethiopia remained free of direct colonial control.[23] In 1883, with French expansion in the northwest and the British invasion of Alexandria in the northeast, the race to partition Africa among the European powers, commonly referred to as the "scramble for Africa," shifted into high gear.[24] Many historians believe that the terms of this scramble were set by British-French rivalry, which began in 1882, reached its apex with the Fashoda Crisis in 1899, and ended with the Entente Cordial of 1904.[25] But some judge this explanation too simplistic, pointing to the fact that French colonization of western Africa began in the late 1870s and that the British occupation of Egypt did not pose a threat to French interests, which were secured in West Africa, Algeria, and Tunisia. These historians point instead to Paris's obsession with accessing the fabled economic wealth of sub-Saharan Sudan, which led them to push further east, triggering a massive French investment in the colonization of Africa in the early 1880s.[26]

Despite the efforts of scholars to distill the shift to new imperialism down to a single explanation, this has proven impossible. However, historians and theoreticians of imperialism—from Lenin to Hobsbawm—do for the most part agree that this period of accelerated colonial expansion was indeed the apex of global imperial competition.[27] What is much more difficult to agree on though is the set of complex human motivations—collective and individual—that have fueled this race for territorial expansion. Perhaps only by acknowledging the near impossibility of understanding the "complexities of human motivation," can we begin to build a more comprehensive picture of the storied motivations behind colonialism in Africa at the end of the nineteenth century.[28]

The Ottoman Empire's reasons for colonial expansion were no less complex than those of the British and the French. A number of factors, economic, political, and ideological, do not add up to a coherent explanation for its participation in the scramble for Africa in terms of clearly defined long-term goals of Sultan Abdülhamid II, his Yıldız Palace advisors, and the various stakeholders in the Mabeyn[29] and the Sublime Porte. Whether it was imagined economic gains, geopolitical advantages, or the empire's "moral duty" to lead fellow Muslims in Saharan and sub-Saharan Africa who had yet to "benefit" from "modern progress" toward a better future, there was no shortage of opinions in newspapers and government correspondence.

With the advantage of hindsight, I believe I can offer an interpretive reading of events to conclude that what was not explicit at the time was perhaps more illuminating of Ottoman motivations than what was explicit; for the truth of the matter is that the last two decades of the nineteenth century afforded the empire a unique incentive in its position as straddling the quickly ossifying divide between rulers and ruled in the world. It was a time when an empire had to participate in the new system of imperialism or risk becoming a "fair target" of European colonialism. The period immediately after the Conference of Berlin offered a short window of opportunity for the empire to liberate itself from the defensive position it had found itself in after the Russo-Ottoman War of 1877–1878.

Domestic Reforms, Global Ambitions

Struggling with financial deficits[30] as well as an influx of refugees from lost territories in the Balkans, North Africa, and the Caucasus[31] and a restive Muslim population dissatisfied with the concessions the Ottoman state had made to the European powers, the Ottoman imperial government undertook a broad array of domestic reforms. In the mid-1970s, after decades of portrayals of Sultan Abdülhamid II's rule as rolling back Tanzimat-era reforms,[32] historians began to take seriously the extensive social, bureaucratic, agricultural, and urban reform programs instituted during this period,[33] finally revealing a complex government apparatus whose flexible techniques of governing ensured the survival of the empire in the latter part of the long nineteenth century. Since then, many scholars of the Ottoman Empire have continued to fill in this more nuanced picture[34] with evidence that the Hamidian regime worked hard to promote a common signifier of "Ottoman-ness" among the various officially recognized "nations" of the empire.[35] Starting in the 1880s, the palace mobilized the rhetoric of a common Ottoman identity as a way to move the Ottoman population from a "passive" and unquestioning loyalty to the sultan to an "active" engagement in a new, carefully orchestrated domestic Ottomanism model.[36] Toward the end of his life, the sultan spelled out the difficulty of his task: "If there were ever a region in the world that never resembled another, it was our poor country. How could I have united the Armenian with the Kurd, the Turk with the Greek, the Bulgarian with the Arab?"[37]

Although the Hamidian-era domestic efforts in the 1880s and 1890s have been well studied, the Hamidian government's foreign policies after 1878 and their impact on the strategies followed on the Ottoman Empire's frontiers have received very little attention. Only a small amount of comprehensive scholarship in European languages has explored the Ottoman perspective, even on issues as necessarily entwined with the fate of the empire as the Eastern Question—what to do about the Ottoman Empire without upsetting the European empires' delicate balance of power.[38]

Some historians whose focus is on the global South have pointedly criticized the Eurocentrism in theories of empire in both early modern and modern periods.[39] This book gives Ottoman imperial history a place in a new kind of global history, one that attempts to move beyond the limitations and assumptions of area studies to explore global trends in imperialism and "webs of inspiration and influence which shaped the historical experience of both colonizer and colonized"[40] across empires. Despite recognition of the need to consider the colonization schemes of non-Western empires, the Ottoman Empire barely receives a passing mention. Scholarship outside of Ottoman studies continues to subscribe to the belief that the empire in the late nineteenth century was at best a defensive one, and indeed, the "Sick Man of Europe."[41] In diplomatic histories of the period between the Congress of Berlin and World War I, little is ever said of the role Istanbul played except to highlight the sultan's impotent response to the blatant European disregard of the empire's territorial integrity[42] or to show that the empire was a tool of European imperial rivalry.[43] The Ottoman Empire is mostly relegated to the position of silent observer, whose territories were merely bargaining chips in negotiations between the Great Powers.[44]

The reality is that Ottoman diplomats were back in Berlin in 1884, not to discuss the division of Ottoman territory or to hand over the fate of part of its population to a European power. They were there to represent the empire as one of the imperial powers deciding on the rules governing the division of Africa. Only five years after the Conference of Berlin and the loss of much of the Balkan provinces, the empire was back in the game of interimperial diplomacy. Its ambassadors, foreign ministers, grand viziers, and even the sultan himself made its position clear on the international stage as they fought for what they believed was their "sphere of influence" in Africa.

Sources play a part here, for even though the Ottoman Archives have been used as a source for over seven decades,[45] research on the history of the Ottoman frontiers in Africa has mostly relied on Italian, English, French, and Arabic records, with the notable exception of the work of Abdurrahman Çaycı and Ahmet Kavas.[46] This book also helps to reverse this trend by relying mostly on Ottoman archival sources together with British archival sources and Arabic and Ottoman-Turkish contemporary newspapers, journals, travelogues, and other publications. The Ottoman Archives bring a new perspective to the logic of Ottoman imperial competitive policies along the empire's southern frontiers.

The Ottomans at the Conference of Berlin, 1884–1885

In November 1884, German chancellor Otto von Bismarck (d. 1898) sponsored the first major European conference to officially make the rules that would govern imperialism in Africa. The Conference of Berlin, also known as the Congo Conference, has often been mistakenly understood as having been called for the purpose of carving up Africa into European colonies. In fact, its purpose was to facilitate conflict-free imperialism in an increasingly crowded market. For the most part, the issue was not territorial division but guaranteeing the "right" of European colonialists to unhindered commercial access to trade routes in light of increasingly competitive imperial activity in the 1880s.[47]

Representatives of fifteen republics, empires, duchies, and kingdoms participated in the conference. Among them were the powers that would later play a significant role in the fate of Ottoman Libya and the eastern Sahara: France, Great Britain, and Italy. Germany and Russia would have an indirect (yet significant) impact on the ultimate outcome for the region and the Ottoman

Empire's position in Africa in general. After several months of discussion and negotiation, all attendees, except for the United States, signed the General Act of Berlin, which not only conferred on European powers the right to African possessions that they had already taken effective hold of before 1885, but also set out rules for claiming additional tracts of land that were not yet under recognized imperial influence.[48]

The Ottoman Empire's agreement to the terms of the act is significant. First, on the one hand with the signing of the act, its right to the Mediterranean coast of Tripolitania and Cyrenaica was acknowledged by other participants in the conference, but, on the other hand, by agreeing to the new rules, it recognized, by default, the right of France to the Muslim-majority areas that were previously Ottoman provinces—namely, Algeria and Tunisia. Second, by signing the agreement, Istanbul essentially agreed to redefine its relationship to an integral part of its empire in order to affirm parity with the European powers' claims to possessions in Africa. In other words, the price for a bid to reenter the ranks of expansionist empires was a rebranding of the special relationship between Istanbul and Ottoman Libya. This meant an end to the empire's historic and religious claims to the Muslim-majority African provinces, albeit exclusively on the level of international diplomacy, something that it would later come to regret. Istanbul used the Act of Berlin as a tool to assert itself as also legally entitled to colonies in Africa well beyond Ottoman Libya.

Instrumentalizing international law was a particularly daring move for the empire, which was in the unique position of being both a member of the Concert of Europe and the object of European imperial designs. The Ottomans were well aware of the extent to which the Act of Berlin was a tool used to justify European colonialism, which meant that the empire's participation might have opened the door to further vulnerability to European imperialism.[49] In addition, the act was meant to apply to what Europeans defined as "civilized" nations only; "uncivilized" nations were kept outside of the rubric of international law. Read backward, this meant that participating in the crafting of agreements assumed a certain level of relative civility.[50]

The terms "civilized" and "uncivilized" may seem like linguistic flourishes, but in nineteenth-century terms they were influential in determining the applicability of international law to different countries. In fact, European jurists used three categories to classify nations: "civilized humanity" (read Europe), "savage humanity" (uncivilized nations), and the semicivilized, or those that fit somewhere in between. In the words of the influential jurist James Lorimer, these last represented "barbarous humanity." The Ottoman Empire, because it seemed to straddle the line between civilized and uncivilized according to these definitions, was often slotted as "semicivilized." For it not to be considered fully civilized meant not only that international law would not apply but that its very right to guaranteed sovereignty over its territories could be questioned.[51] With that in mind, we must understand that the Ottoman Empire was not simply fighting for extra territory; it was fighting to maintain legal standing in the so-called family of nations. If it could use international law to its benefit, then, by default, the empire would be considered a privileged "civilized" nation in an emerging world order split between the "subjects" of history (Europe) and the "Other."[52] Even though the line between civilized and uncivilized had been drawn to suit the aspirations of European colonialists, Istanbul found a crack in the hardening veneer of European assertions of superiority that allowed it to claim a place at the negotiation table. It had little choice but to be a party to this emerging world order because the alternative was its relegation to the ranks of the uncivilized and its subjects' relegation to the category of the invisible native.[53] The Ottoman Empire took advantage of its inclusion in international agreements on "legal" forms of colonialism to make claims of its own as a "civilized" nation, in a sense trying to beat the European powers at their own game.[54]

Neither the Ottoman Empire nor its European counterparts were unaware of the power differential that separated the various signatories. This differential was well illustrated in both the European and the American press, in which cartoons portrayed the Ottoman representatives as small, literally standing in the shadows, fading into the background of the negotiation table (Figure 2). Nevertheless, because the international agreements were binding, in theory at least, Istanbul made the only choice it could: to ignore the extent of their practical applicability. This was a strategic choice that gave the empire a fighting chance at gaining colonial possessions of its own according to the 1885 General Act of Berlin. Such hopes might have been foolhardy, but they were based on what were supposed to be binding protocols. Even though the representatives of the various states and the jurists who interpreted the agreements disagreed on a number of issues regarding the applicability of the laws and their relationship to local and customary laws, one thing was never in question: the agreements bound the signatories to act on an assumed principle of "good faith."[55] Istanbul took this principle seriously, choosing to act and negotiate with the European powers in good faith.

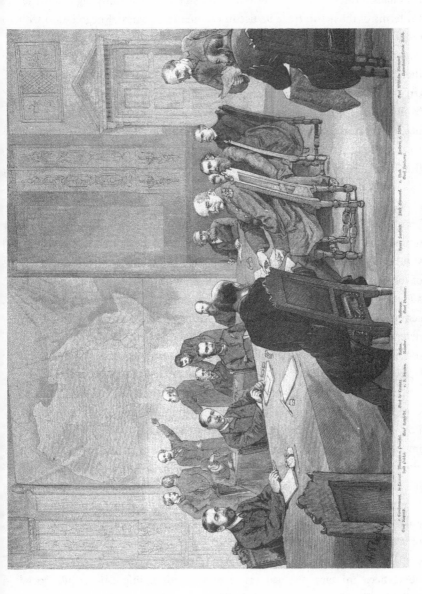

FIGURE 2. Conference of Berlin, 1884 (*Allgemeine Illustrierte Zeitung*, S.308, Am 28).

The General Act of Berlin was a watershed agreement, launching an accelerated partitioning of Africa and the formulation of a legal framework for colonialism under the rubric of international law.[56] I have investigated the legal terms of the act to trace its use in Ottoman strategies of negotiation with other imperial powers over African possessions and the policies of rule along its southern frontiers.[57] *The Ottoman Scramble for Africa* demonstrates just how this "old empire" was in fact ready and willing to develop and practice new tricks in the age of "new imperialism," an age marked by the significance of frontiers in determining the fate of empires, making it an "age of frontier politics" that required empires to adapt to a new reality in which formerly marginal local powers exerted great influence on the outcome of interimperial competition.[58]

Centering the Frontiers

Frontiers are often considered marginal in studies that privilege a structural understanding of empire; this understanding sees imperialism as a web of institutions dotting concentric circles that surround the metropole—the center of imperial power. In contrast, this book views imperialism as a "process of adaptive transformation in which people create, assemble, configure, reassemble, renovate and remodel imperial forms of power and authority under diverse, changing circumstances."[59] Imperialism as process is always unfolding, whether close to the centers of power or further afield along an empire's inherently unstable frontiers. For the best understanding of unfolding imperialism, especially during a time of accelerated territorial expansion (variously described as a "race" or a "scramble"), the African frontiers of the Ottoman Empire in the last two decades of the nineteenth century offer an ideal site of investigation. The twenty-year race that ended with losers and winners strewn along the imaginary web connecting rulers and ruled left the preexisting political map in tatters and paved the way for the great military conflicts of the twentieth century. It was along these frontiers that the imperial presence first took hold, its shape molded through negotiation, violent erasure, and practices of both exclusion and inclusion.

The study of imperialism in a time of expansionist colonialism favors frontiers where "military, political, institutional, cultural, linguistic, ethnic, social and economic frontiers move spatially and temporally at their own pace, so that empire cannot be contained within definite parameters."[60] In visual terms, imperialism as process in Africa was like magma inching along the bottom of the ocean floor, negotiating rough and smooth terrains, avoiding obstacles, redirected by competing local formation, and inhabiting existing crevices and caves. This can best be observed along the moving frontiers during the rare volcanic event: periods of historical accelerated territorial expansion and colonial competition.

Let us pause here to consider the term *frontier*. The very word assumes a certain perspective, a certain vantage point, one that views the horizon from the particular angle of the metropole. It also privileges the perspective of binaries: "imperial vs. indigenous, conqueror vs. conquered, insider vs. outsider."[61] I take this perspective or vantage point seriously, believing that it captures one of the problems that I grapple with in this book: a unidirectional vision of empire from the perspective of the metropole. Admittedly, I adopt the perspective of Istanbul—the Ottoman metropole, the empire's center of power. I do so with full awareness that frontiers are also contact zones between imperial ambition and local political formations. They can be thought of as the very epicenter of certain forms of political life: potentially violent struggle in times of war and productive economic exchange in times of peace. In fact, they are a unique and often complex mix of religious, political, military, and economic formulations that can leave the metropole helpless. They are zones of interaction where cultural, geographical, and political boundaries are blurred as the central imperial state tries to balance stability with state hegemony.[62] These features of frontierhood translate well across empires, whether in North America, Latin America, or East Asia, regions whose rich literature on colonialism I have drawn on to understand the Ottoman imperial frontiers in Africa and Arabia.[63]

Privileging of the metropole's perspective is to a certain extent a reflection of the available sources in various state archives that I rely on. These archives reflect the concerns of the metropole, which engaged with the frontiers only as far as they mattered to its policies and strategies.[64] That is not to say that there is little information about the frontiers in the various imperial archives. To the contrary, microlevel details, from the social to the political, can be found, but they often over-represent times of conflict between the metropole and frontier inhabitants.

Istanbul understood that local regimes substantially influenced imperial strategies and their success or failure. The negotiated expansion of imperial power into the "frontiers" features as one of the main themes of this book. As the British and French empires expanded toward the Ottoman frontiers, the frontiers became interimperial "borderlands," zones of interaction, like frontiers, where lines were blurred and power was contested. However, in the late nineteenth-century borderland, the parties to conflict were imperial powers contesting control of these often vaguely defined zones. The borderlands were part of interimperial conflicts over "territorialized" spaces.[65] Thus, although acknowledging the problematic use of both *frontier* and *borderland*, I employ them to reflect the shift from imperial-indigenous interaction to imperial-imperial competition in central Africa and the Hijaz. In spatial terms, then, this book is about the transition of the Ottoman frontiers in Africa and Arabia into the borderlands of interimperial competition between 1880 and 1900.[66]

In Ottoman studies, frontiers are a subject of research on the effect of state centralization during the reign of Sultan Abdülhamid II.[67] In *Frontiers of the State in the Late Ottoman Empire: Transjordan, 1850–1921*, Eugene Rogan examines the Hamidian government's reach into the Syrian Desert and as far south as Maʿan in what is today the Hashemite Kingdom of Jordan. He defines frontiers as "socio-political orders apart from the institutions of the Empire at large."[68] Once incorporated into the imperial state network, a region lost its status as a frontier, pushing a new frontier deeper into the desert. Rogan offers a nuanced understanding of Ottoman administrative, economic, and military control, which he demonstrates were balanced by measures of accommodation to the local Bedouin population. Expanding on the notion of incorporation of the frontiers in the Hamidian period, he shows that the state's education policies targeted the tribes, one of the empire's most alienated populations,[69] for whom a special school in Istanbul, the Aşiret Mektebi (Tribes' Academy), was established. In addition to teaching modern languages and modern sciences, this school sought to foster an allegiance to the Ottoman state. The education system was tailor-made to incorporate and indeed assimilate the influential sons of frontier tribal leaders from Libya to Kurdistan and from Iraq to the Hijaz.[70]

Yemen and the Balkans were also regions of limited state presence, where the imperial government established new strategies for securing its borderlands. Although these strategies favored cooperation with some Yemeni and Balkan leaders, the Ottoman state had to contend with locals' demands, turning the relationship from one of ruler and ruled into one of partnership between the central state and the local powers.[71]

The question of Ottoman imperialism along frontiers-cum-borderlands is also taken up by Thomas Kühn, who investigates the relationship between imperial officials and locals in the province of Yemen.[72] He argues that Yemen, as a borderland of the empire between 1872 and 1918, showed signs of colonial rule in the state's efforts to align the local population with its centralization plans. What Kühn calls the "politics of difference"[73] adopted by the Ottoman state in Yemen was not a mimicking of European colonialism, despite clear evidence of Ottoman awareness of British and French colonial models.[74] In contrast to European colonialism, Ottoman rule posited cultural, not racial or ethnic characteristics, as a way of differentiating the Ottoman rulers from the local population. Kühn uses the term "colonial Ottomanism" to capture a uniquely Ottoman form of rule in this area that had only some "colonial" characteristics.[75] As Kühn demonstrates, even by 1914 neither ethnic nor legal categories were used by the central government to distinguish "colonizer" and "colonized."[76] The significance here is that the difference between colonizers and colonized was traversable over time and not an essential condition of Ottoman imperial rule.[77]

I have benefited greatly from all of this scholarship, which begins to uncover the Ottoman state's increasing levels of agility and its new methods for consolidating its hold on the southern frontiers in the nineteenth century. It shows that the historical context and the geographic particularities of the frontiers-cum-borderlands necessitated an even wider range of policies aimed at accommodating the particularities of local populations and relational power dynamics. Along the frontiers, the Hamidian regime took an increasingly flexible approach to distinguishing "undifferentiated insiders" and "barbarian" outsiders.[78] The emphasis shifted from asserting central state control over the Bedouin populations along the frontiers to the formation of a partnership with them as a way of consolidating Ottoman hold on the frontiers-cum-borderlands in the face of European challenges to the empire's sovereignty.

Delving into the complex and often fraught relationships among imperial, provincial, and local partners, this book conceptualizes imperial space as a "sphere of a multitude of trajectories of power and influence,"[79] in which individual goals are examined in a wider transimperial context. It highlights similarities and differences between the imperial government's strategic goals, the personal ambitions of imperial intermediaries, and the attitudes of various levels of governmental administrators toward the Bedouin population in the Sahara and the Hijaz. In so doing, it makes a historiographical argument for departing from the oversimplified bipolar relationship traditionally posited between *an* Ottoman government and *a* frontier tribal population. For when we consider the multitude of provincial and local powers and their vision for their regions, which contradicted the vision of the sultan, we come to understand why the much vaunted powerful inner-circle discipline and unity of the Mabeyn did not always succeed in making its vision come true when dealing with Ottoman strategies in provinces along the empire's southern frontiers. Even though Sultan Abdülhamid II shifted executive power from the ministries of the Sublime Porte to the handpicked secretaries in the Mabeyn of Yıldız Palace, his vision did not go unchallenged even there. In fact, it was continuously contested by powers within and without the government rank and file, through official and unofficial channels, leading to many of the problems that were the hardest to tackle and in some cases were the main cause of the failure of Istanbul's plans.

A Road Map

Chapters 1 and 2 of *The Ottoman Scramble for Africa* introduce the history and geography of Ottoman Libya, the Sahara, and the Lake Chad basin. Focusing on the Sanusi Order and the Ottoman state's efforts to reestablish its rule in Ottoman Libya, they set the stage for understanding the context of new imperialism in this part of Africa. They also detail the multifaceted nature of Ottoman strategy and Ottoman participation in the scramble for Africa, alternating between negotiations in Berlin and those in Benghazi.

Chapters 3 and 4 expand the list of competitors vying for control of the eastern Sahara, using a wider lens to examine the impact of intense late nineteenth-century interimperial competition on the empire's southern frontiers on both sides of the Red Sea. In addition to Britain and France, Italy and the Sudanese Mahdist state played a substantial role in determining the fate of Ottoman interests in Africa. Chapter 3 picks up the story at the end of 1886, when the sultan's representative, Sadik al-Mouayad Azmzade, first voyaged to the Libyan Desert; it ends with the devastating diplomatic failures of the 1890s and then examines the change in the empire's strategic and operational focus from territorial expansion to consolidation, and indeed, resistance along the empire's southern frontiers. Chapter 4 traces the impact of the Ottoman Empire's fifteen-year experiment in Africa, and its failure, on its foreign relations and domestic strategies along the southern frontiers-cum-borderlands. Ultimately, the chapter highlights how events taking place in one part of the empire—in this case Ottoman Africa—directly influenced and at times dictated imperial strategy in other parts—in this case Ottoman

Arabia—demonstrating the necessity of a transimperial approach to the study of empire.[80]

Chapters 5 and 6 shift the spotlight to the Arabian frontiers, particularly the Damascus–Medina telegraph line extension project. The telegraph project serves as a case study of Istanbul's shift toward policy making to consolidate its hold on its increasingly vulnerable southern frontiers. It illustrates the intersection of the empire's interimperial competitive strategy and its intraimperial political conflicts. In Istanbul's complex and often conflict-ridden decision-making process, international relations concerns sometimes conflicted with the interests of various imperial and provincial stakeholders. At the turn of the century, seemingly localized problems along the southern frontiers often turned into problems of empire-wide concern. Similarly, intraimperial problems in the borderlands often had global interimperial ramifications.

The Conclusion highlights the importance of not allowing final outcomes to prevent us from looking for unfruitful contingencies and unfulfilled possibilities. Alternative paths that do not accomplish intended goals, even failed attempts, rarely make it into history books. However, this book demonstrates the necessity of exploring these alternative paths rather than justifying the final outcome. In fact, I argue that stories of unfulfilled goals and unfinished plans, which usually disappear into the depths of the archives, are sometimes more telling than stories that seem to fit a neat linear trajectory leading to the end of empire. In the case of the Ottoman Empire, the lost history of Istanbul's efforts to reestablish its presence on the international stage helps us rethink colonial history, international diplomacy, and Ottoman imperialism at the end of the nineteenth century.

Of course, judgments of failure and success, "golden" eras and "dark" ages, and even beginnings and endings are often the privilege of academics who are themselves the product of their local contemporary political and socioeconomic contexts. Similarly, the geographical boundaries of modern area studies are usually the product of contemporary imperial concerns. This has led to an artificial severance of the three regions under study: the Middle East, sub-Saharan Africa, and the Red Sea basin, which, as we will see in Chapter 1, is not a true reflection of the historical reality of these interconnected regions.

1 OTTOMAN LIBYA, THE EASTERN SAHARA, AND THE CENTRAL AFRICAN KINGDOMS

> It is now that travel in the real Sahara starts. . . . Crossing this part of the Sahara Desert, if it weren't for the color difference, one would think that one is on the open seas. No matter how far you move towards the horizon, there it is, the horizon, unchanging. An empty, deep, horizon on fire! No discernible structure, not even a single tree to distract your eye from the fatigue caused by this emptiness.
>
> Sadik al-Mouayad Azmzade,
> outside of Jalu in the Sahara, October 26, 1895

WHAT AN OUTSIDER LIKE Sadik Pasha al-Mouayad Azmzade saw as an ocean of sand dunes and undistinguishable shadows blending earth with horizon was in fact a complex landscape encompassing a multitude of interconnected cultural, political, and religious formations. The perception of the Sahara as a place of exotic "emptiness," literally an unreadable landscape as Azmzade described it, is reflected in much of the scholarship that has treated Saharan and sub-Saharan Africa as spaces separate and isolated from North Africa and the Middle East. This false perception is reinforced by the institutional area studies model, which sets academic inquiry in separate silos to match funding packages that prioritize Western imperial interests in the twentieth century. The result has been an artificial severance of the historical ties that leaves transregional connections between the Mediterranean, the Middle East, North Africa, Saharan/ sub-Saharan Africa, and central Africa greatly under-researched.

The mental separations between the so-called Middle East and North Africa (MENA), the Mediterranean, and Saharan/sub-Saharan Africa are not new, however. They run deep through the historiography of the Mediterranean world from the late nineteenth century, where "Mediterranean Africa (as part of the Mediterranean, or Arab, and hence non-African world) has often been excised from conceptions of the continent 'proper' . . . and the way the Sahara has correspondingly been seen—or rather unseen—as an empty space in between."[1] Azmzade's description of the Sahara as exotic and unfamiliar, for example, is but a continuation of a nineteenth-century tradition of exoticizing the southern reaches of the empire beyond the Mediterranean.

In this chapter, I offer an introduction to this complex geopolitical, economic, and cultural region (Figure 3), stretching from the Mediterranean to sub-Saharan Africa, in an attempt to de-exoticize it for readers who are not familiar with its history. I begin with a brief overview of the political history of the coastal towns of Ottoman Tripolitania and Cyrenaica, starting with the first Ottoman period of rule in the sixteenth century through the years of nominal Ottoman rule by the Karmanlı Dynasty (1711–1835) and ending in the 1840s, when direct Ottoman rule was reestablished and the Sanusi Order began to put down roots in the Libyan interior. Turning the spotlight to the southern reaches of the area under study, I cross the frontiers of the Sahara into the Sudanic belt and the southern reaches of the long-distance trade routes from the Mediterranean Sea, ending along the shores of Lake Chad. There, in the geographic center of the Sudan and the southern African frontiers of the Ottoman Empire, two competing kingdoms had for centuries engaged in productive political, cultural, and economic exchange with the Mediterranean coast. Of course, by "the Sudan" I am not referring to the Republic of Sudan or the Republic of South Sudan. The Sudan in the nineteenth century was what Arab geographers often termed "Bilad al-Sudan," literally "Land of the Blacks"; this is the area that lies south of mostly Arabic-speaking North Africa, stretching horizontally across the continent.[2]

The two kingdoms—often referred to as sultanates because of the adoption of Islam as the official religion of the ruling dynasties—were the Kingdom of Kanem-Borno (often simply Borno or Bornu) and the Kingdom of Wadai (Wadi ʿUlay in some Arabic and Ottoman sources). A third, politically and economically weaker kingdom that survived at different times as a tributary state to either Borno or Wadai or both was the Kingdom of Bagirmi. Together Kanem-Borno, Wadai, and Bagirmi, often referred to as the Central Sudanic Kingdoms, are the focus here, but it is important to note that they were not the only central African polities to influence the extent and nature of foreign imperial presence in Africa at the end of the nineteenth century. There were other kingdoms, sultanates, and caliphates, such as Darfur to the east and Sokoto and Adamawa to the west, but they played marginal roles during the period of focus for this book and therefore do not receive any detailed attention.

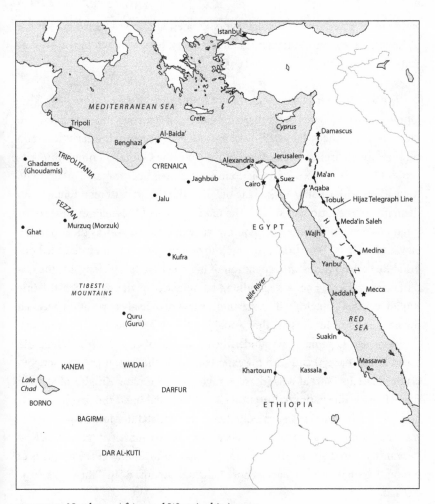

FIGURE 3. Northeast Africa and West Arabia in 1902.

The relationship between the Central Sudanic Kingdoms and Cyrenaica was often mediated through the nomadic populations crisscrossing the eastern Sahara. These were the Bedouins of the Libyan Desert who lived in nomadic and seminomadic tribes that controlled most of the main trade routes across the eastern Sahara and served as human conduits between the Mediterranean coast and the Sudanic belt, tying the two regions together on economic, social, cultural, and political levels.

First, let us turn to the provincial center of power in Ottoman Libya,[3] Tripoli, where the story of Ottoman influence in the region goes back to the early modern period, a time of corsairs, pirates, and the so-called golden age of Kanuni Süleyman (Suleiman the Law Giver), better known in the West as Sultan Suleiman the Magnificent (r. 1520–1566).

The Karamanlı Dynasty and the Central African Kingdoms

Ottoman involvement in the Barbary Coast, which roughly corresponds to the coasts of modern Libya, Tunisia, and Algeria, began in the early sixteenth century. An emerging world power at the time, the Ottoman Empire threw its support behind the coast's corsair commanders, *reis* in Ottoman-Turkish, who were at war with Charles V, the king of Spain and the Holy Roman Emperor, in the name of the Ottoman sultan. The most famous of these commanders—or infamous depending on which point of view one chooses—was the legendary Hayreddin (Reis) Barbarossa (d. 1546), to whom the sultan awarded the honorific Beylerbeyi Pasha in recognition of his role in fighting alongside the Ottoman navy. In 1533 he was appointed commander of the navy with the title Kapudan Paşa (Captain Pasha), starting a trend of official cooperation between the navy and former corsairs that would last through the seventeenth century.[4]

In 1551 the Ottoman navy, under the command of Grand Vizier Sinanüdin Yusuf Pasha (d. 1553) and with the expert advice of the corsair and former governor of Djerba[5] Turgut Reis (d. 1565), routed the crusading Knights of St. John from Tripoli. Interestingly, Turgut Reis was not appointed the first governor-general of Tripolitania. That appointment went instead to Murad Ağa, the former commander of a nearby post.[6] Locals would later sanctify Murad Ağa, who became a revered Sufi figure. The mosque he built in Tajura on the outskirts of today's Tripoli is also his place of burial and has become a Sufi "shrine" (*mezar/mazār*).[7]

For close to seventy-five years, the waters off the Barbary Coast were the borderlands between the Ottoman and Hapsburg empires in the battle for control of the Mediterranean. Initially, with the help of the Barbary corsairs, Istanbul gained the upper hand in the western Mediterranean Sea, prompting some historians to call the sixteenth-century Mediterranean an "Ottoman lake."[8] This status did not last long, however, for as early as the 1570s the empire's hold had begun to weaken, mirrored by the loosening hold on power of a series of Istanbul-appointed governors of Tripolitania.[9]

By the early years of the seventeenth century, Istanbul's tenuous control of the Barbary Coast had been considerably compromised, opening the way for a series of local *deys*,[10] renegades, who took over rule of the area and heavily relied for their economic survival on the slave trade from sub-Saharan Africa and the famous Barbary piracy against European and American ships. This situation continued until 1711, when Karamanlı Ahmed—named in reference to Karaman, a provincial district in central Anatolia and the site of the ancient Emirate of Karaman—led an armed insurgency against the local *dey*, Muhammad Khalil ibn al-Ginn, occupying Tripoli and dismissing the Istanbul-appointed governor-general. Karamanlı Ahmed—also known by his Arabized name, Ahmad al-Qaramanli—was a *kuloğlu* (literally, "son of a slave"). *Kuloğlu* usually meant a janissary who was a son of a janissary, but in the Maghreb it meant the son of a janissary officer and a local woman.[11]

Through a combination of material incentives and deadly force, Karamanlı Ahmed established himself as the paramount ruler of Tripolitania,[12] in the process founding the dynastic rule of the Karamanlı family. He maintained official ties to Istanbul, symbolized by the title Beylerbeyi Pasha bestowed on him by Sultan Ahmed III (r. 1673–1736).[13] Locally, he ensured his monopolistic hold over this autonomous regency (*paşalık*) by massacring most of the influential janissaries in Tripoli who posed potential challenges to his rule. This was a foreshadowing of what would take place in Cairo when Mehmed Ali Pasha followed the Karamanlı example to solidify his rule in the formerly Mamluk-controlled Ottoman province of Egypt.[14]

Despite Karamanlı Ahmed Pasha's major accomplishments, the heyday of Karamanlı rule was actually during the reign of his successor, Karamanlı Yusuf Pasha (r. 1796–1832), who in 1796, following a violent struggle with local rivals, successfully established his dominance in Tripoli.[15] After consolidating his power, he took advantage of the European preoccupation with the Napoleonic Wars to reassert Tripoli's influence in the Mediterranean by intensifying his support for the corsair raids on European and American ships. In the process, he engaged the newly established US Navy along the coast of Tripoli in a battle that ended with the signing of a peace treaty with the Americans in 1812.[16] Yusuf Pasha's ambitions were not limited to the Mediterranean. In the 1820s his financial goals led him south to the Lake Chad basin, where he established a military alliance with the powerful Kingdom of Kanem-Borno.

Borno is the name of a state in the northeast of today's Nigeria southwest of Lake Chad.[17] It was also the name of the ancient kingdom of the Kanuri people of central Africa. Until the first decade of the nineteenth century, the Saifawa Dynasty ruled Borno, whose location at the geographical center of central Sudan made it not only the beneficiary of a multitude of cultural influences but also the trading hub of North Africa, the Nile Valley, and the sub-Saharan region as well as the gateway to the lucrative slave trade.[18] This strategic location also made Borno the object of attacks by aspiring neighbors from both east and west, however. For example, in 1804 repeated raids by the aggressively expansionist Fulani fighters aiming to expand the rule of the Sokoto Caliphate forced the ruling Saifawa family to seek help from a popular Muslim scholar from Kanem, northeast of Lake Chad, named Shehu (Sheikh) al-Hajj Muhammad Lamino (al-Amin) bin Muhammad al-Kanemi.[19] Al-Kanemi came to the aid of Borno on more than one occasion, eventually subduing the Fulani threat.

The long-term consequence of al-Kanemi's success, however, was the weakened legitimacy of the Saifawa *mai* (king)[20] and the eventual takeover of Borno by the al-Kanemi Dynasty. The last of the Saifawa *mais* was executed in 1846.[21] With the al-Kanemi family controlling Borno, the two kingdoms were brought under the same rule, becoming the Kingdom of Kanem-Borno.

The challenge to Kanem-Borno's sovereignty did not end with the takeover by the al-Kanemi family. It continued for the next century, requiring the assistance of allies in Fezzan, Tripoli, and later Benghazi. As early as 1806, while Kanem-Borno was fending off Fulani attacks, Wadai, under the rule of 'Abd al-Karim Sabun (r. 1803–1813), invaded the Borno tributary state of Bagirmi, using the excuse of the religious laxity of its ruler 'Abd al-Rahman Qarun, and took over the capital, Massina.[22] Control of Bagirmi, which for decades had been the main reason for the wars between Borno and neighboring Wadai, would continue to be a security and economic issue until 1817, when al-Kanemi finally accepted the aid of his ally to the north, Karamanlı Yusuf Pasha. Yusuf Pasha sent a military expedition under the command of Muhammad al-Mekani, governor of Fezzan, to assist Borno in its fight against the Fulani rebels that year and again in 1821, when Shehu Muhammad Lamino al-Kanemi (r. 1811–1835) requested aid in subduing Bagirmi,[23] which was once again rebellious.

Karamanlı Yusuf Pasha saw the strategic benefit in aligning himself with Kanem-Borno to solidify his economic ties with the most powerful Sudanic kingdom at the time. This alliance helped him reinforce his hold on the lucrative sub-Saharan–North African slave trade, which was the main export business of Kanem-Borno and a large source of revenue for the Karamanlı Dynasty. Economic and political relations with the regency's southern neighbors acquired special importance after European and American powers forced Yusuf

Pasha to sign agreements to abandon his support of corsair raids, one of his largest revenue sources.[24] The Kingdom of Wadai, Kanem-Borno's main competitor for trade and political domination of central Sudan, continued to agitate for war, at times with great success, eventually reaching and partially destroying the capital of Borno, Kukawa, in 1846.[25]

In addition to the Tripoli-based Karamanlı Dynasty and the Central Sudanic Kingdoms, there was another power to contend with along the eastern trade routes of the Sahara: the "Arab" Bedouins, the masters of the Libyan Desert. Like the tribes that inhabited the Arabian Desert, the Ottoman Empire's other southern frontier, the Bedouins who inhabited the vast expanses of land between the Libyan interior and the Central Sudanic Kingdoms maintained their autonomy under Karamanlı rule and later under direct Ottoman rule. Control of the trade routes was shared with the other masters of trans-Saharan trade, the Tuareg (Tawariq) of the western Sahara. However, because my focus is on the eastern trade route of the desert, I limit my observations to the Bedouin tribes and their role in maintaining the cultural and economic connections between the Mediterranean coast and central Africa during in the second half of the nineteenth century.

One of the strongest of the tribal communities was the Awlad Sulaiman tribal confederation, whose members claimed descent from Banu Sulaim of Arabia, whose origins can be traced back to Khaibar near Najd in central Arabia and later to the Hijaz. Around 978 the Fatimid Caliph al-ʿAziz Billah (r. 955–996) forced Banu Sulaim to migrate to Upper Egypt.[26] In the eleventh century, their descendants, Awlad Suleiman, made their way west through the Libyan Desert to the Mediterranean coastal towns stretching from Tripoli to Benghazi,[27] and by the beginning of the eighteenth century they had established themselves as the main power controlling the flow of goods along the eastern trans-Saharan caravan routes from the Central Sudanic Kingdoms in the south to the Mediterranean coast of the Libyan provinces in the north.[28] In the second half of the nineteenth century, the historic relationship between the Bedouins of the Libyan Desert and the kingdoms of central Sudan helped to facilitate a political alliance between the Ottoman-controlled north and the sub-Saharan interior until the Italian occupation of Libya in 1911.[29] The assertion of direct Ottoman rule in the Libyan provinces in 1835 inadvertently served to solidify these ties when the Ottomans forced the migration of the majority of Awlad Suleiman south to the Lake Chad basin.

1832–1842: A Transitional Decade

In the 1820s, the Great Powers began to pressure the Karamanlı Dynasty to end its support for the Barbary Coast corsairs and enforce the ban on slave trading in Tripolitania. This pressure forced Yusuf Pasha to impose higher tariffs on goods coming from the Libyan interior and to levy special taxes to meet his financial commitments. It was not long before his popularity began to erode in the Libyan interior, most notably in Fezzan, which soon rose up in open revolt. A French blockade of Tripoli in 1830 and a British blockade in 1832 aimed to collect debts that French and British nationals were owed. In response, Yusuf Pasha resorted to the unpopular and ultimately calamitous measure of taxing the *kuloğlu* class. As descendants of janissaries, members of the *kuloğlu* class had traditionally been exempt from taxation by the Tripolitanian government. This desperate measure led to even more social unrest in the coastal areas of the Libyan provinces, eventually forcing Yusuf Pasha to abdicate in favor of his son Ali Pasha.[30]

By then, however, the die had been cast, and the Karamanlı Dynasty's days were numbered. Tripolitania continued to experience a great deal of political and economic turmoil as the dynasty's loss of control led to further internal fighting. The intensifying international pressure to curtail the slave trade and put an end to corsairing, coupled with the collapse of caravan trade routes from sub-Saharan Africa to the Mediterranean coast and the resulting economic crisis, brought the regency to its knees.[31]

In 1835, Sultan Mahmud II (r. 1808–1839) ordered a naval expedition to reestablish Istanbul's control over the Libyan administrative zones of Tripolitania, Cyrenaica, and Fezzan, fearing that sitting idly by while Tripoli faced further internal instability and mounting foreign debts might give France or Britain the excuse to invade.[32] Unwilling to relive the catastrophic loss of Algeria to the French in 1830 and fresh from a humiliating peace treaty he had been forced to sign with Mehmed Ali Pasha, the governor-general of Ottoman Libya's neighboring province of Egypt, the sultan took decisive action, sending in Ottoman troops and starting what historians have come to call the second period of Ottoman rule in Tripolitania, Cyrenaica, and Fezzan.[33]

Ottoman Tripolitania and Cyrenaica[34] or, as they were commonly referred to in Ottoman sources, Trablusgarb and Bingazi, were administrative zones sharing the Mediterranean coast of what today roughly corresponds to the Arab Republic of Libya. I use the somewhat vague term "zone" because, other than the Mediterranean Sea to the north, the boundaries between these administrative and political entities were vaguely defined, stretching and over-lapping along the frontiers of the Libyan and Egyptian deserts and the vast Sahara. The lack of survey-defined borders in the region created a number of contentious issues as territoriality became a defining factor in late nineteenth-century colonialism.[35]

In the early 1840s, only a few years after Ottoman direct rule had been es-tablished for the second time, the coastal cities of Ottoman Libya were chosen as pilot locations to implement the newly announced Tanzimat. The Tanzimat, the brainchild of Sultan Mahmud II and several French-educated men in Istan-bul, were part of a massive top-down project to reform all levels of Ottoman government, often following examples set by other European states. For the next twenty-five years, Istanbul continued to introduce administrative, agri-cultural, and educational reforms in the various administrative zones of Otto-man Libya.[36] A cornerstone of the Tanzimat plan was the centralization of the government's power, prompting the governor-general of Tripolitania to push for more state control deeper into previously autonomous areas of the Libyan interior but meeting with little success.[37] Even though the Ottoman military was largely successful in asserting state control in the coastal cities and towns, it found it much harder to establish dominion in the interior region where, soon after the collapse of Karamanlı rule, the Bedouin tribes reasserted their au-tonomy.[38] Most significantly, Awlad Suleiman, under the leadership of Sheikh 'Abd al-Jalil, had successfully established their dominance over the Fezzan re-gion.

Determined to assert its control over the vast territories of the empire, in 1842 the Ottoman government ordered its military to march south from Tripoli to the renegade region of Fezzan. The armed contingency was dispatched to the *sancak* (a district of the province of Trablusgarb) of Fezzan to punish Awlad Suleiman for refusing to pay taxes and submit to the newly reestablished Ot-toman rule. In the event, Awlad Suleiman suffered a decisive defeat and their leader, Sheikh 'Abd al-Jalil, was killed,[39] convincing tribal elders that they had no choice but to migrate en masse. It was said that they considered two desti-nations in which to take refuge: Egypt and Kanem-Borno. The final decision was Kanem-Borno because of the historic ties between Awlad Suleiman and the inhabitants of Kanem and their familiarity with central Sudan—a clear re-flection of north–south intimate relations. In Kanem, Awlad Suleiman carved out a place of influence for themselves through alliances established with local leaders.[40] Eventually, just as they had done before, within a few decades they had reestablished themselves as major power brokers in the Libyan Desert by aligning themselves with the Sanusi Order, eventually playing a central role in the Sanusi-led military resistance against the French army in central Africa in 1901–1902.[41] This was not a unique development. Another tribe by the name of Awlad Muhammad that had established its trading state in Fezzan in 1550 migrated south to the Lake Chad basin whenever it felt threatened by the state in Tripoli. It was not until the devastating defeat at the hands of the Karamanlı Yusuf Pasha in 1820 that the tribe was all but annihilated.

Understanding the reasons for Awlad Suleiman's resilience in this particular case gives us the key to understanding how the Bedouin tribes maintained their autonomy against the hegemony of imperial forces. Their strength stemmed from the breadth of their networks, which were almost entirely independent from the evolving state system along the coast. The tribes of the Libyan interior established their nodes of political power in the Sahara, outside the purview of the Ottoman state, with leaders of large tribes such as Awlad Suleiman regularly contracting marriage alliances with chiefs, sultans, and kings from the Lake Chad basin east to Darfur. An additional source of resilience was the malleable temporary alliances with other tribes that arose in the face of external threat without causing the loss of a tribe's independent identity.[42] Moreover, the absence of dependence on a single geographical center allowed the tribes to disperse and reorganize with relative ease. If they were defeated in the north, they moved south to safety, relying on alliances far removed from the threat of sedentary states. In their newly adopted home, they rebuilt their society and networks and slowly reasserted themselves in positions of power and as a collective force to be reckoned with. Mobility was their biggest asset in the long run.[43]

The strength that came from alliances among the mobile tribes—a factor too often ignored by historians of nineteenth-century Libya—is fundamental to understanding the strength and influence of the Sanusi Order in the eastern Sahara. The Sanusi Order often catered to and allied itself with major tribal confederations, such as Awlad Suleiman, taking advantage of already established networks of trade, politics, security, and social interactions. The process by which the Sanusi leader emerged as the de facto leader of the eastern Sahara at the end of the nineteenth century tells us much about the Hamidian regime's envisioned method of expanding Ottoman suzerainty deep into the Sahara and the Lake Chad basin after 1885.

The Emergence of the Sanusi Order

Filibeli Ahmed Hilmi Şehbenderzade (1865–1914), an Ottoman intellectual and political writer living in Istanbul, described the Libyan Desert at the end of the nineteenth century as a region full of *zaviyeler* of various orders. In doing so, he consciously chose the Ottoman-Turkish term closest to the Arabic *zāwiya*[44] over the Turkish *tekke* used for most Sufi "lodges" in Anatolia to highlight the distinction between the two. According to Hilmi, the *zawāyā* (plural of *zāwiya*) were at the heart of the quotidian life of North Africans, for the most part filling the void left by absent government services and state-sponsored infrastructure. "[When] one says *zaviye* [in North Africa] one means school, orphanage, old-people's home, a center for assistance and medical help, it means a hospital,"[45] he explained. "The *zaviye* is everybody's religious, political and social reference."[46]

In an area where there was negligible state infrastructure and close to no government social or economic planning, the *zāwiya* fulfilled the practical needs of those who shared this vast space, creating a nodal presence in a seemingly unmanageably large desert marked by the constant struggle for survival in a harsh and often hostile natural environment. A typical Sanusi Order *zāwiya* was a complex of multipurpose buildings serving as school, hospital, trade center, court, and administrative and community center.[47] In effect the Sanusi Order performed the functions of a state through their network of *zawāyā* stretching from Benghazi to the frontiers of sub-Saharan Africa, creating what some scholars describe as a "North African Muslim model" of governance.[48]

The Sanusi Order has been the object of much curiosity, as evidenced by the accounts of Ottoman and European visitors and European military and economic representatives, Ottoman government reports, and contemporary Ottoman and European newspapers and magazines. In the twentieth century, historians from a variety of backgrounds viewed the Sanusi Order from a multitude of perspectives, often producing contradictory analyses of the order and its relations with Ottoman and European imperialism.

Some European historians have investigated the Sanusi Order's organizational structure and the reasons behind its success in the Sahara. Most notably, E. E. Evans-Pritchard, who initially took an interest in the order while on assignment with the British military in 1932, wrote extensively on the Bedouins of Cyrenaica and neighboring areas. His magnum opus, *The Sanusi of Cyrenaica*, and several articles, papers, and essays are still some of the most quoted sources on the topic.[49] Most of the scholarship of the past two decades has attempted to explain the extraordinary influence that this Sufi order exerted on the region, its unprecedented expansion, and the extent of its reach and power. Two of the most prolific writers on this subject are Kunt S. Vikør and Emrys L. Peters. I have relied extensively on their work to produce a background picture of the Sanusi Order before exploring its relationship with the Ottoman state.[50]

In the Arab world, most historians have focused on the "cult of personality" of the order's leaders, their lives, and religious philosophies. The majority of this historical work took place during the height of postcolonial nationalist fervor in the late 1950s and throughout the 1960s, when scholars from the Arab world depicted the Sanusi Order as the forerunner to anticolonial Libyan nationalism.[51] In the 1980s and 1990s, new research produced more detailed knowledge, continuing the discourse of anticolonial nationalism while situating the Sanusi Order of the mid-nineteenth and late nineteenth century as "a strong indigenous Libyan leadership, fully aware of colonial interests in this region."[52] Over the last decade, a new generation of historians—although heavily relying on older scholarship—have reinterpreted the political project of al-Sanusi leadership as promoting a pan-Islamic ideology reflecting millennial populist political thought in the Arab world at the time.[53]

Historians date the beginning of the Sanusi Order[54] to 1843 in al-Bayda' (the White One) in Jabal al-Akhdar (Green Mountain), just outside of the city of Benghazi in Cyrenaica.[55] The order was named after its founder, a religious scholar by the name of Sayyid Muhammad bin Ali al-Sanusi al-Khattabi al-Idrisi al-Hasani (1787–1859),[56] who was born in a village near the town of Mustaghanem on the Mediterranean coast of Ottoman Algeria.[57] For the purposes of this book and to avoid confusion between Muhammad bin Ali and his successors, who were also referred to as al-Sanusi (pronounced "es-Snusi" in the local North African dialect), I adopt the Anglicized version of the name his followers used for the founder, the Grand Sanusi (al-Sanusi al-Akbar).[58]

The Grand Sanusi was educated in several small *zawāyā* before heading to the University of al-Qarawiyyin (Karaouine) in Fes in 1805. In 1824 he took the long journey from the Maghreb to Mecca to perform the hajj,[59] staying there for several years and becoming a very close disciple of Sayyid Ahmad bin Idris al-Fasi (d. 1836).[60] After al-Fasi's passing, the majority of the Grand Sanusi's disciples followed him to the vicinity of Mecca, where he built his first *zāwiya*, which he called Abi Qabis. The Grand Sanusi's time in the Hijaz would prove indispensible to his political success in the eastern Sahara. For example, while living in Mecca he built an important relationship with Muhammad al-Sharif (d. 1858), the future sultan of Wadai, who had come to Mecca to perform the hajj. This partnership would prove crucial to the order's future economic and political success, for Sultan Muhammad al-Sharif and later his son would eventually facilitate trade between Cyrenaica and the Sudan and become strong supporters of the Sanusi religious philosophy, helping to spread its influence to regions of the Lake Chad basin that fell in their orbit of influence.[61]

In 1840 the Grand Sanusi left Mecca and headed back across the Red Sea to the Maghreb, where he built the base of his order's power. There are conflicting accounts of the circumstances surrounding this return to Africa. Some historians believe that he was pressured out of Mecca by zealous local religious scholars (*ulema/'ulamā'*) and local government intermediaries.[62] Azmzade hinted at the pressure the Grand Sanusi felt from the local establishment: "When the late Seyyid Muhammad bin Ali al-Sanusi was in Mecca to spread the 'Sanusiye tarikatı,' he found himself closely watched and facing objections from some elements, even though he never posed any objections to other noble orders."[63] It is also suggested that the Grand Sanusi left Mecca by his own free will, pointing to the fact that his *zawāyā* in the Hijaz continued to operate even after his departure. Evidence from his own writings shows that the Grand Sanusi had begun to see himself as a spiritual guide to the nomadic and seminomadic populations and that very early in his career he planned to return to preach to the Bedouins of the Sahara.[64] According to Azmzade, even in the early period the main target of the Grand Sanusi's mission was the tribes outside of the main urban centers in the Hijaz: "Targeting neighboring tribes, the sheikh was able to save them from ignorance and heedlessness, and the tribesmen were able to attain material and spiritual benefits, and in the process make them follow the path to civility and high standards of good behavior."[65] I believe that both local pressure on the Grand Sanusi and his declared mission led him to leave the Hijaz for the Maghreb.

On the way to the Maghreb, the Grand Sanusi stopped in Cairo before reaching Siwa, Jalu, and Awijja in the Libyan and Egyptian deserts, where he stayed for several months at the invitation of local elders.[66] He then continued his journey northwest toward his declared destination of Gabès (Qabis) in Tunisia, but unexpectedly changed course. His choice of Gabès, so close to French-occupied Algeria, led many historians to speculate on whether the Grand Sanusi's return had anticolonial designs. There are conflicting accounts of his stance on the French occupation of Algeria and the role French colonialism played in his decision to return to the Maghreb. Some historians have even suggested that the Grand Sanusi was one of the main organizers of Algerian resistance against the French in the 1840s and 1850s. Others have suggested that the French were well aware of his movements and from a very early stage planned to combat his influence in North Africa.[67]

I argue that it is only the benefit of hindsight that allows us to assess the Grand Sanusi's actions once he settled in the Libyan interior. There is no evidence of any anti-imperial activities during his lifetime, and it is important that Gabès, and indeed Tunisia, fell to the French more than three decades after his migration from the Hijaz. It is my belief that accounts of the Grand Sanusi's supposed anticolonial activities were intended to imbue the order with an aura of an anticolonial resistance so as to fit it into a latter-day nationalist narration of Libyan history of the mid-twentieth century.

The Grand Sanusi eventually settled in al-Bayda' in Jabal al-Akhdar of Cyrenaica. Much significance is attached to the choice of this location, which would become the "mother *zāwiya*," the spiritual base of the Sanusi Order and the first capital of the independent Kingdom of Libya ruled by the Grand Sanusi's grandson, Idris bin Muhammad al-Mahdi al-Sanusi (r. 1951–1969).[68] Why did the Grand Sanusi choose a location far from the coast? Was it his alleged aversion to the Ottoman state that pushed him toward this remote location? Was it simply a personal choice to live in a remote area that was more conducive to quiet meditation? Or was it that he chose to devote his order to helping the poorly serviced rural population? For me, these questions are not simply a matter of academic curiosity. Rather, they directly impact our understanding of the Sanusi Order's ideological view of the imperial state apparatus and, more specifically, the Grand Sanusi's relationship with the Ottoman state's representatives.

Twentieth-century historians were not the first to speculate on the political significance of the Grand Sanusi's choice to settle in Jabal al-Akhdar. Many contemporary European observers, who were keeping a watchful eye on his actions, pondered his reasons for choosing such a remote and sparsely inhabited region for his first North African *zāwiya*. For example, according to Cecil Godfrey Wood,[69] a Damascene-born British career diplomat and British consul in Benghazi at the time, such a distant location—more than twenty kilometers from the nearest coastal town—served his strong ideological objection to the state-sponsored Western-style reforms of the Ottoman government and its application of the Tanzimat in the main towns along the Mediterranean coast.

More specifically, Wood believed that the reforms introduced by Sultan Abdülmecid and by Mehmed Ali Pasha, the governor-general of Egypt, were in
conflict with the Grand Sanusi's so-called traditional ideology.[70] He went even
further to say that the Grand Sanusi personally warned against "the introduction of European institutions" and "against even contact with Christians."[71] This
opposition, Wood explained, put the Sanusi Order on a collision course with
reform-minded Ottoman officials, leaving the Grand Sanusi no choice but to
physically distance himself from the centers of state control.[72] A closer look at
the context in which Wood's claims were made and the sources he relied on
sheds light on how Wood arrived at such strong opinions.

Cecil Wood's memorandum in which he reported his views in 1889, a year
after being transferred from Benghazi to Jeddah, was largely based on the writings of several French travelers and military explorers who had passed through
the Libyan Desert a few decades earlier. Three books in particular were most
often cited in opinion pieces and diplomatic advisory notes and had a great
deal of influence on public opinion—and not just in France and Germany,
where they were originally published. British and Ottoman diplomats also referred to them in communiqués to their superiors in London and Istanbul.

The ethnographer Louis Rinn's *Marabouts et Khouan: Étude sur l'Islam en
Algérie* (1884) was considered an authoritative guide book of sorts for French
colonial administrators on how to deal with members of local Sufi orders in
North Africa. Writing in the 1880s, Rinn warned that the Sanusi Order was a
very dangerous influence on the political outlook of the local population and
its perception of European colonialists.[73]

The physician Gustav Nachtigal's travelogues, which he based on his trips
through Sanusi territory to central Africa, were also cited in diplomatic reports.
His description of the order and its ideological leanings and of the Central Sudanic Kingdoms in the Lake Chad basin were often Europeans' first introduction to the region as a whole and to the order in particular. His most famous
German-language work, published in Berlin between 1889 and 1900, is a four-
volume study, *Sahara und Sudan: Ergebnisse sechsjähriger Reisen in Afrika*,
which was translated into English between 1971 and 1989. Like Rinn, Nachtigal
saw danger in the order's influence on the locals, warning about the "pertinac-
ity with which these fanatics embrace a great part of Africa in their Jesuiti-
cal web and the threatening selflessness with which they serve their cause."[74]
The most hostile European observer of the order by far was the French adventurer Henri Duveyrier. In his books, published throughout the 1860s, the

Sanusi Order was vilified to a ready Parisian audience who developed a fervent antipathy to it. This fervid hatred might explain the savagery of the French army in annihilating the order and its followers in central Africa four decades later during the French-Libyan War of 1900–1902.[75] Even though Duveyrier's books were little different from those of his European contemporaries traveling through the Middle East and Africa, they are considered much more important because they were widely read by European colonialists and policy makers and thus directly and indirectly affected decisions leading to the course of events during the push for central Africa in the late nineteenth century.[76]

In spite of warnings about the order's hostility toward Christians, the West, and European-inspired reformers, there is little factual evidence to suggest that the opinions of Wood or other earlier European representatives were based in reality. For this reason, recent scholarship revisiting the so-called *légende noire de la Sanusiyya* has determined that these opinions arose from the unquestioned European colonial *mentalité* of the time.[77] I leave the last word on this issue to Evans-Pritchard, the original historian of the order: "Though some writers have made assertions to the contrary, the Sanusis have never shown themselves more hostile than other Muslims to Christians and Jews, and . . . avoided all political entanglements which might bring them into unfriendly relations with neighboring states and European powers."[78]

Unlike the revisionist history of the order's attitude toward Europe and European travelers, a historical revision of Sanusi-Ottoman relations has been slower to happen. I take it on here because these relations are fundamental to an understanding of the Sanusi's role in Ottoman expansionist strategies in the face of European colonialism. I put the inherited knowledge of Sanusi-Ottoman relations under a microscope to better explain how it fits with assumptions about imperial strategy along the southern frontiers of the empire.

The Ottoman Empire and the Sanusi Order: Partnership or Competition?

There is no doubt that the appearance of the Grand Sanusi on the scene a few years after the reestablishment of Istanbul's authority in Ottoman Libya aroused the suspicions of the still young provincial administration. His reputation as a religious leader with a devoted following in the Hijaz and the popular support he garnered in Cairo and several other towns in the Libyan and Egyptian deserts on his way to the Maghreb were probably cause for suspicion about his political intentions and his position vis-à-vis Istanbul's reassertion of imperial rule in the Maghreb.

As mentioned earlier, after changing course from his declared destination of Gabès, the Grand Sanusi did not go directly to al-Bayda'. In fact, he traced his steps back east, first stopping at the seat of the Ottoman provincial government in Tripolitania, Tripoli. There are several accounts of his interactions with Ottoman provincial representatives, many of whom described the Ottoman governor-general, Ali Ashkar ('Ashqar) Pasha (r. 1838–1842), as initially very suspicious of the Grand Sanusi's intentions.[79] However, according to Ahmad al-Sharif (1873–1933), one of the Grand Sanusi's grandchildren and the future leader of Sanusi military resistance against European colonialism, the Grand Sanusi's host in Tripoli, a man by the name of Ahmad al-Muntaser, set out to bring the Sufi leader and the Ottoman governor-general closer together. Al-Muntaser reportedly invited the two to a face-to-face meeting, which led to several subsequent meetings that finally convinced Ali Ashkar Pasha that the Grand Sanusi's plans did not clash with the Ottoman state's Tanzimat-era plans for the area. In fact, the opposite was true: they were complementary to the Ottoman state's reform efforts.[80]

The Grand Sanusi's plans included the promotion of literacy and religious education, support for economic development for the rural population, and, perhaps most important, the promotion of the Ottoman sultan's temporal authority in the region.[81] This matches the 1889 assessment of the order by the British consul in Benghazi, Donald Cameron, in his report to the Foreign Office in London. Cameron wrote that the Grand Sanusi had no aspirations to temporal power or political ambitions,[82] which was no doubt an oversimplification in its assumption of a clear separation between the temporal and the spiritual. Nevertheless, it did reflect the order's official stance as well as contemporary perception on the ground of its purpose in the Libyan interior.

Before we leave Tripoli and the initial dealings between provincial authorities and the Grand Sanusi, it is important to mention that most historians agree that Governor-General Ali Ashkar Pasha himself eventually became a devoted Sanusi, a term which came to denote a follower of the Sanusi *tarikat*.[83] Whether or not the story of his first meeting with the Grand Sanusi is true, it is accepted that the Grand Sanusi eventually left Tripoli on very good terms with Ottoman authorities.[84] In Benghazi he was warmly greeted by the chiefs of a number of tribes from the Libyan interior who had heard of his reputation as a spiritual leader of the Libyan Desert Bedouin tribes from reports describing his stays in Siwa, Jalu, and Awijja.[85]

I am not the first historian to investigate the Hamidian government's relationship with the Sanusi Order. However, I am the first to claim that the relationship between the order and the Ottoman central government was not typical of the usual relationship between an imperial state and local rulers along its frontiers. I argue not only that the Ottoman state's policy and the Sanusi philosophy of administration were ideologically synchronistic but also that their work on the ground was complementary, cooperative, and at times even synergetic. In education, commerce, tax collection, and local governance, a close examination of the programs implemented by the Sanusi leadership in the Libyan interior and the Sahara and those implemented by the Ottoman state along the coast show striking cooperation well before 1885.

Similar to its Russian, Austrian, and Japanese counterparts, the Ottoman Empire during the Hamidian era prioritized the standardization and expansion of state education. As Selim Deringil argues, the purpose of this emphasis on education "was to produce a population which was obedient, but also trained into espousing the value of the center as its own."[86] For the Ottoman Empire, there were two additional incentives for prioritizing education, however. These were the perceived threat of missionary schools, which by the late nineteenth century had expanded to unprecedented numbers in the Ottoman provinces,[87] and the urgent need to staff the empire's changing administrative apparatus that the Tanzimat reforms had significantly expanded, leaving it sorely understaffed by the time Sultan Abdülhamid II took the throne.[88] By the end of Sultan Abdülhamid II's reign, "approximately 9,147 primary (ibtidai) schools, 219 middle (rüşdiye) schools, 104 secondary (idadi) schools, and 18 higher or professional schools [had been] established."[89]

The Hamidian education system also served to emphasize and regulate religious "morality"—an orthodox Muslim state-approved Hanafi morality, to be exact.[90] From the beginning of Abdülhamid II's reign, Yıldız Palace took this task very seriously,[91] even inviting religious dignitaries from around the empire to Istanbul in order to reach a consensus on an interpretation of Islamic political tradition that was favorable to Ottoman ruling interests.[92] In schools the main emphases were "first, the need to pray always to God, second to believe in the messenger Muhammad, and third to obey the sultan."[93] These values were not dissimilar to the ones espoused by the network of schools established by the Grand Sanusi.

By all accounts, education had been unattainable among the nomadic Bedouin population in the Libyan Desert. Now it flourished with the growth of the Sanusi Order and the spread of its *zawāyā* along the various trade routes. According to Lisa Anderson, in spite of the Tanzimat-era reforms that were implemented in Ottoman-controlled Tripolitania and Cyrenaica, in the Libyan Desert schools teaching reading, writing, and simple mathematics, in addition to religious instruction, were being established by the Sanusi Order at a faster rate than were the Ottoman state schools in the coastal cities.[94]

The Grand Sanusi's emphasis on education for the Bedouin population necessitated knowledge delivery systems that accommodated the lifestyle of their target audience. Thus two types of school were established to reach the widest swath of the population. The first was a system of mobile schools in which teachers traveled with the nomadic populations. The second was a system of schools established in *zawāyā* strewn across the eastern Sahara. A French military report from the end of the nineteenth century estimated the number of pupils enrolled in these schools at 15,600. With the addition of the students enrolled in the mobile schools, the total was most likely double that figure because the latter proved very popular, reaching nomadic tribes whose survival depended on their being continuously on the move.[95]

The commitment to the Bedouin way of life was also reflected in the religious education the Grand Sanusi devised for this population. Unlike most urban-based Sufi orders' rituals and philosophies found across the empire, the Sanusi Order's highly informal and uncomplicated rituals and practices did not require much preparation or training. They reflected the Grand Sanusi's understanding of his audience's lifestyle and literacy.[96] The order's evident focus on the practical might also have been part of its appeal to tribespeople who operated outside of the imperial state's system of laws. Because of the emphasis on a form of Sunni Islamic law as a way of organizing daily life, being a *Sanusiyya* follower required very little in the way of complex religious rituals that would have overly taxed a mobile population. The Sanusi Order prioritized organizing principles of day-to-day interaction among individuals, tribes, and the Saharan community at large along with coordinating and supervising commercial activity, particularly long-distance trade, which was the lifeblood of the Libyan Desert tribes.

Sanusi ceremonies of initiation, which the British consul Donald Cameron described in a letter to the Foreign Office on May 12, 1889, illustrate the uncomplicated nature of the order's practices. Two types of initiation ceremonies existed to accommodate pupils' different education levels, both known as "Taking the Rose." The first was taking the "Little Rose," which required three verses covering the basics of the Sunni Islam creed to be recited a prescribed number of times. The second was the taking the "Big Rose," which required a more complex prayer invoking the Prophet Muhammad and his family and hinting at traditional Sufi themes of visible and occult methods of knowing oneself and the divine.[97]

Along with literacy, trans-Saharan trade flourished as the Sanusi Order and its *zawāyā* expanded from Benghazi to the Sudan. With its influence reaching deeper into the desert, most of the tribes traveling the south–north trade routes joined the order. In this way, the arrival of the Grand Sanusi and the order's speedy growth into the Libyan interior and the eastern Sahara provided an approximation of a centralized leadership and administrative coordination, which had not been possible before. By the last two decades of the nineteenth century, the Benghazi–Kufra–Wadai trade route had become the most important of the north–south trans-Saharan trade routes as a result of the Grand Sanusi's efforts.[98] It became especially important after the abolition of the slave trade in Egypt in 1877, leaving the route to Benghazi the only one left for this illicit trade for the next thirty years.[99]

The Sanusi *zawāyā* served as nodal points of mediation and coordination among the various tribes as well as between the Ottoman state and the local population. They facilitated the establishment of customary rules of conduct and guaranteed the safety of the caravans. In addition, they furnished necessary services to long-distance trade, such as caravanserais and storage depots along the routes.[100]

The locations of the *zawāyā* have implications for understanding the influence that al-Sanusi's leadership had among the Bedouins and in turn its claim of neutrality among often warring tribes.[101] Initial research into the siting of *zawāyā* suggested that each *zāwiya* was associated with a specific tribe or subtribal groups and that the geographical distribution of the *zawāyā* mirrored preexisting segmentations and divisions among tribes and tribal confederations.[102] More recent scholarship disputes this theory, arguing that the *zawāyā* were actually intersection points and that their siting in different communities followed the various trade routes taken by different tribes.[103] In many cases, the *zawāyā* were built by the collective efforts of various tribes, and sometimes their construction brought together town notables and tribal sheikhs in rare instances of cooperation, a tradition that started with the construction of the first *zāwiya* in Jabal al-Akhdar.

Even the Grand Sanusi's settling in Cyrenaica was reportedly the result of a joint invitation from both tribal and community leaders from Benghazi. In fact, the Sanusi Order was successful precisely because the Grand Sanusi not only brought warring tribes together but also brokered a rapprochement between various sectors of Cyrenaican society.[104] Part of his power was his ability to both gain the trust of the Bedouin tribes of the eastern Sahara and maintain the respect of Ottoman Libyan society, both urban and rural.

Conclusion

Even though Istanbul had reestablished its rule over the major urban centers along the Mediterranean coast of Tripolitania and Cyrenaica by the early 1840s, its control was effectively limited to a narrow stretch of land. The Libyan interior, including the *sancak* of Fezzan—the homestead of Awlad Muhammad and later Awlad Suleiman—was only nominally in the imperial fold. Tribal structures of power in the desert were rarely interfered with by Tripoli as long as loyalty to the Ottoman "caliph" was maintained and, whenever possible, taxes could be collected. In the second half of the nineteenth century, however, beginning with the arrival of the Grand Sanusi in the Libyan interior, a new sociopolitical order began to emerge. No Sufi order was more successful or had a wider reach of *zawāyā* in mid-nineteenth-century eastern Sahara and central Africa than the Sanusi Order. The Grand Sanusi managed to consolidate the power of the Bedouin tribes and expand his power base by sending missionaries deep into the Sahara. The expanded network brought with it coordination of trade, education, and political activity in the eastern Sahara.

As goods from sub-Saharan Africa began to flow consistently into the Ottoman port cities of Derna and Benghazi, and as exports to Europe and the rest of the Ottoman Empire steadily rose, Istanbul must have begun to view the success of the Sanusi Order in achieving stability with a favorable eye, given that the coordination of economic and social activities, a goal of the modernizing Ottoman state of the Tanzimat era, was indirectly achieved through the coordination of the caravan network across the largest desert on earth. In addition, a single spiritual leader with far-reaching economic, political, and social influence in the eastern Sahara and the Lake Chad basin gave Istanbul a legitimate representative for negotiations on behalf of the Libyan interior's large and diverse population. The Sanusi's relationship with the local population and the order's centralization efforts in the eastern Sahara would take on a global geopolitical importance as the imperial competition over central Africa began to heat up following the Conference of Berlin in 1885.

2 THE LEGAL PRODUCTION OF OTTOMAN COLONIAL AFRICA

Today we performed the Friday prayers in the zāwiya's noble mosque. Even though this noble mosque is not as well designed as the one in Jaghbub, it is very solid and spacious for Kufra . . . In a place this far, when the sermon is read in the name of his excellency the protector of the caliphate, and when upon praying for the holiest of emperors, a group of believers respond with one loud voice: "ĀMĪN!" Can an Ottoman help but shed tears of pride?

Sadik al-Mouayad Azmzade, Kufra, Friday, November 8, 1895

SADIK PASHA'S DESCRIPTION of being overwhelmed with pride because he had witnessed signs of the caliph-sultan's influence in the Sahara showcases the importance Azmzade, a representative of Yıldız Palace on the ground, placed on the strength of political and spiritual ties between Istanbul and the Saharan population. This connection was the cornerstone of an Ottoman-Sanusi partnership in the Sahara after the empire's entry into the scramble for Africa. The long history of cooperation between the Ottoman state and the Sanusi Order combined with the order's far-reaching influence from the Libyan Desert to the Lake Chad basin made the head of the Sanusi order the ideal political partner to allow Istanbul to claim effective control, by proxy, of the "hinterland" of Ottoman Libya.

The logic behind Istanbul's strategy of parallel diplomatic negotiations in Berlin and the eastern Sahara is the focus of this chapter. However, before delving into the empire's "man on the spot" negotiations in the zawāyā of the Sahara and its diplomats' participation in negotiations in the drawing rooms of the German chancellor's residence at No. 76 Friedrichstrasse in Berlin, we go back to Istanbul during the critical years between the Congress of Berlin (1878) and the Conference of Berlin (1884).

From Berlin 1878 to Berlin 1884

Following a series of catastrophic defeats at the hands of an aggressively expansionist Russian Empire, Istanbul found itself in a number of highly disadvantageous negotiating positions. Fearing that the worst might happen—Catherine the Great's old dream of a greater Russian Empire with Istanbul at its center—Sultan Abdülhamid II's new administration signed the Treaty of Berlin in 1878, losing two-fifths of the empire's territories and one-fifth of its population.[1] The treaty indirectly confirmed European interventionism in the Ottoman Empire's ethno-religious separatist struggles, which had begun more than sixty years earlier,[2] forcing the so-called Eastern Question onto the foreign policy agendas of the Great Powers.[3]

The 1880s heralded more Ottoman territorial losses to European interests, only now they took place not in the name of protecting Ottoman Christian subjects or because a dormant national identity of ethno-religious minorities had "awakened." Instead, they took place in the name of protecting European geopolitical and economic interests in Muslim-majority North Africa.[4] Ottoman Tunisia, or Tunus Eyaleti, which had been under Ottoman suzerainty since 1574, was an Ottoman administrative zone that roughly corresponded to the coastal areas of the modern-day Tunisian Republic. According to a contemporary Ottoman geography textbook used in *rüşdiye* boys' schools in the province of Syria, it had a population of 2.5 million and was the largest Ottoman administrative zone in Africa after Egypt and Libya.[5] Similar to what had happened to the Karamanlı Dynasty in Tripolitania fifty years earlier, the Husainid Dynasty's hold on the regency of Ottoman Tunisia began to loosen, opening the way for local tribes to assert their power in the region, which partially manifested itself in cross-border raids into French Algeria. In the spring of 1881, despite Ottoman protestation and with the excuse of stopping these cross-border attacks to protect both the Husainid Dynasty's rule and regional stability, France invaded and occupied Ottoman Tunisia.[6] This sent waves of refugees to Ottoman Libya to escape the horrors of French occupation, as if they embodied the impact of European colonialism as it arrived on the doorstep of the last free Ottoman province.

By early 1882, then, of the three Ottoman provinces in Africa, Trablusgarb Vilayeti, which encompassed Tripolitania, Fezzan, and Cyrenaica, had become the only one not under some form of European rule. In the midst of the tumultuous events of that year, Istanbul designated the office of the governor of Cyrenaica a *mutasarrıflık*, which in late-Ottoman terminology meant that the *mutasarrıf* (the governor of the *mutasarrifiyya*) would now report directly to the imperial center and not to the provincial governor-general in Tripoli. In this way, the sultan's foreign policy advisors could vet all major decisions concerning this administrative zone to ensure that they did not conflict with Istanbul's foreign policy agenda.[7]

It is during the crucial few months between the French occupation of Tunisia in 1881 and the British invasion of Egypt in the summer of 1882 that we begin to hear voices from within the Ottoman ranks urging the sultan to leave the Balkan losses behind and focus on North Africa. A passionate advocate for reorienting Istanbul's geopolitical focus toward the African frontiers of the empire was Ferik Muhammad Zeki Pasha, a divisional general in the Ottoman army.[8] Zeki Pasha played a central role during the 1881–1882 Tunisian crises, when France revved up its threats to invade Tripolitania if the tribesmen who were severed from their kin on the Tunisian side continued their "cross-border" attacks against French borderland military installations.[9] He was part of an Ottoman force sent to Tripolitania after the French invasion of Tunisia, which, according to one French newspaper, amounted to 120,000 soldiers—no doubt an extreme exaggeration. Paris protested Istanbul's actions as provocative, and Istanbul responded with reassurances that it was only trying to ensure security and stability in Tripolitania, which would benefit French interests as well. This was no doubt a cheeky response, alluding to excuses that were employed by the French to justify their invasion of Tunisia.[10]

A letter from Ferik Zeki Pasha encouraged Yıldız Palace to pay much closer attention to the remaining African provinces of the empire, still under direct Ottoman sovereignty. He passionately implored the sultan not to waste time on the past:

> If the efforts needed to carry out the necessary reforms and the development [esbab-ı mamuriyet] projects that this province is in dire need of [şiddetle muhtaç] were spent, it would allow us to control (own) a territory equivalent in size to the size of Rumeli . . . with the strength of one million Muslim inhabitants [milyon müvehidinin küvvetiyle], your humble servant has no doubt that with His good grace [bilütfihi taala] the benefits would compensate for all of our military expenses. . . . This province is truly in need of reform.[11]

Zeki Pasha continued to portray Ottoman Libya as a hotbed of enthusiastic support for Ottoman rule. He claimed that when the locals—with the Bedouin carefully enumerated among them as distinct from city folk—came across Ottoman soldiers, they uttered expressions of support for the sultan such as "May

God make the sultan victorious [*Allah yanṣur al-sulṭān*]" or recited "touching prayers [* adʿiye müesire*] . . . with great eloquence [*kemalı fasahatla*]" for the caliph. Perhaps most important, Zeki Pasha stressed the unique opportunity that this moment in time presented for Istanbul to use the population's anger and their fear of the French threat to reassert the legitimacy of Ottoman rule. The people's anger was due to the French occupation of Tunisia, which sent a flood of Tunisian refugees into Tripoli carrying stories of the horrors the French army had inflicted on them. Thus, the time was ripe, Zeki Pasha argued, for the sultan to publicly assert himself as the legitimate protector of all Muslims and take action to turn the local perception of Ottoman troops from a foreign power to fellow Muslim protectors working to shield the local population from European invaders. Interestingly, he prioritized the construction of an independent telegraph line to tie Ottoman Libya to Istanbul, both as a sign of the empire's commitment to its African province and as a much needed investment in the region's development. This was a foreshadowing of changes that would take place less than a decade later.[12]

Sultan Abdülhamid II eventually took Zeki Pasha's advice to heart, taking steps toward asserting the Ottoman Empire's place in the imperial race to claim parts of Africa but not before the empire suffered further losses. In the summer of 1882, Britain invaded the Ottoman province of Egypt, or Mısır Eyaleti, which held the empire's most populous city, Cairo.[13] British reasoning for the invasion was similar to the French excuse for occupying Tunisia: to stabilize the political situation by protecting the khedival rule from the ʿUrabi Revolt and to secure British interests in the Suez Canal.[14] The ʿUrabi Revolt, which began in 1879, was led by Ahmed Pasha al-ʿUrabi, an army general who had galvanized the Egyptian population against the injustices of the discriminatory rule of the British-backed Turco-Circassian and European elites. By 1882 it had spread to all layers of Egyptian society, posing a genuine threat to the status quo and prompting the British parliament to intervene with an overwhelming show of force by authorizing the shelling and destruction of many neighborhoods in Alexandria, Egypt's commercial hub and second largest city.[15]

Thus in 1884, with the French to the west and the British to the east of Ottoman Libya, Istanbul entered the race for Africa with a plan to expand its territorial claims south into the Sahara and the Lake Chad basin, a region that ran from the Mediterranean coast south along the caravan routes and oases of the Libyan Desert and the Sahara, through the mountain passes of Tibesti, and into the Lake Chad basin and the kingdoms of central Sudan. To appreciate these expanses, consider that the distance from Benghazi to Lake Chad (approximately 2,300 kilometers) is equal to the distance from Benghazi to Berlin, or the equivalent of a three-hour flight. The Sahara, or Sahra-yı Kebir (literally, "vast desert"), was described in an 1881 Ottoman geography textbook as a country (*ülke*) listed only third in order after the Ottoman Empire and Algeria with a population of 1 million made up of a mixture of tribes.[16] If official school textbooks are any indication, it seems that the Sahara was never too far from the minds of the authors of Ottoman textbooks and the collective imagination of a young generation of Ottomans growing up in the new reality of a post-1878 Ottoman Empire (Figure 4).

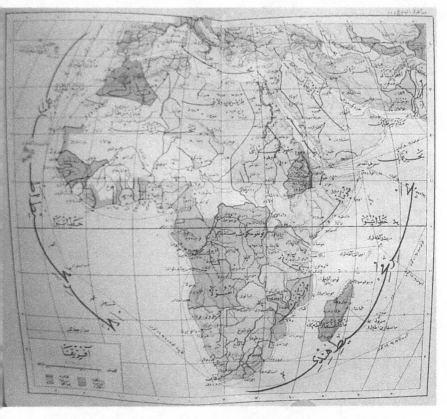

FIGURE 4. Ottoman Africa as it appeared in *Cep Atlası Umumi*, a 1906 Ottoman atlas (al-Zahiriyya Library, Damascus).

The Legal Production of the Libyan Hinterland

The head of the Ottoman delegation to the Conference of Berlin was Said Pasha, the minister of foreign affairs between 1885 and 1895.[17] Conference meetings and discussions went on for several months, eventually producing the document commonly referred to as the General Act of Berlin. Two of the act's articles were of particular significance to Istanbul's bid for expansion into the Sahara and the Lake Chad basin, which Istanbul unilaterally identified as the empire's sphere of influence in Africa.[18] The first was Article 34, which employed the "sphere of influence" concept in legalistic terms for the first time in an international agreement, producing what is known as the "sphere of influence" doctrine.[19] Designed to facilitate the divvying up of what remained of African territories without creating conflict among the European powers, Article 34 stated that an imperial power could no longer unilaterally declare a region within its sphere of influence without meeting a number of criteria set out by the act. These criteria included an explicit declaration of the intention to lay claim to a certain region and in theory required the agreement of the other treaty signatories for a particular sphere of influence to be universally recognized. In effect the act sanctioned the imperial powers' "right" to determine the fate of the African territories without consulting the locals, who were rendered virtually invisible and mute variables in the arithmetic of competitive colonialism. The abstraction of the subjects of European colonial rule was not new. What was new, however, was that the terms of colonialism were being inscribed in international agreements and thus protected under international law. In its early days, international law regulated the ways in which the so-called civilized could exploit the so-called less civilized and the "global North" could exploit the "global South."

It follows, then, that interpretations of agreements such as the Act of Berlin were left to the emerging world powers. For example, Article 34 introduced what later came to be known as the Hinterland Doctrine, according to which "the Power which established a settlement on the coast had the right to assume sovereignty over all the adjacent interior, which is necessary to the integrity and security of the settlement, provided such a territory was unoccupied by other Powers."[20] The term *hinterland* (in German *hinter* means "rear") led to much confusion and conflicting interpretation, particularly regarding how much of the land to the "rear" of a coastal area was to be considered hinterland and what its geographical boundaries would be. Which coastal areas did the hinterland doctrine apply to: the Mediterranean Sea, the Red Sea, the Atlantic Ocean? What about inland waterways and lakes such as the Congo River, the Nile, Lake Chad? What entities could be used to map an area's hinterland: economic ties, historical connections, commercial connections, religious affinities, cultural affiliations, tribal zones, political alliances? Were the hinterland's borders to be drawn perpendicular to the coastline or determined by social and economic relations?

None of the answers to such questions were made explicit in the Act of Berlin, requiring future case-by-case interpretation and negotiations when conflicting interests arose, effectively leaving the final decision to the negotiators. This was no simple oversight. In effect it allowed enough flexibility that when the time came, as would be the case with Ottoman Libya's hinterland, the ultimate decision was left in the hands of those with greater power. This power took political, economic, and military capital to implement. Ironically, the power of the law was also used to protect the privileges of the more muscular empires over the weaker ones.[21]

The second relevant article in the Act of Berlin introduced another problematic concept known as "effective occupation." Article 35 was of great practical importance in that it was supposed to define the sanctioned methods whereby the European powers could legally prove their claims to regions in Africa from 1885 onward. The mere "discovery" or surveying of a territory by an empire's citizen/subject would no longer be sufficient grounds for the imperial metropole to claim control over it. According to Peter Fitzpatrick, "The 'discovery' of territory . . . could not simply be something that a colonizing nation smugly held to itself; it had to be recognized as an effective discovery, be projected forward and secure continuing recognition among the community of nations for it to come into and remain in being."[22] Starting in 1885, an imperial power with colonial intentions would have to demonstrate its effective occupation of an area, signified by "continuous occupation supported by actual settlements or military posts."[23] Here, too, the legal understanding of the term was left vague and would have to be negotiated on a case-by-case basis when a challenge arose.

Most of the regions in Africa over which the Great Powers were competing after 1885 were in the interior and often contained vast swathes of land with harsh environments that proved difficult to colonize. For this reason, actual settlement with a substantial number of boots on the ground in every area that the imperial powers claimed in the vast African interior was a practical impossibility. However, because many interior regions were of essential economic importance to the already established European coastal colonies, they were considered central to the European colonial project despite the difficulty of establishing colonies.

In the case of the sparsely inhabited Sahara, although it had very few natural resources (that were known at the time) to be exploited, the economic viability of other colonial possessions—particularly in sub-Saharan Africa and the Sudan—depended on free access to the trade routes that passed through it. For example, areas south of the Sahara were largely dependent on the long-distance trans-Saharan caravan routes that crisscrossed the eastern Sahara east to west and north to south. The power that controlled these routes controlled the main economic lifeline of the Saharan and sub-Saharan regions of central Africa, not to mention the trans-African route from French-controlled West Africa to the British-controlled Nile Valley.

The post-1885 negotiations were in many ways the catalyst for a redefinition of the concept of effective occupation. They represented a turning point in legal opinion, at which proving possession through actual settlement and direct administration would no longer be the measure of the "legality" of occupation.[24] The change began immediately after the conclusion of the conference, when the emphasis on physical occupation shifted to the "manifestation and exercise of functions of government over the territory."[25] Legal scholar Surya Sharma points out that some contemporary understandings of effective occupation distinguished between territories that were conducive to human settlement (supposedly European settlement) and those that were not. This is of particular importance in explaining the significance of control over the eastern Sahara, the hinterland of Libya. It is also the key to understanding Istanbul's policies in the eastern Sahara beginning in 1885.

In the colonization of the African interior, the emphasis was not on settler colonialism but "upon establishment of minimum governmental authority throughout the areas being acquired in order that existing rights could be protected, trade and commerce carried out, and minimum order maintained amongst the aboriginal population."[26] With this as the standard against which an empire's "legitimacy" of occupation was to be judged, Istanbul set out to solidify its ties to the lands that it believed fell within its "sphere of influence"— the Lake Chad basin north to the Mediterranean coast of Tripolitania and Cyrenaica—using the new language of European colonialism. From this point forward, this region would be described as the hinterland of Ottoman Libya in diplomatic correspondence and in negotiations with the empire's European counterparts. In fact, the terminology of the new imperialism held such rhetorical power and particularity in meaning that *hinterland* was adopted into the Ottoman-Turkish language in its original form because a literal translation was deemed not to convey its contextual power. The weight of colonial possession and the awareness of the novelty of what Ottoman officials were negotiating with meant that there existed no Ottoman-Turkish substitute and the term had to be adopted as is to convey the specificity of the new form of imperial claim.

Phrases such as *"Devlet-i Aliye'nin Trablusgarb hınterlandı . . ."*[27] in official correspondence strictly maintained the terminological distinction between the new colonies (*müstemlekat*)—those being claimed post-1885 in Africa—and those that Istanbul considered to be historical Ottoman territories, provinces, and subprovinces.

Given the harsh natural conditions of the eastern Sahara and the added challenge of winning the loyalty of the autonomous Saharan Bedouin tribes, it must have been a daunting challenge to claim effective occupation of this territory, particularly for a resource-starved empire. This is the reason for my belief that Yıldız Palace worked on forging an alliance with the de facto leader of the Bedouin population and head of the Sanusi Order, the closest thing to a state structure in the Libyan hinterland: to prove effective occupation in that remote region by proxy.[28] To this end, the "Sanusi state" institutions[29] were claimed as Ottoman government institutions of power and as signifiers of its rule. To prove a proxy presence in the Libyan Desert and the eastern Sahara, Istanbul implemented two parallel strategies: building a partnership with the Sanusi leadership and asserting the state's presence in the sparsely inhabited stretches of the Libyan Desert by building telegraph lines connecting the African frontiers to the metropole. I contend that these strategies were carried out by a reinvigorated Ottoman government determined to take advantage of the opportunity that the Conference of Berlin and the resulting Act of Berlin afforded it, in order to reassert itself as a competitor in a new imperial world order.

I borrow the term *proxy* as in "rule by proxy" or "colonialism by proxy" from Moses E. Ochonu, who uses it to describe the Hausa-Fulani imperial agents' rule in the Nigerian Middle Belt during the British colonial period. Ochonu explains the difference between "intermediaries" and "rulers by proxy." An intermediary was a "translator" of colonial rule to the local population. Rulers by proxy, on the other hand, were not simple tools of colonial "indirect rule." To the contrary, they leveraged their positions, often granted and supported by the colonial power, to establish their own style of rule and create their own legacies. Ochonu is the latest revisionist historian to provide a nuanced understanding of the different local imperial agents in Africa. The Ottomans not only allowed but in fact counted on the autonomous power of the Sanusi for the establishment of their suzerainty in what they envisioned to be a colonial possession. In other words, the Sanusi, from an imperial perspective, was a ruler by proxy, but from the local population's perspective he had unhindered autonomy, which he leveraged to negotiate with imperial power. With this in mind, a few months after the conclusion of the Conference of Berlin, Sadik al-Mouayad Azmzade, landed in Benghazi and then headed south to Jaghbub, the seat of the Sanusi Order's leadership at the time. His mission was to provide Yıldız Palace advisors with an assessment of the possibility of a Sanusi-Ottoman alliance along the empire's African southern frontiers,[30] which depended on the state of relations between the Sanusi Order and Istanbul at the time.

Ottoman-Sanusi Relations on the Eve of Azmzade's First Mission

The state's ability to collect taxes from its subjects is often seen as a measure of its ability to exercise its authority, particularly along the frontiers. In the traditional historiography of the Ottoman Empire, Istanbul's ability (or inability) to enforce tax collection has been weighed disproportionately to demonstrate the empire's strength (or weakness), particularly within the theme of post-seventeenth-century "decline."[31] This becomes particularly true given that historians of the nineteenth-century empire have focused on taxation as a measure of the limits of the state's power and in turn as a means of demarcating the imperial frontiers.[32]

Historians of Ottoman Libya have closely examined the relationship of the Ottoman state with the inhabitants of the Libyan interior using the lens of tax collection and taxation enforcement. In fact, they have assumed that Azmzade's visit could have been about nothing other than an enforcement of tax collection on behalf of the imperial government. Because this relationship of the imperial state with the inhabitants of the Libyan interior is of foundational importance for understanding Istanbul's post-1885 strategies along these frontier regions, I, too, devote some time to taxation and tax collection, about which, I argue, some historians have reached the wrong conclusions. Presenting my findings against those in the literature allows me to explain the heretofore missed dimension of the Ottoman relationship with the inhabitants of the

Libyan interior and, more specifically, the Ottoman-Sanusi relationship on the eve of Azmzade's first visit.

A. S. al-Hourier argues that the Sanusi *zawāyā*, in part, operated as quasi-Ottoman governmental outposts, in certain instances even coordinating tax collection while providing public services in the desert that the Ottoman state provided in the coastal cities. Thus, as the *zawāyā* were being built at a steady rate in the Sahara—reaching at least twenty-one by 1860[33]—their sheikhs, known as *khulafā'*[34] (deputies), acted more or less as proxy administrators for the Ottoman government in often hard to reach areas of the desert.[35] The services that the *zawāyā* provided to the Ottoman state were part of an organically developed agreement that was formalized as early as 1856.

Ahmad Sidqi al-Dajani is one of the first historians to provide archival evidence of early Istanbul-Sanusi relations. He shows that in 1856 the Grand Sanusi sent one of his most important *khulafā'*, the sheikh of the Benghazi *zāwiya*, to Istanbul bearing gifts for the sultan and a letter in which he requested official recognition of the Sufi lodges and properties related to the operation of the lodges as religious charitable foundations (*evkaf/awqāf*).[36] This meant that the *zawāyā* and any income they generated would be exempt from taxation. Sultan Abdülmecid consented, issuing a decree[37] granting it special status as a state-recognized Sufi order, in 1856. Al-Dajani also says that Sultan Abdülaziz (r. 1861–1876) issued a second decree in 1870 reconfirming the first one.[38] Al-Hourier confirms this:

> Official recognition of the order's de facto governmental functions came in the form of two decrees. The first issued in 1856 A.D. by Sultan Abd al-Hamid I, was carried from Istanbul to Wali of Tripoli by Abd al-Rahman al-Maghbub, later the Sheikh of the Sanusiyya *zāwiya* in Benghazi. A second firman, issued by the Sultan Abd al-Majid in 1870 A.D. was brought by Abu al-Qasim al-Isawi, al-Maghbub's successor as head of the *zāwiya* in Benghazi.[39]

There are two factual errors in al-Hourier's statement. First, he says that Sultan Abdülhamid I sent the decree in 1856; however, Abdülhamid I ruled between 1774 and 1789, so the decree must have been issued by Sultan Abdülmecid (r. 1839–1861). Second, he states that the first order (1856) was carried from Istanbul by Sheikh al-Maghbub, which is what al-Dajani claims. However, according to Sadik al-Mouayad Azmzade, this first contact was through an envoy sent by the Grand Sanusi himself, carrying gifts and seeking royal permission to build the first grand *zāwiya* in Jaghbub.[40]

Small factual errors aside, I agree with al-Hourier and al-Dajani that plenty of evidence points to a level of coordination between the Ottoman state and the Sanusi Order. As al-Hourier argues, that there were only minor tax rebellions from the 1850s onward was due in part to the Sanusi Order's endorsement of Ottoman tax collection. In fact, the *khulafāʾ* of the *zawāyā* often accompanied tax collectors on their rounds to provide a cover of legitimacy to the local Bedouin population.[41]

There are some historians who doubt the historical validity of the decrees, and there are others who doubt their impact on relations between the order and the imperial state. In fact, the trend over the past few decades has been to argue that the relationship between Istanbul and the Sanusi Order prior to 1885 was one of struggle by the Ottoman state to enforce its centralized power structure through tax revenue, and that the early acknowledgment of the Sanusi *zawāyā* as charitable foundations and the establishment of an official relationship did not necessarily imply true cooperation. This view of the Sanusi Order as a *ḥaraka*—literally "a movement" that is usually political or activist and in this case anti-imperialist—is overemphasized. For example, despite the decrees of 1856 and 1870 exempting the Sanusi Order from taxes and thus implicitly recognizing its status, al-Hourier insists that the Ottoman-Sanusi relationship was one of mutual suspicion, citing the Tunisian traveler Sheikh Muhammad al-Hashaʾishi (1855–1912): "Mistrust between the Sanusi leadership and Ottoman officials was never absent,"[42] and paraphrasing al-Hashaʾishi: "The Turks [*sic*] were ill disposed toward Sanusi and would like to have dealt with him the way they usually handled important Islamic leaders: giving them a palace in Istanbul and seeing to it that they remained there."[43] Al-Hourier bolsters al-Hashaʾishi's statement by drawing an analogy from the Ottoman government's attitude toward other Sufi leaders, such as Abu al-Huda al-Sayyadi (d. 1909), the head of the Rifaʿiyya Order, Sheikh Zafir al-Madani (d. 1905) of the Madaniyya branch of the Shadhiliyya Order, and Jamal al-Din al-Afghani (d. 1897).[44]

If we examine the evidence presented through a historical lens, cracks in this line of argument appear. First, because al-Hashaʾishi's statement was made in 1896, forty years after the decrees were reportedly issued, his contemporary observations do not necessarily reflect the reality of the earlier period. Second, the various Sufi and "Islamic" leaders whom al-Hourier points to were from a variety of time periods, decades apart in fact, and had different relationships with Yıldız Palace—some with well-documented political ambitions and antagonistic stances toward the caliphate in Istanbul. For these reasons, it is prudent to question this evidence, which gives a distorted picture of the relationship between the Ottoman state and the Sanusi Order,[45] but it is not enough to simply question whether any antagonism existed. It is of fundamental importance to prove that tax revenue was *not* the main concern of Istanbul in the Libyan hinterland. In fact, it is my belief that it was not an issue at all, which goes against much traditional historiography.

Michel Le Gall, an authority on Ottoman-Sanusi relations, argues that they can be explained on the basis of Istanbul's serious fiscal concerns. He contends that provincial governors and special imperial envoys like Azmzade were to sent to enforce tax collection in the Libyan interior, *including* the Sanusi *zawāyā*. In particular, he insists that the increasing contact between the Hamidian administration and the Sanusi Order after 1885 indicates intensification of effort on the part of an increasingly centralized state to collect taxes further along the southern frontiers of its empire.[46]

Le Gall goes further, refuting historical evidence of the *zawāyā*'s tax-exempt status as charitable foundations (*evkaf*). He scrutinizes two of the most referenced historians on the Sanusi Order, al-Dajani (writing in Arabic) and Evans-Pritchard, who say that the Sanusi Order's businesses were tax-exempt by royal decree.[47] "All we have at our disposal," Le Gall claims, "are later renditions of, or references to, the original decree. Given the sensitive and potential controversial nature of the issue at stake, any of these later renditions could easily have been the subject of forgery or an about-face by an interested party."[48] Le Gall takes issue with Evans-Pritchard's belief that the royal decree of 1856 "certainly exempted [the Sanusi Order's] properties from taxation and permitted it to collect a religious tithe from its followers."[49] Similarly, he argues that the evidence that al-Dajani presents is not conclusive.[50]

I have investigated the evidence presented by al-Dajani and Evans-Pritchard, and I find it convincing. Most compelling are excerpts from Azmzade's travelogue written during his mission to Kufra in the Libyan Desert. He states: "In the time of Abdülmecid's rule, after spending some time in Medina, Seyyid Mohammad [the Grand Sanusi] returned to Benghazi, where he sent one of his followers, Sheikh al-'Isawi Efendi, to Istanbul and got him to receive royal permission and decree for the establishing and building of *zawāyā* in appropriate places in the *sancak* of Benghazi."[51] Yet Le Gall argues that because this statement does not explicitly state the content of the decree, we cannot be sure that it included tax exemption. In any case, we certainly do not need to rely exclusively on the evidence presented by al-Dajani and Evans-Pritchard. I have uncovered other archival evidence that is quite explicit.

In 1889 the British consul in Benghazi, Donald Cameron, in a memorandum to the Foreign Office in London, reported on the financial status of the Sanusi leader. He wrote that the leader had no personal wealth of his own and that he lived with his family off the sale of produce grown on land belonging to the *zawāyā* as well as donations from Sanusi Bedouins. As charitable organizations, Cameron noted, the *zawāyā* were tax exempt,[52] which confirms what Evans-Pritchard and al-Dajani reported. Moreover, in a document in the Ottoman Archives in Istanbul from 1906, the local governor in Benghazi asked for clarifications on the applicability of the tax exemption and instructions on how to respond to complaints by some *khulafā'* who refused to pay taxes based on an old decree. The governor explained that a *khalīfa* of a Sanusi *zawāyā* had recently come to him, armed with a copy of an old decree, complaining about attempts to collect taxes from the *zawāyā* and *zawāyā*-related properties that were causing violent clashes with the local Bedouin.[53] In answer to the governor's inquiry, the Meclis-i Vükela[54] (Council of Ministers) ruled that the old decrees had indeed rendered all Sanusi *zawāyā* built during the lifetime of the Grand Sanusi as religious charitable foundations and thus were tax exempt, but anything beyond that, including the personal property of individuals or tribesmen affiliated with the Sanusi *zawāyā*, should be subject to taxation.[55] With this evidence, we can be fairly certain that the tax-exempt status of the Sanusi Order well into the early twentieth century is indisputable, allowing us to reopen the file of Azmzade's visit to the Sanusi without preconceived ideas.

The First Mission to the Sahara

At the end of 1885, Sadik (Bey)[56] al-Mouayad Azmzade was trusted with the time-sensitive task of assessing al-Mahdi al-Sanusi's position vis-à-vis Istanbul's plans for forwarding its colonial claim to the Sahara with the full knowledge that it was competing with Paris and London to win the favor of this important ally. Few records of this early mission exist, with the exception of two reports written by Azmzade himself on his return to Istanbul that shed valuable light on the Ottoman perspective on colonialism in Africa and the role it envisaged for Muhammad al-Mahdi al-Sanusi.[57]

Muhammad al-Mahdi al-Sanusi (1844–1901), to whom I refer (as the majority of the literature on the Sanusi Order does) by the name of al-Mahdi al-Sanusi, was born in the small village of Masa in Jabal al-Akhdar, which was close to al-Bayda', the site of the first North African Sanusi *zāwiya*.[58] The eldest son of the Grand Sanusi, as well as his designated successor, he is credited with rapidly expanding the political power and reach of the order, prompting some Libyan nationalist historians to portray him as the father of the modern Libyan state.[59] At the time of Azmzade's visit in early 1886, al-Mahdi al-Sanusi had yet to produce a male heir, designating his nephew Muhammad al-Sayyid Ahmad al-Sharif (d. 1933) as his successor. Ahmad al-Sharif would eventually lead local military resistance against French and later Italian colonialism with the help of the Ottoman military beginning in 1902.[60] Al-Mahdi al-Sanusi eventually produced two male children, the eldest of whom was Muhammad Idris al-Mahdi al-Sanusi (1890–1983), the future king of the short-lived Kingdom of Libya.[61]

It is said that the transfer of leadership to al-Mahdi al-Sanusi was the Grand Sanusi's personal wish. However, it did not take place immediately after the latter's passing in 1859 because al-Mahdi al-Sanusi was only fifteen years of age, causing a minor interruption in the succession. During this transitional period, a council of community leaders, who had helped the Grand Sanusi run the order, oversaw day-to-day affairs until al-Mahdi al-Sanusi was ready to take the reins.[62] In the meantime, the Grand Sanusi's companion, a man by the name of ʿAmran, looked after the Grand Sanusi's two wives and his two underage sons, Muhammad al-Mahdi and his younger brother Muhammad al-Sharif (not to be confused with a nephew of the same name mentioned earlier).[63]

In his report to Yıldız Palace, Azmzade described the reach of al-Mahdi al-Sanusi's political and religious influence over the region's Bedouin population as extending far south into the Sudan and the Lake Chad basin. Many sought his friendship and blessing, including the Egyptian khedive Ismail (r. 1863–1879), who sent him gifts as a sign of his respect and friendship.[64] But we need not rely on Azmzade's words alone for a sense of al-Mahdi al-Sanusi's power. His success is evidenced by the accelerated expansion of the order's zawāyā, starting when he assumed the leadership, which reflected the order's rising regional religious and political clout. The biggest concentration of zawāyā was in Cyrenaica, with a total of forty-five, followed by Egypt with thirty-one, Tripolitania with eighteen, the Hijaz with seventeen, Fezzan with fifteen, Kufra with six, and Sudan with one. These were in addition to the fourteen zawāyā spread throughout central Africa.[65]

Azmzade emphasized that the mission was also successful in the Arabian Desert:

> From the beginning, the late Ahmed bin İdris, with the help of deputies and followers of the Sanusi, have spread the order beyond the city's inhabitants,

reaching out to Bedouin tribes in the desert, many of whom (like the people of Beni Harb and Beni el-Haris) have joined the Order, along with many pilgrims of various orders coming annually from different corners of the world. This way, Sanusi branches spread in Arabia with unusual speed, especially along the coasts of the Hijaz and Yemen.[66]

Azmzade's claims are corroborated by a request from the British Foreign Office in 1889 for an estimate of the reach of the Sanusi Order along the empire's Arabian frontiers in the province of Hijaz. London, much like Istanbul, having taken notice of the order's widespread influence on the Bedouins of the Libyan interior and the eastern Sahara, began to assess the influence of the order even in other territories inhabited by Bedouin tribes. Consul Cecil Wood in Jeddah—who had previously been stationed in Benghazi—assured London that, even though the order's influence was well established in the Hijaz, it was nowhere near what it was in the Libyan Desert and the eastern Sahara. As in the Libyan interior, he said, most Sanusi followers were not in the main cities of the province of Hijaz but rather among the tribesmen who lived along the desert caravan routes. Compared to Ottoman Libya, the number of Hijazi adherents was small but spread evenly among the various clans: "Altogether, the followers of the Senoossia in the Hedjaz may be roughly estimated to be about 2000—They follow the Shar' here as elsewhere very strictly but are not considered of any political importance in these parts."[67]

Interestingly, however, the local Sanusi *khalīfa* was an urbanite from the town of Ta'if who resided in Mecca, the seat of the Ottoman provincial government of the Hijaz. In other words, although adherents of the order were mostly Bedouins, the sheikh of the *zāwiya*, Sheikh al-Sanusi bin Sheikh Hamid Khaira, felt secure enough with the local Ottoman administration to reside in Mecca with other members of the Hijazi elites. This is yet another indication that members of the order as well as its leadership maintained cordial relations, even in the Hijaz, with the Ottoman authorities. According to Wood, "They [the Sanusi followers] would not rise against the Turks [sic] if ordered to do so because the sultan is tacitly acknowledged to be the Caliph."[68]

On this point, Azmzade filed a report on his return from his mission to the Sahara in which he made an impassioned plea to consider al-Mahdi al-Sanusi a political ally of the Ottoman state. He vehemently refuted reports by European journalists and diplomats about al Mahdi al-Sanusi's anti-Ottoman designs, believing that the local population was well aware of the dangers of the encroaching European powers and strongly supported Muslim unity:

> The reality is that because of the guidance of Sheikh Muhammad al-Mahdi, all of the people of North Africa, particularly the Bedouin tribes, with pride and zeal for being Muslim, set out in a unified fashion on the noble path to protect Islam. The Bedouin tribes' aim is to incite fear and anxiety in the maliciously greedy [*garaz-kar olan*] France, Italy, England, and Spain. Since these countries have repeatedly tried to win over the aforementioned sheikh [Sanusi] but again and again have failed, are now trying to make him fall in the eye of the Sublime Porte [ruin his reputation], and through many slanderous publications and letters full made up facts want to portray him as a harmful man. Till today the newspapers continue to advance such [slanderous] screaming proclamations. The truth of the matter is that the aforementioned sheikh [Sanusi] is a hard working leader, and along with the [Ottoman] government will be a bearer of hope and inspiration for Muslims.[69]

Azmzade's report, written on the heels of the Conference of Berlin, makes it evident that this early trip was meant to assess the Sanusi Order as strategic partner in establishing an Ottoman claim to the area, as well the start of a more serious alliance between the order and the empire. Two points were emphasized. The first was the reach of the Sanusi Order—geographically and demographically; the second was the loyalty of the order to the sultan as the caliph of the Muslim world. Because Istanbul was trying to claim effective control over the land, al-Mahdi al-Sanusi's loyalty to the sultan and his official agreement with its objective was of the utmost importance. The local inhabitants' acknowledgment of Istanbul's authority was central to the argument it presented to its European counterparts that the Ottoman government had already effectively extended suzerainty across this region. In the language of interimperial negotiations terms, the empire claimed this area as a legitimate and legal colony, with its sphere of influence firmly established on the ground, albeit by proxy.

The importance of the Sanusi Order in the competition over central Africa was not lost on the Great Powers. After all, its followers controlled the area between the French sphere of influence in the western Sahara and the English sphere of influence in the Nile Valley and East Africa, which was invaluable to the competing empires. Thus, while Azmzade was meeting with al-Mahdi al-Sanusi in Jaghbub to discuss how the Ottoman government could win his support, the European powers were trying to understand the order's power in the region and find ways to harness it or at least minimize the threat it posed to their interests.

Until 1884, most of what Europeans knew about the Sanusi Order came from explorers and travel writers, who had created its hard-to-shake image as a "black legend." For up-to-date information that would be useful in foreign policy making, the British government turned yet again to its man on the spot, Cecil Wood.

Wood described al-Mahdi al-Sanusi as enjoying "unparalleled" prominence in the Muslim world among "Musulmen and ignorant Arab tribes" from Morocco to central Asia. He also warned that the brand of Islam that al-Mahdi al-Sanusi preached was very stringent, anti-Christian, and particularly anti-European, and that this anti-European message resounded with both moderate and conservative Muslims, who were feeling the encroaching European threat and looking for a leader who would help them resist European colonialism.[70] In these early reports, there was no suspicion that al-Mahdi al-Sanusi had any military power to be concerned about. However, his religious and political power, which was a very real threat to British and French imperial interests, was the same power that Istanbul wanted to capitalize on.

European spies were well aware of Azmzade's visit as well; however, they mistakenly saw it as representing a "sudden interest" in the Sanusi Order on Istanbul's part, discounting decades of interaction between the leaders of the order and the previous sultans. Thus, British consul Cecil Wood wrote in 1889:

> Sultans Abdul Mejid and Abdul Aziz took no notice of him [al-Sanusi]. Of late years, the present sultan has sent him flattering letters to which Senousi returns polite answers. Last year Sadık Bey took a present to Senousi, and more recently five chests containing presents were forwarded to Jaghbub. . . . Senousi sent two Korans and two rosaries, and a burnous worn by himself [to the sultan].

Even though Wood's analysis of the background of Ottoman-Sanusi relations points to major blind spots in British intelligence services, reading his reports against the grain allows us an insight into London's perception of the Ottoman government's investment in Africa at the time.[71] As the man burdened with providing an "expert" assessment of what appeared to the British to be sudden Ottoman interest in the Sanusi Order, Wood offered two possible explanations. First, he suspected that the sultan "may be fearful of losing Tripoli and Bengazi; he may desire to unite the Arabs under the Senousi and to show them that Senousi regarded him as Caliph." The Sanusi Order, according to Wood, was the way to reach "an Arab population" in the African provinces. He made no distinction between the Arabic-speaking population of the cities, who were firmly under Ottoman control, and the Bedouins of the desert, who were not. Nevertheless, he managed to explicate what he believed to be the potential benefit that a political alliance between the sultan and al-Mahdi al-Sanusi would have for Istanbul. Al-Mahdi al-Sanusi's recognition of the Ottoman sultan as the legitimate caliph would in turn solidify the legitimacy of Ottoman rule in the eyes of the local population of the Libyan hinterland.[72]

Wood also proposed a second explanation for why the sultan approached al-Mahdi al-Sanusi. He suspected that "in [the sultan's] difficulties with Grand Shereef of Mecca, who is jealous of Senousi, it may be advisable to support Senousi as rival."[73] Drawing a parallel between the leader of the Bedouins in the eastern Sahara and the amir of Mecca in western Arabia (who was often referred to as the grand sharif in British documents) must have been tempting, but it was incorrect. Both were Ottoman-recognized local leaders with much regional political and religious clout, but that is where the similarities end. Whereas al-Sanusi had built his political capital by garnering the support and following of the local nomadic and seminomadic populations from the bottom up, the grand sherif's power came from the top down, with an imperial decree appointing him the amir of Mecca coupled with the legitimacy provided by his bloodline as a member of a Meccan sherifan family. In simple terms, the sultan's authority in the eastern Sahara and the Libyan Desert depended on the legitimization of the Sanusi leadership whereas the amir needed the legitimization of the sultan in western Arabia. Therefore, Wood's assumption that the amir was the leader of the local Bedouin population led him to the wrong conclusions, particularly because he assumed that the Bedouin populations in Africa and Arabia were the same and that their relationships to the local leadership were the same. Indeed, he assumed that the Bedouins across continents were of one mind. This was a common mistake made by many European diplomats and orientalists. Wood moreover made the classic blunder of categorizing locals based on the perception of ethnicity, so to him "the Arabs" of the Ottoman Empire were a single undifferentiated constituency that theoretically could be represented by a single leader, whether the amir in Mecca or al-Mahdi al-Sanusi in Jaghbub.[74]

Where Wood was right, however, was in drawing attention to the transimperial nature of the threat that the Ottoman Empire was facing along its southern frontiers. He understood that the southern frontiers of the Ottoman Empire were vulnerable and that Sultan Abdülhamid II needed the cooperation of the local Bedouin population whether in the Libyan hinterland or in western Arabia.

Conclusion

As the scramble for Africa heated up, the previously marginal territories of central Africa moved to the center stage of negotiations. Just as the Ottomans had identified the Sanusi Order as a key to the region, the British and the French kept a close eye on al-Mahdi al-Sanusi, assessing his popularity and political leanings and attempting to understand what they perceived as Istanbul's sudden interest in him. The Bedouin populations on either side of the Red Sea were crucial to the success or failure of the Ottoman Empire. Archival evidence from the 1880s, both Ottoman and British, suggests that even though the order had some presence in the cities in North Africa and the Hijaz, the vast majority of its followers were Bedouins in the Libyan interior, the eastern Sahara, and western Arabia.

The geographic reach of the Sanusi network was very long, but its main concentration remained in Cyrenaica and the border regions near Egypt and south to Lake Chad. It operated in Ottoman-controlled areas and—more important from a late nineteenth-century colonial perspective—in an Ottoman self-identified sphere of influence. The British were well aware of this and often tried to woo the local population to their side with gifts once they realized they could not gain the loyalty of the Sanusi himself. However, they were not aware of the lengths to which the Hamidian regime was willing to go to hold on to the Libyan provinces, gain the loyalty of the Bedouin population, and expand the empire's claim to the eastern Sahara.

3 THE DIPLOMATIC FIGHT FOR OTTOMAN AFRICA

The Bedouins are taught that their obedience and love for the eternally sublime Ottoman government, along with their obedience and love for the Prophet, are part of their duties as prescribed by the mind and Islamic Law. Similarly, they are advised that they should show respect and obedience to the representatives of the Ottoman government. In addition, when they learn of the Europeans' intentions and desired objectives [*menviyat-ı efkar ve matamih-i enzar*], they [the Bedouins] never gravitate towards them. [Thus], when the French and Italian government sent gifts to the Sanusi, he did not accept them. These valuable gifts were politely rejected by his deputy in Benghazi, the late Sheikh Abdurrahim Efendi, and they then were taken back to the respective countries' Benghazi consulates.

Sadik al-Mouayad Azmzade, Kufra, Wednesday, November 6, 1895

AS THE EUROPEAN COMPETITION for Africa heated up, the Sanusi Order took on greater political and strategic importance for both the Ottoman Empire and the European powers. This chapter extends the inquiry into the scramble for Africa to include an expanded list of competitors vying for control of the eastern Sahara. In addition to Britain and France, Italy and the (Sudanese) Mahdist state now played a substantial role in determining the fate of Ottoman interests. The heightened threats to these interests necessitated a two-track approach by Istanbul. The first was the cultivation of the Ottoman-Sanusi political alliance coupled with the creation of a secret Ottoman-Sanusi military front by channeling Ottoman weapons and ammunition to Sanusi *zawāyā*. The second was a more aggressive diplomatic posture toward the empire's European counterparts. This chapter discusses the trials and tribulations of Ottoman diplomats, international legal advisors, and men on the spot who were fighting for the empire's position in the global struggle for territories and recognition between 1887 and 1895.

The Plot Thickens: Threats from Near and Far

Following the Conference of Berlin, the Hamidian government saw an opportunity to capitalize on the Sanusi's unique influence over the Bedouins of the Libyan hinterland and the Sanusi Order's reach deep into the eastern Sahara. While Azmzade was on a secret mission to Muhammad al-Mahdi al-Sanusi, head of the Sanusi Order, a new front in the competition for the region was to open from an unexpected direction. Just southeast of the Libyan Desert, Mahdist dervish[1] troops in eastern Sudan were on the move west toward Wadai and being closely watched by British and Ottoman men on the ground.[2] Examining al-Mahdi al-Sanusi's intervention in this conflict illuminates the extent of his political power and reveals the first signs of an Ottoman-Sanusi united front. Before delving into the events of 1888–1889, I will provide a brief explanation of the suggestive and often confusing middle name of Muhammad al-Mahdi al-Sanusi and its relation to the "awaited Mahdi" (al-Mahdi al-Muntazar)—the Muslim messiah.[3]

According to Ahmad al-Sharif, al-Mahdi al-Sanusi's nephew, the Grand Sanusi had a premonition that his eldest son might be the awaited *Mahdi*. The story goes that al-Baskariyya, the Grand Sanusi's wife, asked him why he decided to name his son al-Mahdi. He answered with a play on words: "I hope that he would receive all kinds of gifts [jamī* anwā* al-hadāyā] and we pray to God that He makes him a guide [hādiyan] and be well-guided [mahdiyyan]."[4] British consular reports in the 1880s, in explaining the success of the Sanusi Order, attributed much of al-Mahdi al-Sanusi's wide support to his perceived "sanctity."[5] For example, in 1889 Donald Cameron, the British consul in Benghazi, sent a memorandum to the Foreign Office detailing the activities of al-Mahdi al-Sanusi, in which he repeated the story of the Grand Sanusi's anointing of his son the awaited Mahdi and his successor.[6] In a subsequent report, however, he corrected himself, stating that al-Mahdi al-Sanusi was in no way equal to the Sudanese Mahdi and that his name was just that, a name given to him by his father.[7] Al-Mahdi al-Sanusi himself publicly denied being the awaited Mahdi, at one point stating, "I have been told that there are those that have been spreading such a myth" and asking his followers to do all they could to combat this rumor.[8] This repeated denial of sanctity had not only a dogmatic importance but also a significant political meaning because it was in direct conversation with the Mahdist state to the east of the Libyan interior and the Ottoman government's stance toward the Sudanese Mahdi's claims.

Al-Mahdi al-Sanusi's relationship with the Mahdist state went back a few years before 1888. Substantial evidence suggests that Muhammad Ahmad al-Mahdi of Sudan had courted him with the aim of presenting a united front against European imperialism and what he considered the "infidel Turks," which in his terms referred indiscriminately, and with little ethno-linguistic differentiation, to Ottoman imperial forces whether from Istanbul or Cairo.[9]

Al-Mahdi al-Sanusi vociferously rejected the Sudanese Mahdi's religious claims and jihadist philosophy. He also rejected his offer of becoming the Sudanese Mahdi's khalīfa,[10] stating, "I am not even worthy of the dust which got into the nose of the horse that 'Uthman[11]—the blessings of God be upon him— rode in raids accompanying the Prophet—peace be upon him—and thus I have no answer to his letter," sending al-Mahdi's messenger on his way with a clear rejection of the Sudanese Madhi's offer disguised in poetic, self-effacing language.[12] In 1888 Ahmad al-Mahdi's successor sent al-Mahdi al-Sanusi "an invitation for a war of jihad against the infidels," which was also quickly rejected.[13] Al-Mahdi al-Sanusi's anti-Mahdist state views were in line with those of the Ottoman government, which condemned al-Mahdi's religious claims and the aggressive stance of the Mahdist state toward its neighbors.

The Mahdist state's hostility toward "the Turks" was returned, and policy makers and advisors in Istanbul kept a watchful eye on its movements in geopolitically sensitive East Africa. Istanbul's animosity is illuminated by the documented interrogation of a prominent Meccan merchant by Ottoman intelligence officers on his return from Khartoum in 1888.

The questioners, looking for clues to the strength of al-Mahdi's movement and its indigenous support, grilled Sharif Muhammad bin Abdullah al-Madani as though he were returning from behind enemy lines. Al-Madani, who had lived in Khartoum for fifteen years, gave them the impression that the people's only choice was to declare their allegiance to Ahmad al-Mahdi. When asked about the original mission of Muhammad Ahmad elmütemehdi (pretender to Mahdisim)—as Ottoman official documents dismissively refer to him—al-Madani said that it was to eventually take control of Sudan and Egypt and then the Hijaz.[14] What one can discern from the style and language of this interrogation is Ottoman suspicion of the Mahdist state. In fact, it would not be hard to guess that Sultan Abdülhamid II personally viewed Ahmad al-Mahdi as a thorn in the side of the Ottoman Empire, often describing him in terms such as "rebel," "bandit," and "vermin," and compared him to 'Urabi Pasha as another troublemaker. From Istanbul's perspective, al-Mahdi had created the internal instability in the Sudan that the British used as an excuse to maintain their hold on East Africa, and was a menace to the empire's allies in Africa, whether Ethiopia to the south or Wadai to the west.[15] Azmzade called the Sudanese Mahdi *elmütemehdi* and described his army as "thugs," "barbarians," and "enemies" of the empire and its allies.[16]

Like their Ottoman counterparts, British diplomats were closely watching the movements of the Mahdist state when they learned of dervish forces assembled in Darfur with the intention of retaking the Sultanate of Wadai, an ally of the Sanusi Order and the Ottoman Empire.[17] The famous Rabih Fadl Allah al-Zubair (1835–1900), a former slave of a vassal of the Egyptian khedive in Sudan and a self-declared supporter of the Mahdist state, was now the caliph of a predatory state that directly and indirectly ruled over a large part of the Sudan.[18]

In 1888 Sultan Muhammad Yusuf bin Muhammad Sharif of Wadai (r. 1874–1898) wrote to al-Mahdi al-Sanusi asking for both military support against the dervish army and spiritual guidance.[19] According to British consul Donald Cameron, instead of sending soldiers or material support, al-Mahdi al-Sanusi sent messengers to the two warring parties. The first, to Sultan Yusuf of Wadai, stated, "Fear not; if the dervishes are true Moslems they will not attack you. If they are false Moslems they cannot prevail against you."[20] The second, to the recently appointed Mahdist governor of Darfur, the battle-hardened ʿUthman Adam,[21] was a thinly disguised threat that, if the dervish army would not stand down immediately, al-Mahdi al-Sanusi would come to Darfur in person. According to Cameron, ʿUthman Adam held the sanctity of al-Mahdi al-Sanusi in such high regard that out of respect for his authority decided to abandon his mission.[22] Whether or not this account reported what actually took place, it demonstrates the fear and spiritual anxiety that al-Mahdi al-Sanusi invoked, even in his powerful neighbors and enemies.

What we now know is that ʿUthman Adam received an order in April 1889 to demobilize his troops, but whether al-Mahdi al-Sanusi's threat was behind this order is hard to determine. In 1890 ʿUthman Adam invaded Dar Masalit in search of grain for his troops, but failed in this mission because of a cholera outbreak.[23] Borno succumbed to Mahdist troops in 1893 and remained under Rabih's rule until the French invasion of 1900 and the subsequent British occupation of Borno in 1902.[24]

Azmzade reserved a special description for Rabih's army as part unbelievers (*dinsiz*) and part Muslims and estimated it to be 15,000 Bedouins strong, "which he collected from places he had gone through." Azmzade had to reach deep into the history of the Muslim world to find a character ruthless enough to suit the situation. "Like the Tatar Tamerlane," he concluded, "Rabih captured as booty women, men, and children from every settlement he entered and they were driven with him to the next place he was heading. There is nothing to be admired about this kind of treatment of respectable people."[25]

European Reassessments of the Sanusi Order's Power

Continual reassurances that al-Mahdi al-Sanusi's power stemmed exclusively from his status as a spiritual figure failed to calm the fears of the European powers already entrenched on either side of the territory that he controlled. On several occasions, the British, looking for a material reason for al-Mahdi al-Sanusi's power, received reports of secret shipments of weapons to him, but these were always corrected by subsequent reports. British representatives in Benghazi writing to the British ambassador in Istanbul and the Foreign Office in London struggled to explain a notion of power that was hard to grasp and thus harder to combat. Al-Mahdi al-Sanusi's power was not primarily military or economic; rather, it derived from his ability to parlay his religious status into regional political power, which extended well beyond the walls of his *zawāyā*.[26]

In 1889 London asked for yet another assessment of the Sanusi Order's military power and its designs on Khartoum. In his usual confident tone, Cameron advised that al-Mahdi al-Sanusi was more interested in Algeria and Tunisia than in Egypt. That is, his orientation was toward the Maghreb and not the Nile Valley, and thus it was the French and not the British who had reason to be concerned. Cameron's final advice was that, because al-Mahdi al-Sanusi posed no immediate threat to British interests in the Nile Valley, London should not "stoop" to engage him in negotiations.[27]

Cameron's assessment was only partially correct; al-Mahdi al-Sanusi had no intention of marching on Khartoum—that much is true. However, the British consul was wrong on two counts. First, as we see in the following section, Cameron greatly underestimated al-Mahdi al-Sanusi's military power: even though he was not interested in a territorial grab, he would not hesitate to take defensive measures when the time came to fight European aggression. Second, al-Mahdi al-Sanusi might have sympathized with the Muslim people of Algeria and Tunisia suffering under French colonial occupation, but his attention, like that of the Ottoman Empire at the time, was oriented not to the west but due south, toward the eastern Sahara and Lake Chad. As early as 1887, al-Mahdi al-Sanusi was well aware of the secret negotiations under way between the European powers, especially France and Italy, over the fate of the eastern Sahara and the Lake Chad basin. These negotiations were early warning signs for both the Ottoman Empire and the Sanusi Order of what was to come, and they helped to bring the two closer.

Even though the Italians did not invade Ottoman Libya until 1911, Istanbul was already aware of Italian colonial ambitions in 1887, when a secret agreement between Italy, the Austro-Hungarian Empire, and Germany gave Rome, in principle, the green light to occupy Tripolitania and Cyrenaica at some point in the future.[28] That same year, the Ottoman Embassy in Rome and informants on the ground in East Africa confirmed increased Italian military activity in Massawa, a city on the Red Sea coast that had been under khedival rule and thus had been a nominal part of the Ottoman Empire before 1885.[29]

Attacks across the Tunisia-Tripolitania borderland, this time from Tunisia to Tripolitania, by French-armed Tunisian tribesmen,[30] along with reports of secret Italian designs on the Libyan hinterland, prompted al-Mahdi al-Sanusi to request Ottoman military support. Officially, Istanbul refused to send aid, fearing that crucial diplomatic channels with its European counterparts would suffer.[31] However, contrary to Cameron's confident 1889 reports, the Ottoman government had begun to smuggle weapons and ammunition to Bedouin tribes under the leadership of al-Mahdi al-Sanusi as early as 1888.[32] In fact, French intelligence reported that a *zāwiya* had been built in Derna, a port city east of Benghazi, for use as a depot for storing weapons and ammunition being transferred across the desert to Jaghbub.[33]

Similarly, in 1889 the British consul in Tripoli, General F. Drummond-Hay, reported his concern that the Ottoman governor might try to recruit Sanusi-led Bedouin tribesmen to ward off attacks by the French and Italians in the Libyan interior. Soon after, Cameron, again confidently but also mistakenly refuted Hay's reports, assuring London that military cooperation between the Sanusi and Istanbul was not a realistic possibility.[34] One reason for Cameron's confidence may have been the constant reassurance of his informant, a Sanusi *khalīfa* in Benghazi named Sheikh Zuitani. Zuitani's consistent message was that al-Mahdi al-Sanusi and his followers despised "the Turks" and were "friends to the British."[35] A look back allows us to be skeptical of this statement, which points to the possibility that Sheikh Zuitani was delivering false information to the British.

In the two years immediately after Azmzade's mission to Jaghbub, 1887 to 1889, the Ottoman Empire's African spheres of influence came under attack, testing the strength of the Ottoman-Sanusi partnership. Whether it was the Mahdist state in Wadai, the Italians in Massawa, or early signs of Italian and French interests in the eastern Sahara, these years were a turning point for the partnership, changing it from a growing political relationship to a secret united military front. Perhaps the most pointed comment about the relationship between the imperial government and the order during this time came from Sultan Abdülhamid II. He wrote: "If the Sanusis decide to fight, they will force the Italians into a bloody war far worse than the war of the Mahdi of Sudan [against the English]. We have provided the Sanusis with sufficient weapons and cannons and this makes them a redoubtable enemy to be taken seriously."[36] Istanbul was careful to keep the channels of diplomacy with its European counterparts open. However, 1890–1895 would prove beyond any doubt the utter ineffectiveness of the Ottoman Empire on the European diplomatic stage.

1890: A Bad Year for Ottoman Diplomacy

On August 12, 1890, the Ottoman ambassador in Paris reported that negotiations were taking place between Great Britain and France to reach a bilateral agreement on the two empires' respective spheres of influence in Africa and to delineate the borders of their "protectorates," particularly in central Africa. These negotiations were of particular importance to Istanbul because in part they concerned the Central African Kingdoms in the Lake Chad basin: Borno-Kanem, Bagirmi, and Wadai. The British and the French agreed that the area south and west of the basin would be a French sphere of influence, subsuming Kanem, Wadai, and Bagirmi, and that a part of Borno would go to the British. France envisioned a united French colonial territory stretching from North Africa to the Sudan and the Guinea coast.[37]

The Central African Kingdoms were socially and economically tied to Ottoman Libya (indeed, some historians have gone so far as to classify all of them as tributary states of the empire[38]), a connection facilitated in large measure by the Sanusi Order. In this regard, the British-French agreement sent a clear message to Istanbul: land that it claimed as its own based on the rules of the 1885 Act of Berlin—from Libya's Mediterranean coast south to the Lake Chad basin—was to be divided up without Ottoman consultation.[39] The exclusion of Istanbul raised the ire of the sultan, who in response considered and deployed a variety of diplomatic and tactical options.

The Ottoman ambassador to London conveyed the sultan's protest to Lord Salisbury, the British prime minister. Couched in the language of the General

Act of Berlin, his complaint was that the British-French agreement infringed on the rights of the Ottoman government to its own colonies (*müstemlekat*). The original word "province" (*eyalet*) had been scratched out and replaced with "colonies" in the official communiqués—a signal that Istanbul was trying to adjust to a new language when defending its claim to territories in Africa against its European counterparts. These colonial possessions included Wadai, Borno, Kanem and Bagirmi, the subjects of the Franco-British agreement of 1890. In contrast, the language of partnership and unity against encroaching colonialism was used when Ottoman involvement in central Africa was discussed with the Sanusi Order.

I am not suggesting that the Ottomans were playing a game of words. On the contrary, like their European counterparts at the time, they understood that arguments and justifications for expansion differed at different levels of negotiation. Good negotiators, international law experts, advisors, and others involved in crafting and implementing Ottoman strategy understood that the right discursive register had to be employed based on the intended audience, and that the appropriate terminology was fundamental in any successful negotiations.

In response to Ottoman protests, Lord Salisbury sent vaguely worded assurances to the sultan, stating that the British government would protect the interests of the Ottoman Empire but not specifying how the sultan's grievances over colonial territorial claims would be addressed.[40] Perhaps what was not being said spoke louder than what was. An incident almost comical in its absurdity highlights this possibility. While the Ottoman ambassador Rüstem Pasha was waiting in an adjacent office to meet with Lord Salisbury over this very issue, he came across a hand-drawn map of Africa—unintentionally left out on a desk—which he later learned had been drawn up in Rome, marking the possessions of each colonial power with a different color. For Rüstem Pasha, the map's implications were much broader than the depicted territorial claims in the Lake Chad basin. In his words, the area supposedly "under the rule of the Ottoman government around Lake Chad had already been colored to indicate French rule." This episode is a telling example of the pacification of the Ottoman government with empty promises while decisions were being made behind closed doors. Of course, the record shows that Istanbul was well aware of what was taking place but was forced to keep appearances up and diplomatic channels open.[41]

Following this incident, Rüstem Pasha delivered a more strongly worded protest to the British Foreign Office: the Ottoman government would not stand still and allow Borno to be considered part of the British sphere of influence. He reiterated that Borno was directly tied to the Ottoman Empire though its historical and economic ties with the Libyan provinces, and that Istanbul considered it an integral part of the Libyan hinterland.[42] To this protest, the French and British responses were much more direct. The French government assured Istanbul that the French parliament confirmed the Ottoman right to rule Tripolitania but considered the disputed territory to be outside direct Ottoman rule and strongly disagreed with Istanbul's claim to the Lake Chad basin as part of the Libyan hinterland. The French minister, Alexandre Ribot, even claimed that what constituted a hinterland was up for debate, especially because, he said, the German word *hinterland* was not inherently clear. This supposed lack of clarity was often used to explain why the borders of zones of influence were always up for negotiation. Similarly, the British embassy staff in Istanbul told an Ottoman official that they were ignorant of the German language and so could neither debate the meaning of words such as *hinterland* nor comment on the validity of Ottoman claims.[43]

Was the disagreement between British and Ottoman officials really about a foreign word? Of course not. Rather, it was a demonstration that the vague wording of certain articles of the Act of Berlin had been designed to keep the options of the Great Powers open—open for debate and open for their interpretation. The failure of Ottoman diplomatic protests and grievances made it painfully clear to many in Istanbul that facts on the ground were now more important than international agreements.

For example, in a report to Yıldız Palace, military advisor Ferik Şakir Pasha enclosed an Ottoman-Turkish duplicate of a recently produced French map that confirmed what Rüstem Pasha had seen in London, accompanied by a detailed explanation that highlighted the changes in political boundaries and zones of influence expected in Africa during the year 1890 (Figure 5). The map showed the possessions of the Ottoman Empire and the various European empires, as stipulated in the British-French bilateral agreement. The Libyan hinterland, with the exception of the Lake Chad basin, was represented as unclaimed (uncolored) territory, part of which the French were to occupy in the coming year.

Şakir Pasha pleaded with the palace to take immediate action to defend its claim to this territory, particularly because the majority of its inhabitants were Muslims.[44] However, by the end of 1890, after a year of fruitless negotiations over the Lake Chad basin, the French government had become unwilling to

negotiate any further, turning its attention to issues that Paris deemed more relevant. One of these issues was the drawing of a permanent border between French Tunisia and Ottoman Tripolitania[45] and another was to negotiate authority over the trade caravan routes from the Lake Chad basin to the Mediterranean. From the standpoint of France, the taking of areas west and south of Lake Chad was a fait accompli.[46] Istanbul, however, was not yet willing to concede defeat despite the apparent failure of Ottoman diplomacy.[47]

News: The Libyan Hinterland Makes the Papers
In the 1890s, debate over the Libyan hinterland spilled over from private diplomatic negotiations to the public arenas of the international press. As Europe's diplomatic relationship with the Ottoman Empire soured, the popular press took up the competition for the eastern Sahara and presented it to the reading public, from Paris to Washington, couched through the language of perpetually impending "jihad."[48] For example, on August 5, 1892, the Oriental Telegraph Agency of Paris printed a false report that Muslims in central Africa were preparing to declare jihad on Christians who lived there, allegedly on the order of the amir of Mecca,[49] Sharif ʿAwn al-Rafiq. ʿAwn al-Rafiq, in a telegram to Yıldız Palace, emphatically denied these reports filtering in from the Western press, describing them as false and slanderous (iftirāʾ) and meant to cause harm to his relationship with Istanbul.[50]

Other news outlets speculated about Ottoman efforts to increase the sultan's influence in Africa through Muslim missionaries. For example, on July 1, 1894, the Ottoman embassy in Washington sent a report to Istanbul about a news item in the New York Mail and Express claiming that Sultan Abdülhamid II was personally funding missionaries sent to convert locals in Africa. The Presbyterian mission replied to these reports with skepticism, stating that it had not heard of any such missionaries per se from their men on the ground. The closest thing to a corroboration of the story was a statement from Rev. Dr. John Gellespie, secretary of the Presbyterian Board of Foreign Missions: "Five years ago some Mohammadan missionaries were sent out from Turkey and Persia, the two strongest Mohammadan nations, to preach Islamism, but usually Mohammadan missionaries are armed with sword and gun . . . possibly the Sultan is alarmed over the spread of Christianity."[51]

Fear that the Ottoman Empire might lead Muslims in Africa against European colonial encroachment was not just of interest to readers in the West. It was increasingly the topic of newspaper editorials in the empire's two largest cities, Istanbul and Cairo. Yıldız Palace agents kept a close watch on what was being printed within the empire's borders.[52] One story, in the Egyptian daily *al-Qahira al-Hurra*, is a case in point, providing insight into the terms in which the scramble for Africa was being discussed in the Ottoman press.

The front-page story on the role of Christian—particularly Jesuit—missionaries in furthering French colonial interests reported on a contract between the French government and a highly devoted army of Jesuits who were exploring certain parts of Africa and in some cases preparing local populations for French colonial goals, in return for receiving financial support. This partnership, according to the story, had proven successful except in places where Islam was dominant. To prove its point, the story cited an article from the French newspaper *La Revue des Deux Mondes* and a speech by a cardinal stationed in Senegal, both of which emphasized the large number of Muslims in Africa between the Mediterranean and the Niger River.[53]

What makes *al-Qahira al-Hurra*'s story instructive is that it focused on the French government's support of missionary activity not as a matter of ideology but as a tool of colonial domination. The writer explicated the tactical approach of the French by quoting a priest named Isaac Taylor, who claimed in a speech that Paris had for decades accommodated Islam in order to gain the trust and loyalty of the local populations and thus achieve its end goal of entrenching colonial rule. Taylor related a French government debate on opening a large school of Islamic learning in Algeria, fully funded and overseen by the French government, as a means of reaching Muslims in North Africa. Such a strategy could be used successfully by Muslim powers, according to the *al-Qahira al-Hurra* story, which concluded with a call to all Muslims to do more to secure the position of Islam in Africa in much the same way that the Jesuits were spreading Christianity, and it specifically named the caliph-sultan the rightful benefactor, and leader, of such a project. Also, it proposed that committees made up of political representatives and *'ulama'* from around the Muslim world fund and direct African missionary activity in much the same way that European colonialists had been doing.[54]

Public calls for decisive action by Istanbul only intensified as more bilateral agreements between Britain and other European powers were announced, further isolating the empire from any decision making. In fact, the few years that followed witnessed further humiliation on the international stage, culminating in the watershed events of 1894, which was the year that Istanbul recognized that its only remaining hope of resisting European colonial expansion in Africa lay in a military alliance with the local population. By partnering with the Sanusi Order, which would lead the military resistance, Yıldız Palace was finally giving up its belief that international agreements would allow its efforts to expand its territorial claims in central Africa or protect its African sphere of influence.

A Farcical Diplomacy of Denial

April 1894 must have been a month of urgent meetings and endless discussions inside the boardrooms and hallways of the Yıldız Palace complex. In the span of a single year, Istanbul had been shut out of several major agreements that would directly impact its African interests. Events were so serious that in addition to diplomatic protests it was reported that the sultan himself asked Khedive Abbas Hilmi II of Egypt (r. 1892–1914) to "protect" Ottoman domains and cancel an official trip he had scheduled to London as a protest against the exclusion of Istanbul from negotiations.[55]

From the palace's perspective, the most important agreement of 1894 was that between the British and King Leopold of Belgium over the Congo basin which impinged on the sovereignty of the Sultanate of Wadai and the khedive's possession in Equatorial Africa. Khedive Ismail had conquered the area south of Khartoum in the name of Sultan Abdülaziz, but no substantial Ottoman presence was ever established. The area discussed in the British-Belgian agreement was considered part of Egyptian Sudan and an extended region of the Egyptian hinterland. Hearing of this agreement, Sultan Abdülhamid II engaged the Office of Legal Council (İstişare Odası) in Istanbul to determine its legality and asked the Ottoman special commissioner (fevkalade komiser) in Egypt, Gazi Ahmed Muhtar Pasha (1839–1917),[56] for a map showing which African territories theoretically belonged to the Egyptian province, even if they were no longer under Egyptian military control.

Furthermore, the Sublime Porte sent an official order to the khedive to use all means necessary to protect the Egyptian hinterland against foreign incursion.[57] However, while Istanbul waited to hear whether the khedive was willing to abide by Istanbul's wishes (he never responded), the crisis took a serious turn. Despite Ottoman protests in London, an agreement was drafted on April 12, 1894, stating that "Great Britain undertakes to give to His Majesty [King Leopold II] a lease of territories in the western basin of the Nile."[58] It was signed in Brussels on May 12, 1894.[59]

The Ottoman government immediately declared the agreement illegal, arguing that the region subject to it was Ottoman for two reasons. First, the area east of the Sultanate of Wadai fell under the purview of the khedive of Egypt, an Ottoman vassal.[60] Second, Wadai was defined by the Ottoman state as part of the Libyan hinterland. On several occasions in 1894, the Ottoman ambassador to London, Rüstem Pasha,[61] communicated Istanbul's grievances over the British claims to Wadai.[62] He reiterated the empire's claim to all of the hinterland of Tripoli and Benghazi as clearly justified by the Act of Berlin, which had been signed less than a decade earlier.[63]

The British response was more empty promises. Lord Kimberley, the secretary of state for international affairs,[64] communicated to Rüstem Pasha that Britain would protect Istanbul's rights in Wadai, but did not explain how. In an attempt to divert its attention from the crisis in Equatoria, he also advised the Sublime Porte to maintain its vigilance over French and Italian movements in the Libyan Desert.[65] Not long before Istanbul was warned about French designs in the Libyan hinterland, the Italian ambassador to London, Count Tornielli, expressed Italy's concerns about French liberties in the Libyan Desert and requested that the British government inquire into France's plans for the area. Lord Kimberley replied that the British government was well aware of French designs on the hinterland of Ottoman Libya as a way to connect the French spheres of influence west and south of Lake Chad; he advised Tornielli to communicate with his Ottoman counterpart because of their shared interest in the region.[66]

Less than a month later, Lord Kimberley's warnings were confirmed by the Ottoman embassy in London, which reported that new boundaries for the European spheres of influence in the Libyan Desert were being drawn. Specifically, France claimed protector status over two major caravan trade routes from central Africa to the Mediterranean coast. To add insult to injury, the way the borders of the zone of influence were redrawn indicated that the French territories would cut through the third trade route, leaving no route to the west of the Libyan Desert that was not under partial or complete French control. The tone of the Ottoman embassy's report was alarmist, declaring that areas of control, or "protectorates," were being unilaterally established.

Even Khedive Abbas II entered the game of unilateral declarations, designating himself, without Istanbul's consent, the "protector" of several tribes in the eastern Sahara. At the same time, France and Britain were in negotiations to "protect" several tribes and warlords in the area.[67] What the Ottomans had been trying to achieve on a large scale in an alliance with the Sanusi Order, their European counterparts were trying to achieve one tribe at a time.

Competition over the eastern Sahara caught the eye of a reporter from *Le Siècle* in Paris who explained that since the conflict over colonial possessions in Africa had gained the attention of the public already, he would attempt to explicate French policies in the region. He argued that the majority of Saharan trade had fallen under the purview of the Sanusi Order, which he described as anti-Western, citing Gustav Nachtigal for evidence.[68] As a solution to this situation, the author suggested that the French government exploit the competition between Tuareg and Arab Bedouins on the western routes in the Libyan Desert to mobilize the Tuareg against the Sanusi Order, which the majority of the Bedouin tribes followed. This would amount to a rebellion against the Ottoman Empire.[69] Particularly telling about this article is its audience, which shows that French-Ottoman competition in the eastern Sahara had become a subject for public consumption in Paris. Also telling is its understanding that the Sanusi Order was an agent of the Ottomans in Africa and that taking control of a trade route away from the order would be a victory over the Ottoman Empire.

The French were not the only threat to Ottoman interests in Africa. Reports from the Ottoman embassy in Germany warned of secret talks between the Italians, the British, and the Egyptians over Kassala, a district (*sancak*) in the province of (Egyptian) Sudan on the Red Sea coast along the present-day Sudanese-Eritrean border.[70] These talks, which became public in the summer of 1894,[71] led to an agreement between Britain and Italy that granted Italy rule over Kassala (Figure 6), triggering yet another round of official Ottoman protests, but to no avail.[72] An Ottoman officer in Rome at the time provided the Ministry of External Affairs with the latest map of the region resulting from the agreement.[73]

The Sublime Porte's anger and desperation over its exclusion from the Kassala negotiations is evident in an unsigned draft of a note from August 13, 1894 (possibly addressed to the grand vizier): "Just like the farce that took place in the time of Grand Vizier Kamil Pasha that resulted in the Italian occupation of Massawa,[74] now there is another farce [*komidya*], but it is much graver [*vahim*]."[75] The 1894 Italian-British agreement over Kassala,[76] according to the note, was the last straw and should be protested in the strongest of terms because silence would be interpreted as consent. Pointing out that the British and Italians had been questioned about rumors of this agreement, yet they assured the Porte that Istanbul would be involved in any serious decisions to be made.[77] The writer warned that this would not be the only Italian agreement in 1894 to raise the ire of the Ottoman government because Italian negotiations over Libyan territories were also coming to light.

FIGURE 6. British-Italian deal over East Africa (BOA, Y.PRK.ASK-98/54).

By the end 1894, the "secret" Italian designs on the Libyan provinces had begun to be revealed, causing Ottoman diplomats in European capitals to report to Istanbul with a heightened tone of urgency. An excellent example of European discussions and changing perceptions of the Ottoman Empire comes from a poignant German article translated by the Ottoman embassy in Berlin that did not mince words about the tactics of the Great Powers.

"The English and Khedive of Egypt's Position Against the Ottoman Provinces in the Continent of Africa" was published in the *Berliner Tageblatt* on September 25, 1894. Careful to attend to Ottoman sensitivity about the legal status of Egypt in these uncertain times, the embassy had changed the title, which originally read "Khedive's Egypt"; after all, the sultan, not the khedive, was still the sovereign of Egypt. The article's topic was an informal agreement between England and Italy in which Egypt was to be kept out of Italian colonial ambitions in exchange for guarantees that Britain would not interfere if Italy were to make a move for Tripolitania. On Italian justification of its occupation of a region internationally recognized as belonging to another sovereign empire, the writer, with a heavy dosage of sarcasm, said that, for Britain and Italy to "realize their desires, they would try to find any reason or false excuse [*bahane*]." He predicted a scenario in which the Italian government would come to the aid of the Ottomans in order to stop the forcible expansion of the French. If the Ottomans were to say, "We have no need for your help," the Italians would claim that Istanbul obviously was not able to maintain its own internal stability and so they would step in to occupy this land to preserve regional stability. The article continued with this hypothetical scenario, stating that, because of their possessions along the Red Sea coast, the Italians would require a direct path through the eastern Sahara to the Mediterranean, justifying their bid for greater territorial expansion.[78]

Although a rather sarcastic interpretation of the logic of European colonialism, the *Berliner Tageblatt* article painted a prophetic picture of what was to come. It also illustrated with ironic clarity what the Ottoman Empire was experiencing on the global stage and in the arena of international opinion, publicly exposing its weak negotiating position. Other articles in German, French, and British newspapers on possible European bids for Benghazi and Tripoli were promptly reported to the Ministry of Foreign Affairs in Istanbul.[79] When the Ottoman ambassadors in London and Rome asked local officials about them, the response was always to deny their validity and describe them as baseless (*bi asl ve esas*).[80]

In desperation, on October 17, 1894, Rüstem Pasha, the Ottoman ambassador in London, met with Sir T. Sanderson, British undersecretary of state for foreign affairs, and Sanderson's superior Lord Kimberley. He pressed for British acknowledgment of Istanbul's right to the Libyan hinterland's borders, which he said had previously been proposed by Istanbul in 1891 although this right had not been acknowledged by either France or Britain at that time. Sanderson explained that in 1891 Istanbul was claiming areas to the south and west of Lake Chad against British objections but there would be no reason for the British government to object if the empire were to claim only the land to the north of the lake. However, he said that he could not predict how the French might feel about this and that Istanbul's ambassador in Paris should discuss Ottoman claims to the eastern Sahara with his French counterpart.[81]

Of course, the British were playing diplomatic games. Foreign press reports, particularly in Paris, contradicted all official British promises. On December 29, 1894, the Ottoman ambassador to Rome, Mahmud Nedim Bey,[82] met with the Italian minister of foreign affairs, Baron Blanc,[83] to discuss an article in Le Journal claiming that Italy and England had signed a secret agreement regarding the occupation of Tripolitania. Baron Blanc said that the claim was false and that the Italian government supported the Ottoman position in Africa, including its right to Ghoudamis. Lying on the border between Libya, Algeria, and Tunis, Ghoudamis was a city particular geopolitical importance as well as a point of contention with areas south of Tripoli. Blanc added that if the French ambassador were in the room, he would repeat his statement to his face and that any movements that Italy might make in Africa should not in any way worry the Ottoman government[84]—a bold statement that would prove to be an outright lie.

Conclusion

Ottoman diplomats in the last decade of the nineteenth century were witnesses to a game of diplomacy of denial. They were forced to pretend that they did not know they were being lied to when the Great Powers claimed not to be engaged in secret dealings that would harm Istanbul's interests in Africa. The more Istanbul confronted its Concert of Europe "partners" with rumors of negotiations taking place behind its back, the more false reassurances were given. Sultan Abdülhamid II, a strong believer in the power of international agreements, must have felt a huge sense of disappointment at this state of affairs. Article 34 of the General Act of Berlin seemed not to apply to the Ottoman case in Africa, and Istanbul was systematically excluded from decisions related to its spheres of influence. In particular, the hinterland and sphere of influence doctrines seemed to be legally worthless when used by Ottoman diplomats. The empire had no cards to play, and the European powers knew it; indeed, the international press knew it and held up Istanbul's weakness against European disregard for international agreements for the whole world to see. Even the Libyan provinces, the last of the Ottoman provinces in Africa, were now on the table as targets of European colonial occupation.

The year 1894 was a turning point for the Ottoman Empire. Evidence shows that the empire began shifting its efforts toward support of Sanusi-led military resistance in central Africa and consolidation of its hold on the frontiers of the Libyan provinces. Throughout the 1890s, following bilateral negotiations between London and Paris, the Central Sudanic Kingdoms were being divided up into French and British zones of influence. These territories had deep ties to the Ottoman Empire and the Sanusi Order and had been explicitly identified by the Ottomans as an essential part of the Libyan hinterlands. In the decades that followed, they would be dissected along the newly created borders of the colonial central African nation-states of Chad, the Central African Republic, Niger, Nigeria, and Cameroon.

Ottoman partners, whether in London, Paris, or Rome, used the almost farcical diplomacy of denial to appease Ottoman diplomats, but actions spoke much louder than words. As the diplomatic route became less effective in defending Ottoman claims to self-identified zones of influence, and as the specter of European occupation of the Libyan Desert grew, the bond between the Istanbul and the Sanusi Order grew stronger, changing from political cooperation to covert military alliance.

RESISTANCE AND
FORTIFICATION, 1894-1899

> In spite of Wadai's distance from the sea, the people of Wadai are well aware
> of the European greed and blind drive [*hırs ve inhimak*] to occupy the African
> coast and that their [the Europeans'] determination to move further inland
> would definitely affect them. Thus, from the beginning, knowing that they
> will have to protect their country from the probable European occupation,
> they have desperately hoped for the supply of new weapons. However, due to
> prohibitions on importing weapons, their wishes have remained unfulfilled.
>
> Sadik al-Mouayad Azmzade,
> somewhere between Taylamun and Benghazi, Saturday, November 30, 1895

AZMZADE WAS NOT SIMPLY REPORTING on the unfulfilled wishes of the of Wadai people; his comments were in conversation with the Ottoman government's secret program to supply weapons to central African resistance fighters under Sanusi leadership. Chapter 3 discussed the decade-long process that led to Istanbul's exclusion from negotiations over the fate of central Africa. In this chapter, we witness how the strategic and operational focus of the Ottoman Empire along its southern frontiers took a decisive shift from efforts at territorial expansion to consolidation and, indeed, resistance along the empire's southern borderlands. What becomes clear as the nineteenth century came to a close is that the empire's position on the global stage forced its painful transition from one attempting to negotiate the delicate position it found itself in: straddling the line between subject and object of colonialism, to one who became a clear target of the Great Powers' predatory territorial ambitions. Expanding the panoramic lens of inquiry, this chapter shifts the focus from Ottoman participation in the scramble for Africa to the impact this participation had on Ottoman foreign relations as well as domestic policies along the empire's southern frontiers on both sides of the Red Sea.

The empire's position in Africa was also a reflection of wider developments in the world at the time, for between 1894 and 1896 it witnessed what came to be known as the Hamidian massacres of Armenians in the Anatolian heartland. The result was further direct European intervention in the empire's internal affairs with the stated aim of guaranteeing the safety and rights of its Armenian subjects.[1] Additionally, the period between 1896 and 1898 witnessed a number of rebellions in the Ottoman province of Crete, which were supported by the Kingdom of Greece. The Ottoman minister of foreign affairs in 1897, Tevfik Pasha, worked tirelessly to win the support of the Great Powers to block Greek military and political intervention in the island's affairs, but to no avail.[2] Despite Istanbul's best effort to defend its sovereignty in Crete, the European powers' position oscillated from promises to stop the Greek invasion to increasingly forcing Istanbul's hand in curtailing its defensive efforts until most of the Ottoman troops were withdrawn from Crete and governorship of the island was handed over to Prince George, the second son of King George I of Greece (r. 1863–1913). This effectively meant the handing over of Crete to the Kingdom of Greece in all ways but name. Istanbul's protestations about this situation paralleled its diplomatic complaints about its exclusion from the decisions being made vis-à-vis central Africa.[3]

Allies in Peace, Brothers in Arms

After 1894 the Hamidian regime turned to its ally, al-Mahdi al-Sanusi, to mount and support local resistance against the impending European occupation of central Africa. Evidence of this turn comes from reports of the British consul Justin Alvarez in Benghazi,[4] who reported on a letter his spies had intercepted that included specific instructions from Istanbul to al-Mahdi al-Sanusi to commence military operations against any European maneuvering in Africa. More specifically, Istanbul instructed al-Mahdi al-Sanusi to use his influence over various tribes to coordinate a united front against impending European military action. In response al-Mahdi al-Sanusi called an emergency meeting with his deputies from the various Saharan *zawāyā*.[5] The mounting threat to Ottoman interests in the Libyan hinterland also prompted an urgent mission to the Sahara by none other than Sadik Pasha al-Mouayad Azmzade. Simultaneously, Istanbul embarked on an emergency project to create facts on the ground in its African provinces. In particularly, through the building of telegraph lines to the southern frontiers of Ottoman Libya, Istanbul hoped to establish an undisputable link between the Ottoman's African frontier and the empire's capital.

In the time since Azmzade's first mission to meet al-Sanusi a few years before, the Ottoman position on the global stage had taken a serious beating. For his second mission, in November of 1895, the destination, much further south in the Sahara, was the oasis of Kufra, the new headquarters of the Sanusi Order and al-Mahdi al-Sanusi's new residence. A significant difference between his last mission and this one was that Azmzade was now equipped with new record-keeping technology and one of his hobbies: a camera. Thus, compared to his first mission, we have many more details about this trip, both textual and pictorial. Azmzade, one of the first Ottomans to write a book on photography,[6] was careful to document every stage of his journey, which unlike his first one in 1886, was not kept secret. In fact, Azmzade's travels were detailed in a series of articles published in a popular magazine and later printed as a travelogue in Istanbul in 1899, with both the manuscript and a printed copy presented to the sultan as gifts.[7]

On his return from the 1895 mission (Figure 7), Azmzade filed a report on the state of affairs in Benghazi and its hinterland. In this report, which was a much more frank account than the one he offered in his travelogue, he described in detail an area that, according to his assessment, continued to be very loyal to the sultan even though it was desperately poor and required much more attention from Istanbul than it had been receiving in terms of economic investment and infrastructural development. Despite the noted neglect from the Ottoman government, Azmzade was surprised at the welcoming attitude of the Saharan people, particularly toward him as a uniformed representative of the Ottoman government. The people's recognition of and affection for the Ottoman presence, notwithstanding the fact that "no Sublime Porte representative has ever been there, nor have the people ever seen an Ottoman banner before," had a great impact on Azmzade.[8]

What Azmzade did not mention was that the two Ottoman banners he was proudly carrying with him were meant for the gates of the *zāwiya* of al-Mahdi al-Sanusi's residence in Kufra but that, according to the governor of Benghazi in 1908, al-Mahdi al-Sanusi declined to install them. How do we reconcile this with what Azmzade was reporting on local support?

Despite the enthusiasm and support for the Ottoman sultan described by Azmzade, al-Mahdi al-Sanusi must have found it prudent not to appear as though he and his order were becoming an arm of the Ottoman state. In fact, maintaining a public image of autonomy would be beneficial to both the Ottomans and the Sanusi because the power of the Sanusi leadership, which the Ottomans were banking on, would have been compromised if the order were to be seen as a puppet of an imperial power.[9] Moreover, planting a flag would not

جوال الصحرى

FIGURE 7. Azmzade on his way back from his second mission to Kufra in the Sahara (Nadir Eserler Library, Istanbul University, 779/64).

have been enough in the post-1885 era to declare sovereignty; such symbolic declarations were no longer sufficient to send a message to the French and British, who were well aware of the Ottoman-Sanusi alliance. For this reason, the Ottoman government's "effective occupation" of the eastern Sahara remained a source of tension between Europe and the Ottoman Empire. Moreover, the lack of a substantial physical Ottoman governmental presence in the Libyan Desert remained a concern for Yıldız Palace. Speculations about Ottoman attempts at military occupation to establish a presence triggered British consular reports from Benghazi and Tripoli.[10]

In his formal report, Azmzade addressed the importance of al-Mahdi al-Sanusi's autonomy to the success of Ottoman strategy and offered two recommendations that spoke to this issue. His first was that no Ottoman *kaymakamlık* (administrative district) be established in Kufra or in any area south of it, arguing that the Sanusi Order maintained the peace in those areas and so kept trade routes between Wadai and Benghazi open and secure. In his travelogue, he described the importance of this accomplishment:

> In reality . . . the Wadai–Kufra–Benghazi route, for fifteen years was unusable until the father of his holiness Seyyid Sanusi invested a great deal of effort to secure it and subsequently, using his own money, had a water well named Bushra dug up between Wajanga and Kufra, in a benevolent effort meant at easing the hardship of travel. Today, this road is referred to as "Es-Seyyid es-Sanusi Way." The current level of security and peace is astounding to such an extent that it can be said that one does not find this level of security in the most developed of places. Traders from Tripoli always prefer this route now, and so they travel by sea to Benghazi and then south on this road to the Sudan.[11]

Azmzade argued that any overt Ottoman presence would ultimately do more harm than good for the empire's objectives in the area, and that the Sanusi Order was sufficiently protecting Ottoman interests.[12] He also stressed the necessity of better coordination between Istanbul and the Sanusi Order to establish a legitimate presence on the ground without undermining one or the other's political authority. Why was the question of authority such a concern, especially after describing how loyal the population and al-Mahdi al-Sanusi himself were to the sultan? His second recommendation combined with a report from British consul Justin Alvarez holds the answer.

A few months before Azmzade left Istanbul for Kufra, on April 4, 1894, Alvarez, in a letter to the British ambassador in Istanbul, Sir Philipp Currie, reported rumors of an Ottoman military expedition headed to Kufra to establish an Ottoman administration—*kaymakamlık*. He wrote that the Ottoman government had not previously been in full control of the region, whose location at the crossroads of several trade routes made it of high economic and strategic importance. Alvarez reported that the expedition was made up of three hundred men on camelback.[13]

Azmzade reported on a similar expedition that he had witnessed in the hinterland of Benghazi, where he encountered a very tense situation on arrival. After a round of attacks and counterattacks between Bedouin tribesmen and an Ottoman regiment, the governor's men seized camels from the tribes and other locals as a form of collective punishment. Learning of this, Azmzade ordered the camels to be returned to their rightful owners and brought Ottoman representatives and sheikhs of the tribes to a meeting to begin the process of reconciliation. With that, the situation returned to normal and Azmzade continued on his way.[14]

After recounting this story, Azmzade, in a tone that was rather sympathetic toward the Bedouins, gave his second recommendation, suggesting that instead of giving the Bedouins honorary decorations (*nişanlar*) and gifts, a more consistent system of taxation should be followed, one that would be perceived as fair and serve to avert incidents like the one he had witnessed. He also recommended opening more schools in the region because they were sorely lacking and predicted that the Bedouins would be very interested in attending them.[15]

Azmzade was in fact recommending an Ottoman presence in the area but not a military one. He advised that the palace would gain goodwill with the local population by providing social services and supporting the local Sanusi establishments. The existing system of governance, he argued, had established a bad precedent of military action, and sending more soldiers or establishing a new *kaymakamlık* would only serve to turn the local population against the Ottomans.

Compared with the language he used in his field reports, Azmzade's language in the official report was reserved and diplomatic in its criticism of the provincial government. In his field reports, a much more unreserved Azmzade named names and pointed his finger at Ottoman officials. For example, in a memo summarizing the two field reports he had sent while on his way to Istanbul from Kufra, he was particularly critical of an expedition sent from

Benghazi against Bedouins, most probably for tax collection. He blamed the governor of Cyrenaica, Ahmad bin Hamed Taher (r. 1893–1904), for ordering the expedition, which led to ten deaths on both sides and seven Bedouin men injured. Azmzade wrote that such poorly thought out actions only helped raise suspicions of the Ottoman government despite the medallions and gifts sent to the chiefs of the tribes. He insisted that the impacts of Ahmad Pasha's decisions and actions were not limited to Benghazi but had transimperial ramifications. This meant that a decision to send a military expedition like the one he reported on should not be made by the *mutasarrıf* alone.[16]

Azmzade was not proposing a new administrative system; rather, he was simply insisting that the rules of governing Cyrenaica as a *mutasarrıfiyya* be followed. As discussed earlier, a *mutasarrıfiyya* was a category of provincial administration reserved for localities given varying levels of autonomy and placed under the direct purview of Istanbul because of their status as zones of global geopolitical significance. Prime examples of administrative zones designated as *mutasarrıfiyya* included Jerusalem and Mount Lebanon.[17] Azmzade argued that what happened in Benghazi's hinterland held implications for the entire empire and therefore only an informed imperial government should be making potentially fateful decisions concerning it. In other words, Cyrenaica as a *mutasarrıfiyya* should be taken out of the provincial orbit of Tripoli and the local overview of Benghazi and placed in the hands of strategy experts in Istanbul. Al-Mahdi al-Sanusi sent a letter to Sultan Abdülhamid II, dated April 22, 1895, in which he emphasized his loyalty and allegiance to the caliph-sultan and acknowledged the support his *zawāyā* had been receiving from him. However, he also expressed support for Azmzade's argument, complaining that provincial administrators were causing strife and instigating conflicts between the sultan and himself.[18]

Ahmad bin Hamed Taher, the *mutasarrıf* of Cyrenaica and the object of Azmzade's criticism, also sent a letter on December 12, 1895 to Istanbul. He wrote that a deputy of al-Mahdi al-Sanusi from Benghazi, Sheikh Abdul Aziz Efendi, and several notables from the region accompanied Azmzade to Kufra and back. They provided him with safe passage and helped him secure what was needed for the difficult journey. For that reason, Taher Pasha requested that honorary medals be sent to these men and their relatives as a sign of gratitude for their service to the sultan.[19] Indeed, ten days later, Taher Pasha sent another letter fishing for a "gold" Mecidiye medal (first-class Mecidi Order)[20] as a reward for his support of Azmzade's mission.[21]

The lack of coordination between Istanbul and the provincial governors caused more than just administrative inefficiencies. In the frontier regions, actions that might turn the locals against the empire meant that the first line of defense against European imperialism was compromised. Because Abdülhamid II counted on the Bedouins' loyalty, shortsighted actions such as Mutasarrif Taher Pasha's expedition to collect tax revenue ultimately threatened the Ottoman state's security and, in the case of the volatile frontiers, its very sovereignty.

The disconnect between the strategy objectives of the center and the administrative objectives of the provincial powers was not limited to Cyrenaica. It seems to have been built into the system of intraimperial relations, and we encounter it when we examine other Ottoman southern frontiers in western Arabia in Chapters 5 and 6. In this region, provincial, local, and imperial authorities were not only disharmonious on the policy level. The provincial and local authorities viewed Istanbul's efforts to consolidate its hold over its geopolitically sensitive frontiers as antithetical to their own goals, and they worked tirelessly to undermine Istanbul's authority, in the process compromising Istanbul's strategies for fending off foreign intervention.

News: Africa in the Ottoman Press

By the close of the nineteenth century, Ottoman imperial interests in the Sahara were being publicly debated in Istanbul. An article in the semiofficial newspaper İkdam from January 1897 sheds light on the public's interest in the empire's involvement in Africa.[22] The article's writer began with a brief description of what had been taking place in Africa since the middle of the 1880s, drawing the general reading public into discussions of the interimperial competition taking place on the doorstep of the empire's African provinces. He analyzed the positions of the various European players in this competition and where the empire fit in. He argued that the empire had an advantage over the Europeans because it shared a religion with the local inhabitants, which allowed Ottoman missions to the eastern Sahara to avoid the "catastrophic" fate of some European missions. Additionally, he said, the empire was no stranger to Africa; it already had large tracts of land in North Africa that allowed it easy access to the Sahara.

The writer did not stop there, however. He discussed ways that the empire could develop the economy of the region, taking advantage of Tripolitania as the gateway to the Sahara. He proposed a railway to connect sub-Saharan Africa with the Mediterranean coast so that the empire could both develop the region economically and gain from becoming the linchpin of trade between the sub-Saharan region and Europe. Interestingly, the writer then declared that such economic development would bring civilization (*medeniyet*) to the continent: "With the efforts of the Ottoman government in Tripoli, it can occupy an important position in the history of the development of Africa [*tarih-i medeniyette pek muhim bir mevki işgalı*]."[23]

It is important that the rhetoric of bringing "civilization to the locals" was not presented in a culturist sense. The writer was not arguing for a "white man's burden," or a *mission civilisatrice*. Rather, he was making the implicit argument that economic and technological development would help "modernize" Muslim African society. In fact, civilizing improvements as an outcome of economic and technological development—*not* cultural assets brought to the locals by a colonizing Ottoman ruler—lay at the heart of discussions taking place in Istanbul.

Another *İkdam* article from October 1898 discussed a sudden upsurge in French public support for a railway from the Lake Chad basin to the Mediterranean that France saw as essential to the economic success of its African colonies. The article questioned whether this was a matter of simple economic interest or strategic geopolitics, pointing out that this idea had been proposed fifteen years earlier, at the time of the Conference of Berlin, but had been shelved because of internal squabbling in Paris. The article additionally suggested that the French would have a great deal of trouble dealing with the local Bedouins, who would be very hard to convince that the train would not take away their source of livelihood, the camel caravan trade.[24]

The Beirut daily newspaper *Lisan al-Hal* reported on the French railway proposal in 1899, after the project had won the approval of the British in February of that year. *Lisan al-Hal* devoted several columns each day to European colonialism in central and eastern Africa, like other newspapers in the empire.[25] As we see in Chapters 5 and 6, various stakeholders in the Ottoman Empire were debating telegraph line and railway projects as well, such as the extension of telegraph lines through Bedouin territories in the Hijaz and the Libyan Desert.

It was through the press that interimperial competition over Africa, particularly Muslim central Africa, entered the Ottoman public domain. Newspapers did not simply report what was taking place; they critically engaged with events, offered recommendations, and passionately encouraged action by the government. Given the wide distribution of these newspapers, it is safe to assume that at the turn of the century the scramble for Africa was being discussed in the saloons of Beirut and the *hamams* of the Ottoman capital as well as in the hallways of Yıldız Palace and the offices of the Mabeyn and the Sublime Porte.

Aman My Pasha! Time Is Precious and Short

In 1895 al-Mahdi al-Sanusi moved from Jaghbub to Kufra. In line with inter-pretation of the Grand Sanusi's original choice of al-Bayda' in Jabal al-Akhdar as inspired by an assumed animosity between the Ottoman government and the Sanusiyya (see Chapter 1), al-Mahdi al-Sanusi's relocation so far south was assumed to also be a result of Ottoman pressure. However, nothing could have been further from the truth. In fact, in the five years between 1896 and his death in 1901, al-Mahdi al-Sanusi and Istanbul drew ever closer, finally form-ing a military alliance in which Ottoman military support proved crucial to the central African resistance. According to Azmzade, the establishment of a *kaymakamlık* in Jaghbub might have influenced al-Mahdi al-Sanusi's decision to move to Kufra given that his local authority among the Bedouins appeared to be challenged by Tripoli-appointed officials. Azmzade considered the Jagh-bub *kaymakamlık* a poor strategic move because the rule of al-Mahdi al-Sanusi in these areas was already sufficient to support Ottoman interests.[26]

That the very large Jaghbub *zāwiya* remained in full operation indicates that the order was not under threat after the Ottoman *kaymakamlık* was established in 1892. In fact, for a few months after al-Mahdi al-Sanusi's move to Kufra, his brother Muhammad al-Sharif oversaw operations in Jaghbub until the middle of 1896, when the *zāwiya* was mostly shut down and, according to British con-sular reports, the remaining members left to join the order in Kufra.[27] The oa-sis of Kufra by that time had become the nodal point through which caravans passed on their way to Wadai and Borno,[28] two sultanates in the imperial cross-hairs of British and French ambitions.[29]

In August 1896, British consul Justin Alvarez reported that Major Hakki Bey, the military inspector of accounts in Benghazi, was meeting with al-Mahdi al-Sanusi in Kufra on a secret mission commissioned by Istanbul to entice al-Mahdi al-Sanusi to use his influence, "temporal and spiritual," to diffuse the tense situation in the south. The hope was that the Sanusi Order could recon-cile Rabih al-Zubair in Borno and Sultan Yusuf in Wadai in order to present a united front against the increasingly emboldened English and French in the Lake Chad area and to maintain control over the caravan route from Lake Chad to the Mediterranean.[30] However, Alvarez mistakenly reported that guides along the road refused to guarantee Hakki Bey's safety, forcing him to abandon his mission.[31] I could find no reference to such a mission in the Ottoman Archives, and I believe Alvarez's intelligence was inaccurate because, as evidence shows, al-Mahdi al-Sanusi did manage to reconcile the regional leadership. In fact, by the end of 1899 he had moved his headquarters further south, into the town of Guru in the heart of the Lake Chad basin, in order to lead the local resistance.

The cries for combating French and British movement in the eastern Sahara grew more urgent in 1899. In a letter to the palace, Tripoli's former head of the court of appeal, Ahmed Mustafa Pasha, wrote: "For my country, my people, my sultan, and with good intentions and with neither lax nor imperfect service, I have tried to describe and explicate what I have seen and heard and investigated in my surroundings [*meşhudat ve mesmuat ve tahkikatımı tevsi ve teşmile çalıştım*]: Ottoman Africa has gained an overwhelming importance and delicacy." He continued:

> It is being said that the French have reached the great city of Zinder, which is the key and entryway to the land of central Africa, where thirty million Muslims await the arrival of the Ottoman banner of victory. The merchant caravans from Tripoli to Sudan can't continue on their route, due to the clashes taking place along the way, forcing them to return to Ghat. After passing the sub-provinces under Tripoli rule, including Jebel al-Gharbi, Garyan, Urfali, Sirt and head south, there is nothing but the mention and thoughts of Seyyid Sanusi, along with that of the sultan of Wadai. There is word that he himself went there. . . . If nothing were done, crying over a missed opportunity would not be accepted by those deserving the protection and friendship [of the sultan]. Aman my Pasha! Time is precious and short. . . . In a little while [it will be too late] and everything will be lost.[32]

This impassioned plea reflected Ottoman officials' fear that the opportunity for redemption on the global stage, after fifteen years of effort, seemed to be slipping right through their fingers. The agreement between France and Britain over the eastern Sahara was about to take effect. France in particular felt emboldened by an 1899 agreement with the British to solve the Fashoda Crisis, and the French military was already on the move toward central Africa.

The Fashoda Crisis gave rise to yet another major European agreement that raised the ire of Istanbul, expressed through diplomatic protests to which the European powers responded only with more empty assurances. However, it was different from other episodes of Ottoman exclusion from negotiations over

African land claimed as colonial possessions by Istanbul. The Fashoda Crisis and the resulting London Declaration of 1899 marked the end of the road for the Ottoman expansionist experiment.

Since 1895 French colonialists had been urging their government to challenge Britain's claim to the Nile Valley. A slow three-year march from French West Africa to the Nile Valley ended in Fashoda—a town on the White Nile in southeast Sudan—with French and British forces coming very close to an all-out confrontation over colonial possessions. The decade that began with concerted efforts to increase the economic prosperity of competing European imperialists under the rules laid down by the Act of Berlin had by 1899 turned into a clash of colonial interests between two Great Powers, which, because of its vital importance to Ottoman interests in central Africa, was closely followed by the Beirut daily *Lisan al-Hal*. Beyond the details of the conflict, and later the agreement to end it, the paper devoted pages to explaining the complexity of the issues involved, which, although manifested in the Nile Valley, concerned global interimperial disagreements from fishing rights off the coast of North America to rights to the island of Madagascar to ship-refueling rights in Muscat.[33]

As the French and British armies prepared for battle, negotiations in London led to the pivotal bilateral agreement of 1899, which demarcated territorial possessions without the approval of the imperial powers directly affected. This in essence rendered the Act of Berlin null and void and gave the French the green light to invade the sultanates west of the Lake Chad basin.[34]

Known as the London Declaration, the agreement was signed on March 21, 1899. It gave Paris the "right" to occupy central African territories north of the fifteenth parallel in return for giving up its claim to the Nile valley for good.[35] The area handed over to the French was none other than the domain of al-Mahdi al-Sanusi and by proxy the territories claimed by the Ottoman Empire, stretching north from Lake Chad as far as Tibesti. Interestingly, according to the *Geographical Journal*, published by the British Royal Geographic Society, "Tibesti . . . naturally belongs to the Hinterland of Tripoli, and the present recognition of French claims will not, of course, be binding on other Powers."[36] Yet the Ottoman Empire by that time was not counting on invoking international agreements or registering diplomatic complaints. The time for diplomacy in the Libyan Desert and indeed on the empire's southern frontiers had passed. The empire's hopes of reinventing itself on the international stage had been dashed, and it now had a mere supporting role in the eastern Sahara, providing weapons to the Sanusi Order. While the order led a military resistance against the French in the eastern Sahara, Istanbul's attention turned to securing its provincial borderlands in Ottoman Libya and the Hijaz.[37]

1900–1902: *Sanusi Resistance in Central Africa*

In 1899 the military alliance of the Ottoman state and the Sanusi Order was put on display, with al-Mahdi al-Sanusi now being invited to official military inspections as a member of the Ottoman elite. In February 1899, for example, British consul Justin Alvarez wrote to the British ambassador in Istanbul that Taher Pasha, the *mutasarrıf* of Benghazi, had ordered an inspection of the troops in Berka and that al-Mahdi al-Sanusi was in attendance as the guest of honor.[38]

Similarly, in November 1899 Sheikh Muhammad Suleiman Pasha of Alexandria, a third-generation religious scholar and Muslim missionary, wrote two letters to the sultan in which he described a journey he had undertaken in the eastern Sahara. He said that traveling through the territory under Sanusi control made it clear to him that al-Mahdi al-Sanusi and all his followers were "publicly and privately" truly loyal to the caliph and that love of the caliph was instilled in all Sanusi followers in Africa right from childhood. However, he warned the sultan that the Europeans were intent on occupying the eastern Sahara and Lake Chad basin and their plan was to divide the Muslims and create a wedge between the sultan and al-Mahdi al-Sanusi. Suleiman Pasha warned of rumors not just from European sources but from sources in Istanbul: those "in high-up positions, who are untrue and don't know their religion [are] promoting such rumors."[39]

The sultan was already convinced of al-Mahdi al-Sanusi's loyalty, according to his memoirs: "If there is anybody who is able and willing to defend our rights in Africa, it is al-Mahdi al-Sanusi."[40] The *mutasarrıf*'s invitation to al-Mahdi al-Sanusi to inspect the Berka troops was just one sign of Istanbul's trust. In fact, by the beginning of 1899 the Sanusi Order was establishing even more *zawāyā* and trade routes deeper into the Lake Chad basin, strengthening its presence in areas under immediate colonial threat, while the Ottoman state was filling the power vacuum left behind in Kufra and other areas in the Libyan hinterland. For example, after al-Mahdi al-Sanusi's move to Guru, Kufra was left exposed to British and Mahdist threats from the east. The sultan ordered the governor of Benghazi to request al-Mahdi al-Sanusi's consent to establish an Ottoman *kaymakamlık* there, apparently taking the advice of Azmzade.[41]

At the same time, according to British intelligence sources, al-Mahdi al-Sanusi was in negotiations with the sultan of Darfur to open a new trade route from Darfur through Kufra and on to the Mediterranean coast in anticipation of a possible French takeover of the western routes.[42]

After the signing of the London Declaration in 1899, it was only a matter of months before the French army moved into the Lake Chad basin. In preparation, al-Mahdi al-Sanusi sent two missions south of Guru, so far south, in fact, that they reached areas where "Arabic was not spoken."[43] The purpose of these missions was to set the stage for al-Mahdi al-Sanusi's arrival to establish a united local military front against the French. In 1900 reports from British dragomans in Istanbul, and from Alvarez in Benghazi, indicated that al-Mahdi al-Sanusi's negotiations with the local tribes and sultanates had consolidated his hold over the southern regions of the eastern Sahara.[44] The sultan of Darfur, for example, declared his allegiance by accepting al-Sanusi's offer to build three Sanusi zawāyā in Darfur.[45] Evidence points toward Ottoman-Sanusi coordination of military resistance against the invading French army, particularly after al-Mahdi al-Sanusi's move to Guru.[46] Support for Sanusi-led local militias armed with Ottoman weapons came from the highest officials of the Hamidian regime.

Sultan Abdülhamid II himself supported the Sanusi Order's preparations for military resistance. For example, in a report sent to London, the British ambassador in Istanbul, Sir Nicholas R. O'Conor, paraphrased an anxious letter he had received in which the sultan declared that it was in the British Empire's best interest to help the Ottomans repel French attacks on Ottoman territories in Africa. The sultan relayed his confidence in the strength of al-Sanusi and his loyalty to the empire, and rejected rumors reported in the French media that al-Mahdi al-Sanusi had asked for or accepted French protection. This vote of confidence would seem to corroborate reports from Alvarez about Ottoman arms being shipped to Derna and then transferred by caravans to Sanusi hideouts in zawāyā further south.[47] Nevertheless, despite substantial evidence of Ottoman tactical and material support of the Sanusi leadership, there is no evidence of any direct Ottoman military intervention in the looming war. Resistance against the French invasion was led by al-Mahdi al-Sanusi and manned locally by the various tribes.

In 1902, after the death of Muhammad al-Mahdi al-Sanusi, his nephew Ahmad al-Sharif al-Sanusi took over leadership of the order, becoming the de facto head of resistance against French and later Italian colonialism in the

Libyan interior. Ottoman support of Sanusi-led resistance continued even after the reign of Sultan Abdülhamid II. When al-Sharif al-Sanusi fled to Istanbul in 1918, he was received as a hero and was settled with his family in a mansion in Bursa. He continued his resistance to Libyan occupation in exile until his death in 1933.[48]

Technologies of Resistance

Even though Istanbul continued to support Sanusi resistance well into the twentieth century, Ottoman archival records point to a decisive shift in its strategic focus, from expansion to fortification, starting as early as 1895. Efforts to consolidate the empire's hold on its Libyan provinces became evident during the planning of a comprehensive North African telegraph network, through which the empire intended to assert its hold on its provinces by connecting Libyan provincial borderlands to Ottoman administrative centers on the Mediterranean coast.

In September 1899, the Ottoman Ministry of the Interior sent a request to the Ministry of Telegraph and Post for urgent action because of recent reports of European competition over areas in the Libyan Desert and rumors of British and French plans to build a telegraph line to connect this highly coveted region with their respective metropoles in Europe. Fearing that "imperial executive rights" (*hukuk-i tasarrufiye-yi sultaniye*) would be threatened if these foreign lines were built, the Ministry of Interior asked that the Ottoman telegraph network be extended south and west from the Mediterranean shore to ensure that the Ottoman government's "effective occupation"—to use the already lapsed terms of the General Act of Berlin—would be fortified.[49]

By 1899 construction of the Hijaz telegraph line took up all the resources of the Ministry of Telegraph and Post. That is why it was not until 1901 that a comprehensive plan was presented to the Sublime Porte, including cost estimates, for an extensive network that would connect Tripoli, Sirt, and Benghazi with the Libyan interior.[50] Budgetary concerns were part of the picture, but the project's high strategic importance meant that it would be executed despite the expense and risk involved. Inspector Rahmi Bey, director of telegraph services in Kosovo and the first director of the telegraph office in Salt in southern Syria, was transferred to Tripoli to oversee construction of the first Tripoli–Fezzan line.[51] Soon after, a decision was made to replace the Benghazi–Alexandria submarine line with an overland connection to Tripoli, which would be extended to Crete and then on to Istanbul. This, many thought, was a line to nowhere because connecting with Sirt and then with Tripoli meant traversing long stretches of uninhabited desert. Although no revenue was expected from this line, Alvarez reported to London that the sultan "now attaches great importance to the construction."[52]

Alvarez criticized the line as a waste of money, considering that it would go through the territory of Bedouins who might cut it down and make off with the poles.[53] However, in light of the importance of technological and infrastructural projects in the late nineteenth and the early twentieth century, the logic behind this decision is obvious. Yıldız Palace was determined to establish an independent infrastructure, avoiding foreign technical expertise and capital, throughout its threatened frontier regions. Istanbul went as far as diverting money from a second cable to the all-important Hijaz line to the Libyan lines.[54] In fact, as if asserting their Ottoman-ness, the telegraph stations in Ottoman Libya were equipped to send and receive telegrams in only two languages, Arabic and Ottoman-Turkish.[55]

The empire's experience in Africa had led to a loss of faith in international agreements and thus Istanbul's pursuit of a strictly independent and indeed isolationist approach to ensure the security of its domains. As the Ottoman experiment in new imperialism wound down, attention shifted to the empire's other vulnerable frontiers-cum-borderlands in western Arabia. European exclusionary policies and heightened tensions between the empire and the Great Powers manifested not just in Africa but also in Ottoman Arabia thousands of kilometers away.

In 1893 a French company proposed a partnership between the Ottoman and French governments for the extension of a mutually beneficial telegraph line to the southern reaches of the Red Sea. According to the proposal, the French and Ottoman empires were facing the same problem of having to rely on British-controlled telegraph lines to communicate with their respective government outposts in the Red Sea and the Indian Ocean. For the French, the main concern was reaching their isolated colony in Madagascar off the British-controlled African east coast. For the Ottomans, it was reaching their province of Hijaz. The proposed scheme would connect Marseilles to al-ʿArish or Gaza by a submarine line and then extend a line down the east coast of the Red Sea to Madagascar and out to the Indian Ocean and beyond, making the British lines unnecessary.[56]

Three years later, in 1896, an update of the French proposal was back on the table. The Ottoman special commissioner to Egypt, Gazi Ahmed Muhtar Pasha, wrote to the Sublime Porte emphasizing the danger of relying on British lines and raising the specter of intentional delays of Ottoman messages or sabotage of the line. He believed that it was of the greatest urgency that alternatives to the British lines be studied.[57] This strong sense of urgency from the Ottoman special commissioner to Egypt requires further investigation, especially when we take into consideration British protestation over what appeared to be unannounced Ottoman naval maneuvers off the coast of Egyptian Sudan during the same period. The Ottoman government claimed that the navy's presence was simply for the purpose of repairing the submarine telegraph line, although it happened to coincide with the handing over of Massawa to Italy by the British, despite Istanbul's vehement protestations. Muhtar Pasha also reported disagreements between Ottomans and Egyptians over the use of the telegraph line. Furthermore, he reminded the Porte that the Ottoman-French joint telegraph venture, which had been proposed more than three years earlier, was still awaiting approval or rejection. His frustration was thinly masked when he hinted at "some" in the government who seemed to delay or avoid making such decisions.[58]

Muhtar Pasha's push to reconsider the now updated French proposal led the Sublime Porte to assign Émile Pasha, the former director of the Damascus telegraph office, as head of a commission to investigate the benefits of the proposal, which called for a submarine cable that would be strung from Marseilles to Jaffa and from there an overland line to ʿAqaba. The Société Industrielle de Paris would financially sponsor the portion of the line over Ottoman land, and after its completion it would be under the control the Ottoman Ministry of Telegraph and Post. An underwater line would continue to Bab al-Mandab and from there to Madagascar. Émile Pasha suggested that the revenue generated from the proposed line could be spent on independent lines connecting the Hijaz, Tripoli, and Yemen with Istanbul.[59] In early 1899, the Ottoman government announced a clear rejection of the updated proposal, stating that a decision had already been made to build an entirely independent overland route to the Hijaz, which would make a second line unnecessary.[60] However it is no coincidence that 1899 was the year of the Fashoda Crisis and the subsequent London Declaration. The relationship between events such as these in Africa and Arabia offers a new explanation of the logic behind Istanbul's foreign strategies and their ultimate impact on domestic policy.

Conclusion

The French telegraph proposal is just one example of the decline in Ottoman relations with the Great Powers from a high point in the early 1880s to a low point in the mid-1890s. As early as 1888, the European powers had systematically excluded (and eventually isolated) the Ottoman Empire from European negotiations over the division of the African territories. Even though the Ottoman experiment in colonial expansion in central Africa had failed, Istanbul's resolve to assert its independence only grew stronger. The military alliance with the Sanusi Order was maintained, although an open declaration of war was never made because it could not be made. The Ottoman military was no match for the forces of the Great Powers. All that could be done was to provide weapons and tactical support to the local resistance. In 1900, following the calls of its military and political advisors, Yıldız Palace embarked on a large-scale telegraph project in the Libyan Desert and the Hijaz, and its attention shifted to its important Arabian frontiers. In Chapters 5 and 6, I also shift the focus across the Red Sea to the Hijaz, following policy makers and negotiators sent from Istanbul, such as Sadik al-Mouayad Azmzade, as they moved their field of operations from Africa to the deserts of the Hijaz at the turn of the twentieth century. Even though the Great Powers robbed Istanbul of its dream to rejoin the ranks of the great empires of the time, it would take another fifteen years and a world war before the Ottoman Empire fell to European colonialism. It is important to remember that the empire did not survive simply because the Great Powers desired to maintain a balance of power. As the following two chapters demonstrate, Istanbul's strategies for maintaining its independence and agency in resisting European hegemony deserve much more academic attention than they have garnered up to now.

5 TRANSIMPERIAL STRATEGIES FOR AN INTERCONTINENTAL EMPIRE

While the camel caretakers were sitting around the fire and talking, one of their stories caught my attention: A person from Jalu walked by himself to Kufra; which was also our destination. This journey is a distance of at least 150 hours on foot. 150 hours walking in an ocean of sand by himself! We could not even fathom such a march of fools.

What wonder! [*Sübhanallah!*] In Europe, a man travels with money in his wallet, a pre-planned route, regular breaks in his travels during the day, and nights spent in hotels, inns, villages, or houses. He gets to eat and drink all that he desires and to enjoy his time in restaurants that he happens upon along the way. His travels from so-and-so-city to so-and-so-city become the concern of the press, and journalists follow him, and send telegrams whenever he departs or arrives at a place. Millions get to learn the traveler's name and he gains admiration and fame. Meanwhile, here we are, three days since we left Jalu [and we are still nameless], and despite all my efforts to learn the name of this wretched soul [from Jalu] . . . I am not able to attain that information. . . . For the Bedouins, all of this [travel] is just business as usual.

Sadik al-Mouayad Azmzade,
on the road from Jalu to Kufra, Saturday, October 26, 1895

SADIK PASHA, who was assigned to lead the construction of the Hijaz telegraph line a few years after his journey to the Sahara, observed the difference between European-style travel and his, praising the Bedouin travelers for their "strength and steadfastness." He lamented the anonymity of the everyday heroic feats of travelers like him who did without the comforts afforded European travelers and adventurers and had no reporters along to tell the world of their journey. But this anonymity, which he experienced in the Sahara, would be all but lost during his mission to the Hijazi Desert. With the Hijaz telegraph lines connecting one of the most remote corners of the empire to Istanbul, Azmzade was able to report on his progress almost in real time, much as European travelers could advertise their adventures in London, Berlin, or Paris. Moreover, he, too, would be celebrated as a pioneer and adventurer through triumphant telegrams to Istanbul via telegraph lines newly built with the help of Bedouins, whose service he relied on. These reports, often published in popular newspapers, at times also served as advertisements for successful government efforts in far-off places.

This chapter turns the spotlight on the Arabian frontiers-cum-borderlands by focusing on the Damascus–Mecca telegraph line extension project, the construction of which Azmzade was assigned to lead. I chose it as a case study of Istanbul's shift toward policy making that prioritized the consolidation of its hold on its increasingly vulnerable frontiers. This "line in the sand" was meant to tie Istanbul, figuratively and literally, to the government nerve center of the province of Hijaz, and to Mecca, the spiritual heart of the Muslim world. I argue that the Ottomans' fifteen-year participation in and ultimate exclusion from the scramble for Africa informed their strategic policies along the Arabian frontier.

The extension of the Hijaz telegraph line paved the way for the more complicated and expensive construction of the Hijaz Railway between 1902 and 1908. Despite the many attendant technological, financial, and security challenges of the construction of the railroad, the telegraph line was in many ways even more challenging to complete. As the first stage of a project of unprecedented scale in the Ottoman Empire, through trials and many errors, the extension broke ground for the railway, giving the Ottoman government firsthand experience with the difficulties of dealing with the Hijazi Desert and local politics. According to William Ochsenwald, an authority on the Hamidian Hijaz Railway, "The telegraph served as a test of efficacy of the plans for the railroad."[1]

I provide here a detailed account and analysis of the telegraph extension project—the considerations evaluated, the interests at stake, and the ultimate decisions made. By mostly following correspondence containing the solicited and unsolicited opinions of imperial, provincial, and local power brokers, I explicate policy deliberations in late nineteenth-century Ottoman government and explain how the decisions made pointed to Istanbul's changing strategic priorities in securing its sovereignty in light of its failures in Africa. This close examination of the complexity of decision making includes a reassessment of the dominant image of the Hamidian state as an autocracy that revolved around Abdülhamid II's whims and personal inclinations. To borrow historian Halil İnalcık's words in questioning accepted knowledge about the decision-making process in the Ottoman government: "How absolute the power of the sultan really was?"[2]

A Brief History of the Ottoman Hijaz and Telegraphy

The province of Hijaz, Hicaz Vilayeti,[3] had a colorful history that spanned continents. Immediately after its conquest by the Ottomans in 1517, it became part of the larger province of Ethiopia, Habeş Eyaleti.[4] In the sixteenth and seventeenth centuries, the capital of Ethiopia was Massawa and then Suakin on the western shore of the Red Sea. It was later moved to Jeddah on the eastern shore;[5] however, during this time the Hijaz region in general and Mecca and Medina in particular were only nominally under Ottoman control. The effective ruler in the Hijaz was the local amir of Mecca (also referred to as the *sharīf* of Mecca or, as British diplomats referred to him, the grand sharif), who traditionally hailed from one of two powerful Meccan families, 'Awn and Zaid.[6]

The first period of Ottoman rule lasted until the invasion of the Wahhabis from Najd in 1806, which prompted Sultan Mahmud II, in 1812, to request the help of Mehmed Ali Pasha in reasserting his authority.[7] Khedival rule over the Hijaz lasted until 1840, when the second period of Ottoman direct rule began, coinciding with the second period of its direct rule in Ottoman Libya, as discussed in Chapter 1. The office of amir of Mecca was gradually incorporated into the Ottoman administrative structure starting in 1850s. With the implementation of the centralizing Tanzimat, the amir had to be an Ottoman vizier and as such was given the imperial honorary title of pasha.[8] Additionally, he had to prove his loyalty to the sultan and gain political and administrative experience by serving in the imperial government in Istanbul, often as a member of the Şura-yı Devlet (Council of State), the highest advisory and legislative entity in the post-Tanzimat empire.[9]

During the Hamidian period, the Ottoman state attempted more direct control over the Hijaz. However, even then many of the privileges that Medina and Mecca traditionally enjoyed, such as exemption from taxes and army conscription, remained until the end of Ottoman rule.[10] In fact, Istanbul continued sending subsidies to the two holy cities and surrounding regions, which had no known natural resources at the time, to ensure good relations with the local Bedouin population, particularly during the busy hajj caravan season.

However, because the amir of Mecca was allowed to tax the local population on his own, the efforts of the provincial and imperial administrations were often thwarted.[11] Istanbul's lack of control over the local distribution of subsidies and taxation had a large impact on the effectiveness of the Ottoman strategy in the Hijaz at the turn of the twentieth century.

Unlike the Hijaz telegraph project, the Hijaz Railway project has for decades been the object of much academic attention. For this reason I undertake a representative, but by no means comprehensive, summary of published studies on it. In English Ochsenwald's research remains authoritative. His work on the railway's social, economic, and political impact illustrates the Hamidian regime's mobilization of the full resources of the state to extend its control to an important frontier of the empire. Other historians have focused on the railway's political, social, and military aspects and the government's use of it as a tool of pan-Islamic propaganda.[12] In Turkish there are several thoroughly researched studies relying mostly on Ottoman archival material. Ufuk Gülsöy bases his research on previously unavailable material that provides new details about the individuals involved in the planning of the railway as well as about post-Hamidian efforts to extend it to Mecca and Jeddah.[13] Since Gülsöy's work in the 1990s, other historians have taken this research to a much finer level of detail, incorporating increasingly abundant records from the Ottoman Archives.[14] Several studies in Arabic have made use of archives from former Ottoman provinces of the Arab lands for a local perspective on this trans-imperial project.[15] My research has greatly benefited from all these works and the detailed research and data they contain.

Analytically, I take a similar approach to Ochsenwald's on the planning and construction phase of the railway; I also emphasize the heated discussions between competing schools of thought in the Ottoman government to better understand imperial policies and intraimperial politics during this time. By following these discussions, I construct a nuanced picture of important strategic and operational decisions in Istanbul. Additionally, I view the Hijaz telegraph line and railway as a trans-imperial project that was part of the foreign policy revamping that had started more than fifteen years earlier in Berlin. In this way, I transcend the limitations too often imposed on the study of empire by adopting the perspective of contemporary nation-state politics and geography.[16]

Even though the first Hijaz telegraph line was not constructed until 1882, the Ottoman government was introduced to telegraphy as far back as 1839, when Samuel Morse's agent in the Ottoman Empire and Persia visited Istanbul to promote the new technology but was turned away. In 1847 Morse sent two specially designed instruments to Istanbul with the president of the American Scientific Association, John Laurence Smith, who was heading to Istanbul to consult on the empire's mining operations. Smith set up a demonstration at the Beylerbeyi on the Asian shores of the Bosphorus, the favorite summer home of the royal family,[17] that impressed twenty-six-year-old Sultan Abdülmecid. However, like other world leaders who were approached by Morse at the time, Abdülmecid was hesitant to invest, although he did award Morse the Order of Pride (Nişan-ı İftihar)—reportedly the only Ottoman decoration ever bestowed on an American citizen.[18]

Ultimately, it took a war to prove the usefulness of telegraphy to the Ottoman government. In 1855 the first telegraph line was built and operated by the British army during the Crimean War. It extended from Varna to Balaklava in the Crimean Peninsula via Istanbul.[19] At roughly the same time, the first Egyptian line between Alexandria and Cairo went into service.[20] A decade later, after purchasing the Varna–Balaklava line from the British, the empire became the third signatory to the International Telegraph Convention of 1865. This was the first step toward connecting all Ottoman territories through telegraphy.[21]

By 1877 a vast network of telegraph lines stretched over seventeen thousand miles of the empire.[22] It was constructed by foreign contractors, and either remained under their supervision or was operated jointly by Ottoman and foreign governments. Such was the case in 1860, when London and Istanbul collaborated on a project to construct a line across Anatolia and southern Iraq to Fao (al-Faw). Fao, which sat on an inlet of the Persian Gulf, was the southernmost town in the province of Basra at the border with the Persian Empire. Passing through Ottoman territories, the network had been initiated by London to create the first line of communication with the Indian subcontinent. The Ottoman Empire had use of the line to connect Istanbul with towns and cities in Anatolia and Iraq.

Even though the British and Ottoman governments were in agreement over the mutual benefits of this project, and although the topographic and economic conditions seemed favorable, the trans-Anatolian line proved unreliable. The reason was that its planners had largely underestimated the importance of obtaining the buy-in of local tribes. Tribesmen in Basra were frequently engaged in an open conflict with the Ottoman provincial government, and the telegraph lines were often the first targets of retaliation against government raids. In the 1870s, the line proved so unreliable that the British government was forced to build an alternative overland line from the Persian Gulf via Persia to connect to the Russian telegraph network.[23]

However, by the late nineteenth century, when the Ottoman government was considering the best route for the first Hijaz line, it did not limit its options to terra firma. In fact, submarine telegraphic experiments had been carried out successfully as early as 1840, and by the second half of the century, such lines were relatively common.[24] The most famous of these was the transatlantic line, which was completed in August of 1858 but failed soon thereafter. The cable was redesigned and successfully relaid in 1865.[25]

Several options were available to the Ottoman government, including submarine, underground, and overland, as well as various combinations of these. The choices available, in addition to the logistical, technical, and geopolitical considerations involved, made deciding on the right option very difficult. Once European colonial threats and Ottoman colonial ambitions are added to the list of considerations, it becomes easy to understand how even the simplest of decisions on the southern frontiers had potentially complicated and far-reaching implications, which were felt most strongly in Istanbul. To understand the decision-making process and its shifts based on imperial strategic priorities, the story of the Damascus–Hijaz line cannot begin in 1900, when actual work on the project commenced. Instead, we have to reach back twenty years, to 1880, when the first Hijaz telegraph line was being debated.

The First Hijaz Telegraph Line

One of the first proposals considered by the Ottoman government to connect the Hijaz to Istanbul was presented by the British Eastern Telegraph Company, in 1880.[26] This was a plan to construct a submarine line connecting Jeddah across the Red Sea with Suakin, an important port city on the coast of Egyptian Sudan and a former Ottoman provincial capital of the ancient province of Ethiopia. From Jeddah the line would extend inland to Medina and Mecca and south to the province of Yemen and from there to British Aden and on to the Indian subcontinent.[27] The proposal attracted much heated discussion in government circles, with the majority of opinions decidedly against it. A closer look at the negative opinions reveals the concerns that ultimately weighed most heavily in the government's decision making in 1880.[28]

A report from the Council of Telegraph and Post (Meclis-i Telgraf ve Posta)[29] summarized the main challenges facing the proposed project. A primary concern was the technical difficulty of a submarine line given a history of failed attempts to conquer the rugged terrain of the Red Sea floor.[30] However, the 1860s saw several technological advancements in submarine cable reinforcement and insulation. Moreover, two major projects had been successfully completed: the Persian Gulf line in 1864 and the second transatlantic line in 1865,[31] and by 1870 the Eastern Telegraph Company had successfully laid submarine cables connecting London to Lisbon and Lisbon to Gibraltar, Malta, and Alexandria, continuing overland to Suez, through the Red Sea to Aden, and on to Bombay.[32]

A factor that weighed even more heavily on Ottoman officials was the lack of domestic expertise with submarine lines, which meant relying on British contractors for construction and maintenance of this critical tool of communication, essentially leaving it at the mercy of a foreign entity.[33] A related concern was the high cost of such a large undertaking, which would not only further burden an already bankrupt treasury[34] but also line the pockets of British contractors instead of those of local contractors. There was no choice but to hire British contractors, however, who had a virtual monopoly on the laying of submarine telegraph cables at the time.[35]

Another concern about foreign partnerships was the probable necessity of having to conduct telegraphic communication in what the Council of State referred to as "foreign tongues" (*elsine ecnebiye*) as opposed to Turkish and Arabic because the lines would be shared with the British imperial government.[36] The Morse code for the English alphabet was different from that for the Ottoman-Turkish alphabet, as were the extensive language-specific abbreviations that were regularly used.[37] What made this more than a simple matter of practicality was Ottoman insistence on the use of the empire's languages as a signifier of imperial pride and sovereignty.

Technical and foreign partnership concerns were dwarfed by worries about the Bedouins in the Hijaz and the fear that local authorities could not guarantee the safety of the telegraph lines passing through their territories. To drive the point home, the Council of State, which was debating the issue in 1880, brought up the trans-Anatolian line running through Bedouin territories in Iraq, which, despite the best efforts of the Ottomans and the British, were regularly attacked.[38]

Thus it is clear that Ottoman officials' concerns were of two main types: an expressed aversion to foreign dependence with an emphasis on maintaining Ottoman sovereignty, and domestic security threats to telegraph line. To deal with these concerns, the special Council of Telegraph and Post proposed awarding a contract to the Eastern Telegraph Company to build a submarine line for the *exclusive* use of the Ottoman Empire, which would have complete control of its operation and so could mandate use of the Ottoman-Turkish alphabet and abbreviations for transmissions. As for the route that the line would take, the council recommended connecting Jeddah to Suez and using a second cable to connect Suez to Yanbuʿ, a coastal town on the Hijaz Red Sea coast approximately 300 kilometers north of Jeddah. A submarine intra-Arabia connector that would run along the Hijaz coast south to Yemen was also suggested. The council's reasoning was that such a project would ultimately be a more useful and secure investment than the joint venture with the British government proposed by the Eastern Telegraph Company.[39] The council's objective was a compromise in which contracting a British company would be necessary but without sharing a line with the British in order to preserve Ottoman control over its operation. Additionally, the recommended line would minimize overland connections because the port cities along the Arabian coast would be connected underwater.

The Ottoman government did not question the decision not to use overland connections, accepting that Bedouin tribes in the Hijaz were more of a danger to the success of the project than foreign contractors. Nevertheless, it did refuse to accept the council's recommendations without requiring specific route modifications. Thus, on April 2, 1882, the Ministry of Telegraph and Post announced its decision to build a submarine line connecting Jeddah in the Hijaz to Suakin—effectively the original British proposal. The basis of this decision was not made explicit, but letters from the Hijazi government to the Ministry of Interior offer some clues.

In Council of State archival files, there are letters advising against the underwater Suez route recommended by the Council of Telegraph and Post.[40] These were from the governor-general of the Hijaz, Marshal Osman Nuri Pasha, who was a close advisor to Sultan Abdülhamid II, and from ʿAbd al-Mutalib Pasha, the newly appointed amir of Mecca. Because ʿAbd al-Mutalib Pasha had recently replaced Amir Hussein Pasha, who had been accused of conducting unauthorized negotiations with the British government, his advice against tying the Hijaz to British-controlled Suez is easy to understand. However, other geopolitical factors were also at play. By the beginning of 1882, the ʿUrabi Revolt was in full swing in Egypt, and Britain's intention to invade the country in order to protect the Suez Canal was known to the Ottoman government. For these reasons, a long-distance line to the Suez, which was the declared focus of British imperial interests, was too risky.[41] In his 1882 memoirs, Sultan Abdülhamid II wrote that Britain was on course to take full control of the Suez Canal and would eventually push even France's interests to the side.[42]

Suakin, a port town on the Red Sea lying directly across from Jeddah and still under Ottoman sovereignty, provided a viable alternative to the Suez as the final destination for the telegraph line. It was already connected overland to the Egyptian telegraph network, which had been expanded in the 1860s under Khedive Ismail Pasha (r. 1863–1879).[43] The Egyptian line connected Suakin inland to Berber on the Nile and followed the Nile north toward Lower Egypt to Cairo. In 1872 it was run to Alexandria and Istanbul, affording the Ottomans an alternative to reliance on a European line.[44] Also, the submarine section of the line would require insulation to protect against the harsh undersea elements, making it the most expensive component of the Jeddah–Suez connection. Thus choosing the shorter Jeddah–Suakin submarine connection meant considerable savings.[45]

It is safe to conclude that in the early 1880s concerns about threats to domestic security in the form of Bedouin attacks ultimately weighed more heavily than concerns about dependency on foreign expertise. Yet it would become painfully evident that the decision to rely on the Egyptian network would come to haunt the Ottoman government. Soon after the line was completed, complaints from the Ministry of Telegraph and Post were raised, mostly stemming from the lack of control over the operation and maintenance of the bulk of line.

Initially the problem was Egyptian mismanagement of the line between Suakin and Cairo, which caused regular service interruptions. Also, dispatch priority was given to Egyptian and British telegrams, creating noticeable delays for Ottoman messages.[46] Delays were common during this period because of the mechanics of long-distance transmissions. Messages were often sent along a network of intermediate transition points, and at each point they had to be retranscribed and retransmitted. Such bottlenecks in the chain of transmission caused not only delays but sometimes even loss of a message along the way.[47]

The unreliability of Egyptian telegraph services threatened to cause an intraimperial altercation between Cairo and Istanbul. Ottoman authorities sent an official complaint to the khedive, asking for his intervention in the matter. A quick telegraphic reply stated that Cairo would communicate to Suakin authorities that special care must be taken in handling Ottoman dispatches. Istanbul also instituted a special procedure for official telegrams sent from Jeddah to Istanbul in which messages were to be copied by the telegraph office and bundled copies be sent on a monthly basis by mail to make sure that no official correspondence was lost.[48]

It is not clear whether the khedival government actually took any measures to alleviate the problem of delayed and missing messages, but there is evidence that the problem was not solved. Thus, in late 1883 the Ottoman government decided to take matters into its own hands, dispatching the head of telegraph operations in Damascus, Émile Bey, and some of his staff to Cairo to ensure that its telegraphic interests were being protected. These reassignments were supposed to be temporary, but they lasted for months and even years.[49] Istanbul would soon recognize that an alternative solution would have to be found for its ongoing telegraphic woes.

In addition to technical and bureaucratic difficulties, military and political conflicts in Egyptian Sudan and along the Red Sea coast were further complicating the situation; Mahdist forces were attempting to take over the rest of the Sudan while the Italians were vying for Massawa. After their occupation of Egypt in 1882, the British pressed the khedive to give up direct control of Massawa and Suakin, two important Red Sea port cities that were in the crosshairs of the Mahdist state as well as those of Britain and Italy. By 1885 the Italians had taken Massawa, but did not officially declare their annexation of the city in order to avoid an unnecessary public confrontation with Istanbul. Mahdist forces took control of Egyptian Sudan with the exception of Suakin, which remained under British control.

Such maneuverings rendered the overland telegraph line on which the Ottoman government relied virtually unusable and necessitated diversion of telegraph traffic coming from the Hijaz to the British Suakin–Suez submarine line,[50] which had been laid after the British invasion of Egypt in 1882.[51] The delicate balance of diplomacy and realpolitik would continue to play havoc with Ottoman-British relations as the decade came to a close, but not before more immediate technical issues affected telegraph operations, highlighting the reliance of the Ottoman government on foreign technical expertise.

In March of 1884, the Ministry of Telegraph and Post drew up preliminary budget and routing plans for a new connection to the Hijaz that would bypass all foreign networks. The plan at that early stage called for connecting Muzeyrib[52] in Darʿa, where the Syrian line ended, to Medina and Mecca via ʿAqaba.[53] Even though the Ottoman government did not announce its intention to build this alternative route until the 1890s, documents from 1884 indicate that the new route would be completely independent from foreign-controlled networks. The pressure on Istanbul to find an alternative to the Hijaz line increased as demand for the telegraph rose, creating more stress on the existing network.

After 1885 the pressure on Istanbul to improve its telegraph network and expand it further into remote areas of the Arab provinces grew. For example, in 1886 officials of the province of Syria and the *sancak* of Zor—a district of the province of Syria close to the present-day Iraq border with Deir al-Zor as its main town—wrote to the Ministry of Telegraph and Post requesting the construction of a line between Deir al-Zor and Damascus. They argued that quick communication between the provincial capital and remote Zor was necessary for the effective control of the "wild tribes" in the Syrian Desert.[54] In the same year, the army sent a request to the ministry for a line connecting Damascus to Masmiyya, a settlement in the middle of a large swath of the desert approximately 55 kilometers south of Damascus. Even though, at the time of the request, the army was still relying on horseback messengers,[55] it took almost a year of discussion and a full cost analysis for the Damascus–Masmiyya project to be approved by the Council of Ministers (Meclis-i Vükela).[56]

By the beginning of 1889, the need for an alternative to the Hijaz–Suakin line had become even more pressing. Messages from Hijaz now were either carried on horseback to Muzeyrib to be sent via the Damascus or Beirut telegraph lines, or sent by slow, but more reliable, post.[57] The diverted Hijazi telegraphic traffic, coupled with the increased use of the telegraph generally, caused noticeable strains on the network further north. To mitigate these strains, line repairs, new line construction, and staff increases were approved for Diyarbakır, Aleppo, and Damascus.[58]

Problems were also brewing under the sea, for in addition to regular wear and tear on the submarine cables necessitating repairs by foreign contractors,[59] the water entry points for telegraph lines on the Red Sea coasts were becoming highly problematic. On both sides of the sea, the lines had been laid too close to the harbor and at shallow depths, increasing the risk of damage or complete severance by docking ships, particularly during stormy weather. That was exactly what happened in 1897, when the *Elektra*, a ship owned by the Lloyd Austria Company,[60] damaged the submarine line while docking in Suakin harbor. The Ministry of Interior and the Ministry of Telegraph and Post sued Lloyd for damages and repair costs, but later dropped their suit on the advice of Ottoman international law experts.[61] Besides the risk of severed cable, there was the constant worry over reliance on British firms for maintenance of the aging line,

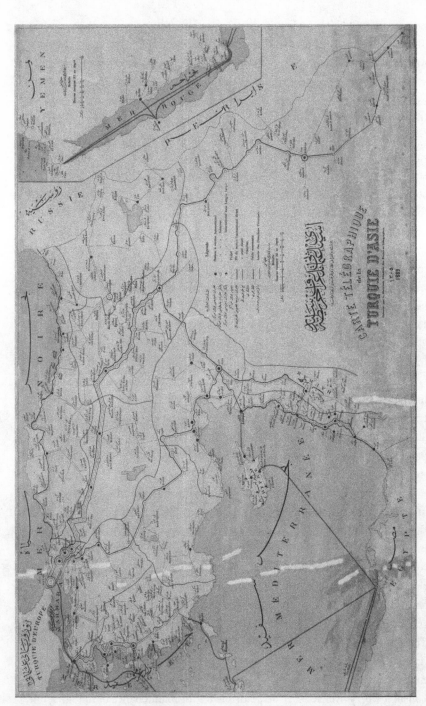

FIGURE 8. Telegraph lines in the Ottoman Empire as of 1889 (BOA, HRT-H-366/1).

prompting the ministry to complain about the poor quality of the cables used for the "only method" by which to reach the Hijaz (Figure 8).[62]

The pressure on the financial, technical, and military resources of the government and the importance of connecting the Hijaz with Istanbul were very high, and it was in this context that an independently funded, built, and run telegraph line was being debated. Foreign proposals that offered financial and technical relief, even though they meant the involvement of European imperial competitors, must have been very tempting.

Reading the Fine Print

In September 1888, John Pender, the chairman of the Eastern Telegraph Company, hand-delivered a proposal to the Minister of Telegraph and Post in Istanbul which outlined the details of what looked like a financially favorable deal for the Ottoman state. Pender proposed a submarine telegraph connection between Jeddah and Hudeidah that would connect the province of Yemen with the rest of the empire's network, with two-thirds of the cost of construction to be covered by the Eastern Telegraph Company.[63]

Despite the favorable financial terms and the strategic benefits of tying the empire's internationally sensitive southern frontier to the capital through a secure submarine line, Yıldız Palace took less than a month to reply with a firm rejection, in the process closing the door on any future bids from British firms.[64] The rejection letter stated that the Ottoman government would continue with plans for an "envisioned" overland connection for which it had already ordered a scientific and technical assessment, adding that it would contact the Eastern Telegraph Company if its services were to be required in the future. A subsequent letter to Pender himself from the special Council for Telegraph and Post was more explicit; it stated that the sultan himself was entirely committed to an overland line and therefore Pender's services would not be needed.[65] This rejection of the head of the largest telegraph company in the world, controlling the vast majority of long distance telegraph lines, was decisive. The question is why the Ottoman government replied in such a way to a company it had contracted with less than a decade earlier.

Pender's proposal must have seemed financially attractive initially, and with the security problems associated with an overland line passing through the Hijazi Desert there must have been a great deal of pressure to use a submarine line instead. However, the proposal contained an important stipulation that made the offer impossible to accept: Pender wanted a concession to operate the Istanbul–Fao line, which connected London with British-controlled Karachi and ran through the heart of Anatolia and lower Iraq. An independence-conscious Istanbul, intimately familiar with the novel rules of new imperialism as a participant in the scramble for Africa, found such an offer a threat to its sovereignty for two reasons.

Giving a British company the rights to a line that ran through the middle of Anatolia and represented one of Istanbul's main arteries of communication with its eastern provinces gave rise to fears of repeating the experience of delayed and lost messages on the British-controlled Egyptian telegraph network if the trans-Anatolia line were to also fall under British control. Also, there was the danger of allowing a foreign entity to have rights over physical infrastructure on Ottoman soil. In the General Act of Berlin of 1885, a very relevant stipulation in Article 35 introduced certain conditions necessary for a European government to claim rights over land in Africa (see Chapter 2). A telegraph line was often the most effective and cheapest form of making such a claim, allowing colonial powers to literally plant their stakes in the ground. According to Claudio Canaparo, the telegraph is a "highly efficient" way for an imperial state to convert a "terrain" into a colonial "territory." It was especially effective in expanding a state's frontiers and annexing further terrain by marking it with state-sponsored infrastructure.[66]

Even if the growing "Armenian question" is taken into consideration, Anatolia was not in immediate danger of colonization, nor was it a frontier like the Arabian Desert and the Sahara.[67] Nevertheless, the logic of colonial possession in the age of high imperialism still held, particularly at a time when the Ottoman Empire was increasingly becoming the soft target of European colonial interests, and so independence from foreign control over imperial projects was taking on new meaning as a nonnegotiable requirement. In addition, the connection between telegraph technology and British imperialism had by then become a clear and well-established one, which the Ottoman Empire was adamantly determined to avoid.[68] John Pender and his monopolistic hold over the submarine telegraph industry is a case in point.

John Pender was a Manchester cotton magnate who had served in the British Parliament and went into the business of laying submarine telegraph cables at a time when most investors shied away from it. His early risk paid off, giving him an advantage over other telegraph entrepreneurs. He made a name for himself by laying cables connecting Great Britain with the Mediterranean in the 1870s, when most companies stayed away from submarine lines because of the disastrous Red Sea failure in 1858. After 1893 the British government began subsidizing cable construction in return for control of both the cable and the rates for official telegrams. Pender took advantage of such subsidies and also enjoyed British naval support in surveying ocean floors and British diplomacy in pressuring foreign governments to award him cable landing rights.[69] Pender's telegraph companies, as private outfits, were favorably positioned to get around the regulations of foreign governments that viewed British companies as suspect. Even when competing imperial powers refused to hire British contractors, Pender was able to set up shell companies that seemed to be non-British owned, but which archival records show were in fact tied to him.[70]

Collaboration between British telegraph companies and imperial governments reached its apex immediately after 1885. While the major European powers were agreeing on ways to divide up Africa, communication technology was taking on a different dimension. As mentioned earlier, the rules of "effective occupation" for vast areas that could not be directly colonized with boots on the ground called for some form of infrastructure that would tie the colony to the metropole. Telegraph lines were one of the most practical and cost-effective ways to achieve this goal, a fact that both the Ottoman Empire and the Great Powers realized. Overland telegraph lines had the added benefit of acting as the visible presence of an often distant and hard to imagine colonial authority.

Mirroring its efforts in Africa, the British government attempted to incorporate both Persia and the Ottoman Empire into its "informal electronic empire." Through a series of agreements between 1868 and 1892, it succeeded with Persia, effectively controlling the Persian national telegraph system. However, despite its best efforts, it was not successful in doing the same with Ottoman system. British companies could only provide technical support to the Indo-European network and the Ottoman Telegraph Agency to ensure continued operation of this network, which connected Britain to India, in this way appeasing the Ottoman government and maintaining an "informal empire."[71]

Conclusion

By early 1882, British imperial ambitions in Egypt and the Red Sea had come to light. The Ottoman government found it wise and cost effective to lay a line connecting Jeddah with Suakin on the Egyptian-Sudanese Red Sea coast and linking to Berber and then to Cairo overland. However, although this route offered an alternative to complete dependence on the British-controlled submarine network, Istanbul could not have predicted how fast geopolitical reality in

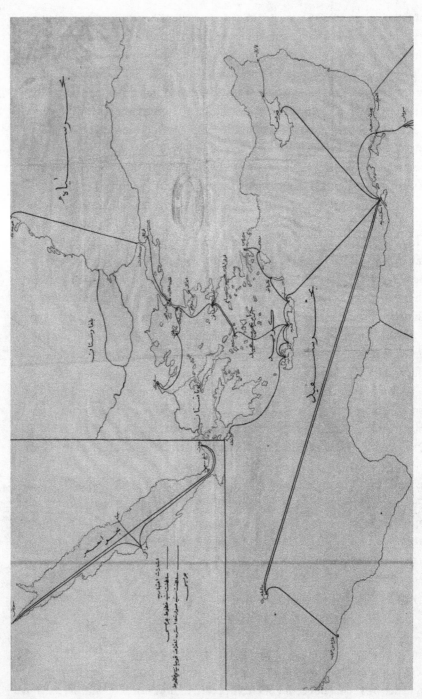

FIGURE 9. Submarine telegraph lines in the Ottoman Empire as of 1923 (BOA, HRT-H-135/1).

the Sudan and along the Red Sea coast would change in the following decade. By 1885, imperial competition in the Red Sea, the Mahdist state's success in expanding east toward the Red Sea coast, and the ineffective relay of messages in the Egyptian telegraph network made the Jeddah–Suakin line highly unreliable. There are numerous examples of money spent to patch and repair the Ottoman line in the Red Sea when what was needed was a long-term solution. Frustration over unreliable service was being channeled away from complaints about technology toward anger over Istanbul's apparent inability to avoid over-dependence on foreign powers for communication with its southern regions. The lines from Istanbul connecting Tripoli via Malta and Jeddah via Egypt both passed through British-controlled telegraph lines that depended on British companies for their operation and maintenance. Perhaps Sultan Abdülhamid II said it best: "We should keep track of the Great Powers' policies when it comes to their offers to construct railways . . . as we might end up making a big mistake and falling in harms way if we [give] a contract to the wrong party."[72]

Thus, the Ottoman government benefited from lessons learned during the preceding fifteen years in two ways. First, its severely strained relations with Britain and France in Africa led it to reject both French and British offers to build the telegraph line extension, despite seemingly favorable operational and financial terms. Second, as the following chapter demonstrates in more detail, the successful partnership with Bedouins on the Saharan frontiers between 1885 and 1900 dampened the Hamidian regime's hesitation to partner with some of the Bedouin tribes on the Arabian frontiers in 1900–1902, in this way avoiding reliance on European powers.

6 THE LOCAL MEETS THE GLOBAL ON AN IMPERIAL FRONTIER

In order to complete the information I have given so far about the Sanusi
zawāyā, I believe that a discussion about the state of affairs in Arabia would not
go to waste. . . . In both Africa and Arabia, [the order] saved [the Bedouins]
from the lure of Europeans' ostentatious demonstrations of progress that [were]
meant to attract and eventually use Muslims, especially the impressionable
and gullible ones amongst them. . . . Europeans who have political designs on
the region, have kept their eye on the order's zawāyā in Africa, where many of
the African Muslims stay when they pass through the vast territory which falls
under the guidance of the sheikh, on their way to the Hijaz.

Sadik al-Mouayad Azmzade, Kufra, Wednesday, November 6, 1895

AZMZADE'S FOCUS on European designs in both Africa and Arabia reflect
the empire's vigilance and its acknowledgment of the importance of local populations of the imperial borderlands in the interimperial competition that was
raging at the time. An anxious Istanbul understood the global ramifications
of what seemed to be exclusively local issues along the southern frontiers. In
places like the Hijazi Desert, domestic issues such as the Bedouin question and
global concerns such as competitive colonialism merged, often in unpredict-
able ways. Events surrounding the Hijaz telegraph line illustrate the complexity of intraimperial politics and contingencies that became disproportionately
important on the transimperial stage. In the midst of debates over the planning
and construction of the Hijaz line, Istanbul's international strategic concerns
come into stark relief against the individual concerns of the multilayered structure of the Ottoman government.

This chapter delves into Ottoman intragovernmental relations that fore-
grounded the main issue along the frontiers, that is, Istanbul's relationship with
Bedouins in the context of interimperial competition in Africa and Arabia.
The back and forth of debates over the telegraph line—tedious as they may

appear—outline the interactions between the various levels of the government that had a major impact on Istanbul's strategies along the empire's frontiers-cum-borderlands. Even though Yıldız Palace continued its policy of cultivating relationships with Bedouin chieftains, the Hijaz would prove to be a much more complicated web of powers and individual interests to navigate.

Many officials were involved in decision making concerning the extension of the Hijaz telegraph line, but only a handful had vested interests in its success (or failure). First, there was the palace with Sultan Abdülhamid II, serving as the main arbitrator, and the special telegraph council headed by İzzet Pasha al-Abid (in Arabic ʿIzzat Basha al-ʿĀbed), who was a close advisor to the sultan and the man responsible for many of the financial schemes behind major infrastructure projects at the time. A fascinating character, İzzet Pasha rose from *katib* in his native Damascus to the sultan's right-hand man, often referred to by adversaries and the Istanbul press as *Arap* İzzet Pasha (*Arap* was a thinly disguised racist term for a person with dark skin).[1] İzzet Pasha was famous for his negotiating skills and for the backing of Sultan Abdülhamid II, which made him legendary and later notorious in fin-de-siècle Istanbul.[2]

The Ministry of Telegraph and Post, the Ministry of Interior, and the Ottoman army were responsible for the day-to-day planning and execution of the telegraph project, an already difficult job made even harder by scarce resources and complicated intragovernmental squabbling. Finally, and perhaps most important, provincial stakeholders proved to be the project's game changers, altering the course of the line, physically and figuratively. Some of them, such as the governor-general of the province of Syria, supported it and provided resources in its service. Others, such as the commander and governor-general of the province of Hijaz and the amir of Mecca, did their best to derail it.

All of the players in the second Hijaz telegraph line, in attempting to negotiate their vision into reality, shaped the debates surrounding it. This was a typical feature of Ottoman governmental decision making at the end of the nineteenth century, and to understand it we have to return one more time to the last five fateful years of the century, when the project's planning and construction exposed internal rifts among the various levels of the Ottoman government.

Debating the Second Hijaz Telegraph Line

In 1896 the main areas of contention over the telegraph line were tactical, stemming from budgetary limitations and the balancing of security with geopolitics on the sensitive frontiers of the Hijaz. A special council was created to provide information about all aspects of the project—budgetary, technical, environmental, and security—to the Council of Ministers. While in private the feasibility of the project was being debated, a public relations campaign had been ongoing from the beginning. One of the earliest press releases to appear was about a "gift" of wooden poles, including thirteen thousand from "the people of Damascus" and five thousand from the "people of ʿAjlun." The Ottoman Ministry of Forestry, Mines, and Agriculture had authorized these donations, which represented more than two-thirds of the estimated poles required. This "gift" was reported in the daily newspaper, İkdam, which at times acted as the mouthpiece for the imperial government's campaign, emphasizing the united support for the telegraph extension and giving special mention to the Bedouin tribesmen who helped transport the poles.[3]

For the remainder of the expenses, an itemized budget estimate was submitted to the Council of Ministers for approval. Documents from this early planning stage show Jerusalem, which had been connected to Istanbul in 1865,[4] as the point from which the telegraph would take an overland route to ʿAqaba, ʿAynuna, Wajh, Yanbuʿ, and then Medina—all cities lying along the Red Sea coast. The original plan also called for a submarine line to connect Yanbuʿ and Jeddah. Although acknowledging that the ultimate decision lay with the Council of Ministers, an unnamed military source recommended connecting the line with one of the four hajj caravan routes to Mecca that would start in Jerusalem and connect with Maʿan–Tabuk–Medaʾin Saleh–Hadiyya–Medina and end in Mecca.[5]

The Council of Ministers eventually produced a decision paper in 1896 in which the telegraph council's recommendations were summarized and several crucial budgetary items were added. These items highlighted the substantial cost of security personnel to guard against attacks during and after construction. A portion of the security budget was allocated to the atiye (in Arabic ʿaṭiyya), a gift (or bribe depending on one's point of view) to be given to key Bedouin chiefs along the proposed route in order to secure their support for the construction and operation of the telegraph line. The rest was to cover the cost of permanent installations of armed guards for the protection of the line and the telegraph stations. The ministers' report warned that the wooden poles donated by Damascus and ʿAjlun, might not withstand the harsh natural environment of the desert. Depending on the recommendations of a provincial environmental inspector, it was acknowledged that iron poles might be required, in which case the cost of construction would double.

The report turned to another issue of considerable importance. This was the vehement opposition of Hijazi authorities to the project. In a letter to the grand vizier, the governor-general of the Hijaz, Ahmed Ratib Pasha, wrote that he did not recommend the project as proposed because the provincial government could not prevent Bedouin tribesmen from attacking the line. The Council of Ministers, citing the alleged impossibility of guaranteeing the safety of the telegraph line did not recommend the continuation of the project as it stood at that time.[6]

Further investigation into the council's decision leads to a number of letters written by the head of telegraph services in the province of Hijaz, Şefik Pasha, to Governor-General Ratib Pasha and a later letter from Ratib Pasha to the Sublime Porte. The first set of correspondence came in response to an official visit to Istanbul by Suleiman Pasha, a *sheikh al-mashāyekh* (head of chiefs; in Turkish *Şeyhülmeşayıh*) from Wajh on the Red Sea coast that was on the initially proposed path of the telegraph line. Reportedly, in an effort to show his support for the sultan, Suleiman Pasha had made the long journey to personally guarantee protection for the telegraph line that would go through his jurisdiction. Years later, the governor-general of Syria, Nazim Pasha, recommended that Istanbul honor Suleiman Pasha for "his help in moving a large amount of columns and equipment, and for his help in defending the line, and his friendship to the Ottoman government."[7] However, in 1896, Suleiman Pasha's goodwill and political showmanship were interpreted as violating the provincial chain of command, which triggered the ire of Şefik Pasha and the loud protestation of Ratib Pasha.

First, Şefik Pasha wrote a long letter to Ratib Pasha in which he outlined much of what appeared in the final Council of Ministers' decision as evidence against the telegraph council's proposal and as an implicit criticism of Suleiman Pasha. In addition to recommending the use of iron poles, he provided the governor-general with the key argument against the extension, sarcastically suggesting that even if Suleiman Pasha could protect the line in Wajh, the danger of attack in the less inhabited areas would remain. He also suggested that the proposed path be completely scrapped (*sarf-ı nazar*) and made some guesses about a better route: in short, that the Jeddah–Suakin line be replaced with a submarine Yanbu'–'Aqaba line with overland connections from Yanbu' to Medina, Mecca, and Jeddah. This, he claimed, would minimize the exposure of overland lines to Bedouin attacks.[8]

In turn Ratib Pasha wrote to Istanbul echoing Şefik Pasha but embellishing the danger of Bedouins in the region in a dramatic and essentialist ethnocultural way:

> Since most of the Bedouins who inhabit the Hijaz have not yet escaped the world of savagery and tribalism [alemi vahşet ve Bedeviyetten kurtulmayıp], they are ignorant and unaware [cahil ve gafil] of the benefits of the telegraph or of similar means of prosperity and civilization [mamuriyet ve medeniyet]. . . . In general, the line could not be kept away from the harm they might cause. Understanding that there are studies underway, we also found and brought experts in the form of two chiefs from Wajh and Rabigh to ask their opinion on this matter. [They informed us that] in order to avoid the Bedouins' interruption of the government's work, an appropriate sum of money has been given. However the money that would be given to combat the ignorance of the tribes' members [kabilelerin efradının cehaletlerine karşı] will not provide any guarantees. If the extension of the line would continue in the direction of Medina, the logic of how the ignorance of the Bedouins' works will be uncovered to the government [hukumetten mestur kalmayacağı], who will start to see its destructive impact.[9]

Finally, declaring that the province could not guarantee the safety of the line, Ratib Pasha recommended instead that the main portion of the line be underwater, away from the desert's "harsh nature and men"; the only safe overland portion would be the route between Mecca, Medina, and Jeddah because it was well traveled and Ottoman forces were stationed on it.[10] We see in the following section just how wrong Ratib Pasha was, because the most dangerous and ultimately impassable road would prove to be the one between Mecca and Medina.

Reading the letters of Şefik Pasha and Ratib Pasha, it becomes easy to understand where the Council of Ministers must have gotten their information. The advice of an Ottoman governor-general, based on his experience with the "locals" in a "distant" land was powerful enough to lead the ministers to reject the telegraph council's proposal. Ratib Pasha spoke for the provincial and local powers in the Hijaz, which included the amir of Mecca and others who had an interest in blocking the telegraph line to prevent Istanbul's meddling and to protect the status quo.[11]

The Route to Mecca: Weighing External versus Internal Threats

Despite the ministers' decision, because of Yıldız Palace's unwavering backing not all was lost for the telegraph project. Four months later, the minister of telegraph and post wrote to the minister of interior, who wrote to governor-general of the Hijaz. Their message was that, despite the council of ministers' rejection and the governor-general's complaints, construction of the line was to go ahead, albeit with slight modifications. In his letter to Ratib Pasha, the minister of interior outlined the logic behind this decision, which provides us with our best indication of Istanbul's priorities. He wrote that despite the high financial cost involved and the governor-general's valid concerns, the benefits of running the line overland outweighed the risks because this was the only way the empire could execute the project independently, using local resources and expertise, allowing Istanbul to demonstrate its self-reliance to fellow Ottomans and to the world at large. Moreover, this decision would in the long run prove financially and politically profitable. The minister wrote that he did not want to downplay the risks and cost involved in an overland line, in both military resources and total expense, which was estimated at six or seven million *kuruş*, but he assured the governor-general that solutions would be found if problems arose.[12]

The letter to Ratib Pasha could not have been timelier. Along with the ever present maintenance expenses of the Hijaz–Suakin line, another submarine line connecting Cyprus with Latakia had recently failed and an emergency budget had just been approved to immediately begin repairs.[13]

The minister of interior's sentiments were echoed by Hussein Hilmi Pasha, who would soon be governor-general of the province of Yemen (r. 1898–1902),[14] in a well-timed letter complaining about the lack of reliable telegraph connections to Istanbul. He cited the Jeddah–Suakin line as an example of money that would go into the pockets of foreigners if the government chose a submarine line. Hilmi Pasha also wrote of the renewed imperial pride that was asserting itself on the international stage. He recommended an overland line regardless of the dangers and costs because it would keep the empire's important communication out of the hands of a foreign company. In what would prove to be the rallying cry of Yıldız Palace as it campaigned for Ottomans' support and donations from the Muslim world, he concluded that showing the world that Ottomans could do it on their own would have "material and spiritual" (*maddi ve manevi*) benefits that outweighed any risks.[15]

Thus, much complicated negotiation and arm-twisting were involved in a government project of this magnitude. That the buy-in of all stakeholders was critical was proved repeatedly as construction got under way. Even though Istanbul had appointed both the governor-general of Hijaz and the amir of

Mecca, it did not control their local influence. Additionally, even though the overland route seems to have been forced through despite the Council of Ministers' reservations, it was a strategic choice, not the arbitrary wish of the sultan because of his well-known distrust of the British. In part, it symbolized the empire's retaking control of its infrastructure, in an effort to boost the morale of imperial subjects. Also, the telegraph project would prepare the way for the much more expensive and ultimately more complicated Hijaz Railway. Keeping in mind that Istanbul had just recently been elbowed out of the colonial race in Africa and upstaged by the Great Powers, the decision to undertake such a bold project was one way that Yıldız Palace attempted to reassert its sovereignty, particularly along its southern frontiers.

Consultation continued, this time tackling the path of the telegraph line through the difficult and often dangerous Hijazi Desert. The cost estimate provided by the army and the Ministry of Telegraph and Post was for the original path that would start in Jerusalem and connect with the Syrian hajj caravan route. However, once this path was announced, opinions—solicited and unsolicited—flowed into Istanbul, questioning the estimated budget for transportation of materials and warning of the Bedouin threat. These opinions were considered by the telegraph council, which changed its recommendation, dropping the long and sparsely inhabited route from Jerusalem to 'Aqaba. In a more conservative approach, the line would now be built in several phases, with the first phase testing the feasibility of security and the accuracy of the cost estimates. At the completion of each section, the plan would be adjusted according to revised recommendations.[16]

This final decision was approved by a special council representing a "Who's Who" in the imperial government. Its membership comprised the minister of external affairs, the head of the Council of State, the minister of education, the director of religious endowments, the head of the Treasury, a representative from the Imperial Armory, the minister of internal affairs, a grand vizier's consultant, Şeyhülislam, the minister of justice, and representatives from the army and navy. Their collective approval sent the message that the time for (open) opposition to the project had passed.[17]

The route to the city of Ma'an was the only one not in dispute, while the rest of the route continued to be debated. The main question was whether to build the line along the Red Sea coast or further inland. Yet again two camps emerged over the Bedouin issue. Ratib Pasha advised the Sublime Porte that the line should follow the coastal route—Ma'an-'Aqaba-'Aynuna-Wajh-Yanbu'-Jeddah, with connections to Yanbuʿ–Medina and Jeddah–Mecca because there was far less of a Bedouin presence along the coast. Yıldız Palace backed the telegraph council in its choice of the Syrian hajj caravan route further inland, which followed the route taken by the sultan's *surra-yı hümayun* carrying the annual *muhammal*.[18] Because the Syrian route was already one of the most secure routes in the desert thanks to this precious cargo and, according to the palace, because it was far from "external dangers" that might come from the Red Sea, a special decree (*İrade Hususi*) was issued confirming this route as the sultan's will (Figure 10).[19]

What danger from the Red Sea? As I discussed in Chapter 5, by the end of the nineteenth century, European designs on Ottoman frontiers were coming to light. The construction of the telegraph line was the first step toward the construction of a railway to connect Istanbul with the Hijaz along the same path. On choosing the location for the railway, Sultan Abdülhamid II had this to say:

> One has to take care and be careful. The railway has a large strategic importance, because it could be used to provide means of quick military transportation. Thus, it could be used as an effective weapon if an enemy was to take it over, where it would be used to facilitate the occupation of the lands the railway passes through. For specifically this reason I opposed the placement of the route close to the borders. . . . One has to only look at central Asian countries to see how railways can be used to their detriment. If these countries did not let Russia expand its network through their land, Russia would not have been able to expand its influence into their land as quickly as they did.[20]

Once again, international geopolitical considerations trumped fears about dangers posed by Bedouin tribes on the western frontiers of the Hijaz province. However, these dangers were not completely ignored, as a closer look at the schedule of expenses for the telegraph line makes clear. The special council was betting on a strategy of appeasement with a line item of 5,000 Kuruş to be given to the chiefs of every tribe in the region as a cost of doing business on the frontiers. Other line items were for army expenses and salaries for station guards.[21]

At the end of 1898, the final decision was made. Taking into account the price of foreign intervention and the moral benefits of self-reliance, an Ottoman-built line was agreed on with the acceptance that challenges would come up along the way. However, construction of the Damascus–Medina line was not to start for another eighteen months.

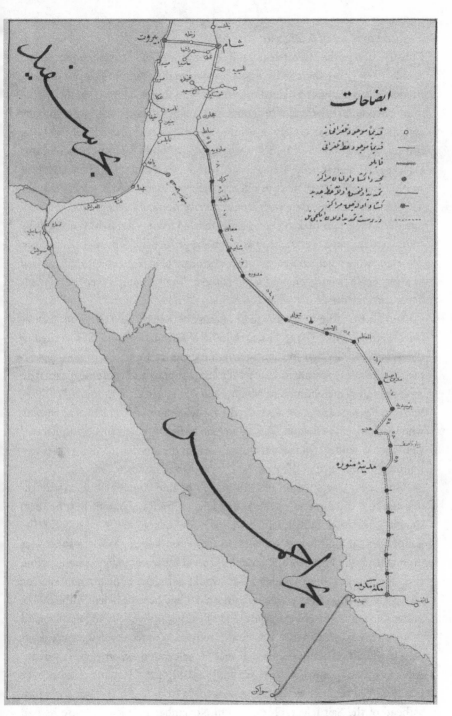

FIGURE 10. Original Hijaz telegraph line planning map (BOA, HRT-H -475/2, HRT-H-476/1).

The Logistics of a Difficult Project

Construction of the Hijaz telegraph line began with official assignment orders sent to none other than Sadik Pasha al-Mouayad Azmzade. In April of 1900, Azmzade was appointed to lead the project with four generals from the special army telegraph corps under his command. Eighty infantry men were initially assigned to the project, sixty of whom were dispatched immediately with the rest to follow soon after. In acknowledgment of both the importance of this project and the hardship it entailed, it was decreed that all of those involved would receive their pay twice as often as their colleagues and at triple the regular rate. Additionally, they each would receive honorary recognition on completion of their tour of duty.[22] Azmzade traveled from Istanbul to Damascus by train, arriving on May 2, 1900.[23] His entourage included one assistant officer, one captain, two lieutenants, and two engineers of sublieutenant rank, as well as a physician, a surgeon, and a pharmacist. The remainder were regular officers and enlistees.[24]

For construction of the line to be successful, well-trained telegraph technicians were required. The technical training of Ottoman telegraphers started in 1855–1856, and the first formal training program commenced in 1861. Nevertheless, operators remained in woefully short supply, and those with expertise were in high demand. Initially, Morse code was adapted for Ottoman-Turkish, but later "İzzet code" was developed by a telegraph operator in Kastamonu, who rearranged the dots and dashes to match the Ottoman-Turkish alphabet.[25] Convincing skilled civil servants to move from the comfort of larger cities to a remote location such as the Arabian Desert proved difficult.

On June 13, 1900, with 200 kilometers of line completed, Azmzade requested that the director of the Beirut telegraph office, Hamdi Bey, be reassigned to the town of Salt, which was to house a large telegraph office.[26] The announcement of this appointment, in İkdam on July 2, 1900, was somewhat premature,[27] for Hamdi Bey's orders included an accompanying note stating that "the Pasha who is moving to Salt" would not receive any extra money for relocation and his salary would remain what it had been in Beirut.[28] The title of pasha was sarcastic here, the equivalent of calling someone of high self-regard "your highness." Apparently, Hamdi Bey refused to move without proper compensation and so Azmzade insisted that his relocation expenses be covered.[29] After negotiating moving expenses and hardship pay, Hamdi Bey must have finally agreed to move to Salt, because records from two years later show him as head of the Salt telegraph office. On November 10, 1903, because he had "demonstrated good service on the Hijaz telegraph line extension," he received a raise and the relocation costs of his transfer to the Urfala–Benghazi telegraph office on the frontiers, where someone of his expertise was needed.[30] This incident tells of the difficulty in finding qualified staff for posts on the Arabian frontier. It shows that in the early twentieth century Istanbul did not have the power to move civil servants at will but had to negotiate to secure skilled staff to take posts in the critical yet remote regions.

Project financing also ran into problems. Initially, line construction proceeded at an impressive rate, but speed meant that staff and equipment for telegraph stations were needed earlier than expected, just a few months after the start date,[31] and the result was another controversy over expenses and financial responsibilities. The British consul in Damascus, William Richards, reported a private discussion with the governor-general of Syria in which the governor-general criticized spending so much money on a telegraph line that would almost certainly require a great deal of repair without having a "locomotive" (he was referring to the railway that would be built soon after) or the infrastructure to protect and repair it.[32] Richard's reports are corroborated by Ottoman documents detailing the governor-general's protests about expenses, which led to the division of expenses among the various military regiments and provinces rather than automatically charging them to the Syrian provincial government.[33]

The newspapers in Istanbul were interested only in reporting on the successes of the project. In particular they described the pomp and circumstance surrounding laying the telegraph in Salt on June 28, 1990,[34] and its arrival in Karak city center on July 30, 1900.[35] This rapid progress took most observers by surprise, especially given the financial complications and the expected difficulties with the Bedouins in the region. However, at this early stage the public was only told of Bedouins' cooperation in official publications such as the weekly *Suriye*.[36] On July 31, 1900, Richards reported that the rapid progress of the line between Damascus and the Hijaz and the coming railway construction meant that Syria would soon regain its former political and economic importance in the empire. He took this opportunity to request raises for himself and his staff, arguing that their positions were about to become even more crucial to the interests of the British Empire.[37]

The celebrations in Istanbul in 1901 followed shortly after a large ceremony commemorating the sultan's silver jubilee, during which the base of a column commemorating the Damascus–Hijaz telegraph line was laid.[38] Designed by Raimondo D'Aronco, the Ottoman court architect, this column, which is covered with Ottoman-Turkish writing and topped by an unusual replica of the Hamidiye Mosque, still stands in the middle of Marjeh Square in the Syrian capital (Figure 11).[39] Newspapers in Istanbul and Damascus described it with pride, boasting that it stood in the "very center of the city."[40]

Myth and legend surround many Ottoman-era monuments whose history has been obscured or forgotten, much like the telegraph monument that still towers over the commercial heart of Damascus. For example, according to İklil Azmzade, the great-grandnephew of Sadik Pasha, whom I interviewed in Damascus in 2009, the column has many stories associated with it. One is that Sadik al-Mouayad Azmzade was at the unveiling and was honored for building a

FIGURE 11. Column commemorating construction of the Hijaz telegraph line, Marjeh Square, Damascus (author's collection).

telegraph line to the holy cities. Mr. Azmzade also said that this symbol of pride for the "Ottoman Pasha" was an easy target of vandals after the fall of Abdül-hamid II. According to family legend, in the fervor of celebrating the deposition of the sultan, the crowd attempted to topple the giant column. When they failed, they tarnished its white veneer with tar, forever blackening the stone. According to art historian Klaus Kreiser, however, the column was constructed of cast iron, making it a heavy column indeed but also a black column from the beginning.[41]

Even though the telegraph line eventually reached Medina, the celebrations were premature, for in spite of the rapid progress financial obstacles continued to mount, forcing Azmzade to plead for additional funds.[42] This caused a great deal of internal squabbling because the money had to come from the budgets of the various ministries and provinces involved.[43] In one case, the head of the telegraph council, İzzet Pasha al-Abid, along with Marshal Şakir Pasha, minister of telegraph and post, Hussein Pasha, and Reşid Pasha, chief of ministry finances, presented a report making the case for additional monies for Azmzade and the Fifth Army regiment.[44] The report demonstrated that, even with the additional money requested, the telegraph line was still expected to turn a profit.[45]

This was only the beginning of a number of successful proposals initiated by İzzet Pasha, who continually provided cost-cutting recommendations while managing to meet project demands. İzzet Pasha would be credited with keeping the money flowing for the telegraph line and later for the railway as the head of the Hijaz Railway Commission, which was founded in 1901.[46] He was successful in obtaining large donations from provincial dignitaries from Yemen to Beirut in return for honorary medals and public acknowledgment in newspapers. He would employ this method to fund the Hijaz Railway, and for a number of years the front page of *İkdam* was reserved for the acknowledgment of generous contributors to the railway living in the capital and the provinces and even Muslim subjects of European empires.[47]

From Temporary Agreements to a Permanent Partnership

While İzzet Pasha dealt with budgetary and tactical issues in Istanbul, Sadik Pasha was in the Syrian Desert dealing with the various obstacles impeding progress. As construction continued south toward the Syria-Hijaz provincial border, stories of interactions with Bedouin tribesmen appeared more frequently in his dispatches. The following story is just one example of the telegraph council's coming face to face with the social realities of the desert.

In a letter to Şakir Pasha, a leading military advisor for the telegraph council, Azmzade described an incident near the Syria-Hijaz provincial border in which he became involved when asked to mediate a dispute between two local tribes. The Beni ʿAtiyya and an unnamed rival tribe had agreed that each would return the booty taken from the other during the previous hajj season. When the rival tribe reneged, a revenge killing took place. Following tradition, the various area tribal chiefs then gathered to decide the punishment for this crime. The Huwaytat tribe, which had a blood tie with Beni ʿAtiyya, had to be present at the gathering, but its chief refused to attend,[48] insisting that his tribe would not interfere in the matter. His refusal led to an impasse, and Azmzade was called in to mediate.[49]

Sadly, the outcome of his mediation was not recorded.[50] Regardless, the case is significant as an instructive example of the Ottoman government coming into a world outside of the state system with its own rules of justice and ways of resolving conflict. It also tells of Azmzade's not trying to impose the Ottoman state's laws on the Bedouins, instead, involving himself in the tribal system of justice. This example demonstrates how the relationship between the Bedouins and the Ottoman imperial government was not inherently confrontational. Indeed, for Azmzade—a representative of the sultan—being asked to mediate was a high honor.

Azmzade's story exemplifies the Hamidian regime's approach to managing its relationship with the Bedouins of the southern frontiers after learning from its experience in the eastern Sahara. Its negotiations entailed culturally sensitive diplomacy and partnership building with a balanced combination of accommodation (of course, always backed by the implicit threat of imperial military might). The Ottoman state had centuries of experience in negotiating mutually beneficial agreements with the tribes in the region, mostly for the safe passage of the hajj caravans.[51] What was new about the Hijaz telegraph line was its physical permanence and the host of issues that this permanence was to bring up.

Traditionally, agreements between the Ottoman state and Bedouins were made annually at the beginning of the hajj season, when some tribes living along the route were hired to provide transportation and safe passage to the large pilgrim caravans passing through their territories. This made the relationship between the Ottoman state and the Bedouins episodic, contractual, and seasonal. However, the permanence of the telegraph line necessitated a new kind of relationship.[52] Agreements could no longer be temporary and now had to tackle the delicate issue of permanent security and the continued operation of the telegraph line in Bedouin domains. Istanbul had to find a way for the local tribesmen to accept the landscape-altering presence of the Ottoman government in the tribes' domains, which traditionally had been outside the purview of the imperial state. The poles, telegraph offices, and low-voltage lines that dotted the Hijazi desert landscape, the home of the Bedouin tribes, were permanent "facts on the ground."

I use the term *landscape* to refer to the desert as an "experienced world, not as an empirical backdrop."[53] Thus for the inhabitants of this space, the landscape constituted an idea rooted in a specific lived political and sociological context. It had its own "complex symbols and images of its 'inhabitants' and 'users' . . . and [was] impregnated with symbols and imagery that [had] an explicit and insidious impact in spatial practices of everyday life."[54] Altering the Bedouin landscape—one pole at a time in an unbroken line stretching to the distant all-powerful imperial capital—was a transformation of the familiar into a "hegemonic space" of imperial power. What might seem to the outsider as nothing more than an empty space crisscrossed by telegraph lines could be easily interpreted by the Bedouins as signs with existentially threatening messages.[55] Acknowledging the desert landscape in the Hijaz as part of the quotidian experience of its inhabitants allows us to better understand the impact that the telegraph lines must have had. The Bedouins could have easily read the changes in the desert landscape as a sign of Ottoman colonization of their space, which was a new interpretation of their "social and political relations with the empire and its representatives."[56]

Although the physical presence of the telegraph line was essential to the empire's claim to the frontiers in the face of European colonial expansion, the telegraph council was committed to carrying out its mission in partnership with the Bedouin tribes. In fact, the new line had to send conflicting messages to different audiences: to its European counterparts the message was that the Ottoman imperial government controlled the desert; the message to the Bedouins was that the government desired a partnership with them so that imperial infrastructure could be built through their domains.

Evidence shows that Yıldız Palace and the telegraph council understood the necessity for delicate and skillful negotiations not only to allow the productive involvement of Bedouins during construction but also to persuade them to be invested in the maintenance of the successful operation of the line by offering financial rewards, employment incentives, and honorary medals. However, as Yakup Bektaş shows, bribes alone were not enough. Financial incentives had been tried and had failed in the building of the Istanbul–Fao telegraph line.[57] Istanbul now had the more difficult task of presenting the telegraph line as a permanent symbol of partnership, a source of employment, and a sign of the Bedouins' own agency, not as a signpost pointing to a colonized space. Azmzade was relatively successful at negotiating this partnership until he encountered trouble on the Medina–Mecca route.[58]

Istanbul conducted face-to-face negotiations similar to those it carried out in the eastern Sahara with the help of al-Mahdi al-Sanusi. It also capitalized on Azmzade's experience in sensitive dealings along the frontiers when it assigned him to supervise construction of the line. What was not taken into consideration, however, was that in the Hijaz there was a lack of leadership support such as that al-Mahdi al-Sanusi provided in the Libyan Desert. In other words, there was no willing leader in the Hijaz to act as a local representative of the Ottoman-Bedouin partnership. Tackling the Bedouin "tribal question"[59] therefore required a coordinated effort on all government levels to reach out to the key Bedouin chiefs.

Some of the tribes along the route had done business with the Ottoman Empire for several generations. Based on this and possibly strengthened by the imperial government's experiences in the eastern Sahara, the opinion of the telegraph council on dealing with Hijazi Bedouins was outlined in a report written by Marshal Şakir Pasha. Şakir Pasha believed that a clear and consistent policy was essential and that an understanding of local traditions and a respect for boundaries would avoid some of the anticipated resistance. He acknowledged the realities on the ground and the formidable power of the Hijazi Bedouins:

> In order to get the Bedouins that live next to the railway and telegraph lines to work [on this project], they should always be treated well [*daima hüsnül-müamele*] and should be paid their daily wages in full. In addition, some of the tribal chiefs should be given a red *çoha* [an honorary wool ceremonial cloth] and be assigned an appropriate official position along the railroad. . . . These measures done consistently over time will then be enough to guarantee that we can get the benefits of their services as has been done for a long time.[60]

Thus, Marshal Şakir Pasha offered three seemingly simple yet very telling recommendations. First, show respect for the Bedouins and their authority over their domain. Second, honor financial agreements with promptness and consistency. Third, systematically involve tribal chiefs in the imperial network, tying their fate to the success of the state's plans through honorary gestures and positions appropriate to their status. Above all, ensure consistency; timely payment of agreed-on amounts for services rendered—to establish long-term trust. Deviating from this advice would prove to be one of the telegraph council's downfalls.

Official adoption of Şakir Pasha's recommendations did not always translate to action. In a project of the telegraph's magnitude, the differences between plan and implementation were often great, and ideals were often set aside in favor of cheap and speedy solutions. For example, financial agreements were not always honored, a fact that was conspicuously absent from Ottoman field reports yet reported in detail by the British consul William Richards.[61]

On July 31, 1900, for example, Richards reported on the progress of the line to the Foreign Office. He wrote that construction thus far had been mostly the product of the forced labour of villagers and Bedouins, and that families were required to supply two wooden poles as an ad hoc tax imposed to raise funds. If the poles supplied were deemed inadequate, the authorities charged an additional lira (or more).[62] Richards's dispatch was early proof that in order to meet deadlines and tight budgets, corners were cut at the expense of the ideals laid out by Şakir Pasha. Ottoman records are silent about the moral economy of the rapid progress of the line, but generously enumerate the medals awarded.[63] The Istanbul press painted a rosy picture of the project, praising the harmony, mutual respect, and even appreciation that governed relations between Bedouins and Ottoman soldiers.[64]

As construction leader, Azmzade must have been aware of the ill treatment of some Bedouins, so it could not have come as a surprise that after a relatively incident-free five months, sabotage began to be reported. Lines were cut in July and August of 1900, and two thefts of lines and wooden poles in the province of Syria were reported in 1901.[65] As early as September 1900, Hussein Nazim Pasha, governor-general of Syria (r. 1896–1908) and the *kaymakam* of Karak were reportedly at their wits' end. Nazim Pasha told Richards that telegraph poles were being pulled down as soon as they were erected.[66] In his quarterly report, Richards speculated that behind the Bedouins' actions was a desire to blackmail the government. He wrote that in seven months over eight hundred Turkish pounds had been sent to the region for distribution among the tribes.[67]

On inquiring into the Bedouins' complaints, Richards was told that the Bedouins claimed that the poles caused their camels to behave with "curiosity and terror," which both Richards and Ottoman officials brushed off as native superstition. Interestingly, reports of Caribou herds acting strangely when telegraph lines were first put up in British Columbia in the 1850s were similarly dismissed.[68] Almost a hundred years later, however, scientific research showed that extremely low-frequency electromagnetic fields like telegraph lines disrupt ruminants' internal polar magnetic alignment, causing them to become confused and disoriented.[69]

A Man-Made Impasse on the Medina–Mecca Road

Despite hurdles, construction continued, and by October 1900 the line was running 368 miles south of Damascus. In early November 1900, it reached Meda'in Saleh in the region separating Syria and the Hijaz. This meant that the border between these provinces had to be formally established for the first time. Negotiations were complicated because the new boundary would affect the fees for telegrams sent from the two provinces. An agreement came in March of 1901, but was later changed when the governor-general of Syria managed to have the southern border moved to Salt, arguably increasing telegraph revenues and decreasing provincial operational costs. This is just one example of how the arrival of technology reorganized the economy of space and necessitated continual negotiation of the rights and responsibilities of provincial and imperial powers.[70]

When the sultan was informed of the arrival of the telegraph line in Meda'in Saleh, he congratulated Nazim Pasha and expressed his wish that his good service and commitment would continue in the next phase, the construction of the Hijaz Railway, which was due to start early in 1901. The railroad project was more formally organized and overseen than the telegraph project. There were two commissions: one in Syria headed by Nazim Pasha and the other in Istanbul headed by İzzet Pasha al-Abid. The Syrian commission oversaw the operational side of the project, while the Istanbul commission oversaw tactical and fund-raising matters. Major decisions were to go up the chain of command from Nazim Pasha to İzzet Pasha and then to the sultan, but that was rarely the case. In reality, İzzet Pasha made most of the decisions, for which he became the target of attacks from both Istanbul and the provinces. Supervision of the telegraph line construction, which lasted only two years, was ad hoc in comparison to the commission-driven construction of the Hijaz Railway. It is safe to assume that the telegraph line was the training ground for the railroad.[71]

The sultan finally gave the authorization for continuation of the telegraph line into the border areas between the Hijaz and Syria. What neither the council nor the sultan could have predicted at the time was that this would prove to be the most difficult phase of the project.[72] In the first few days of 1901, Azmzade had the honor of sending the first telegram from Medina to Istanbul. In Damascus William Richards expressed his astonishment at such rapid progress, especially considering the construction team's "inexperience" and the difficulties and hostilities it faced. According to his calculations, since November 1900 the rate of progress was close to an impressive three and a half miles per day.[73] What seemed like a success story in January 1901, however, soon turned into story of Azmzade's failure to extend the line south of Medina.

In the twelve months that followed the first telegram, as Azmzade attempted to push for the extension of the line toward Mecca, reports of escalating violence on the Medina–Mecca route spiked.[74] Out of fear for their safety, workers were instructed to wait in Medina until the road to Mecca was secured. More painful to receive were reports of sabotage of completed lines between Biyar Nasif and Medina on the Hijazi side of the Syria-Hijaz border. In April 1901, Azmzade, who had remained in Medina to negotiate with local authorities, received the disappointing news that forty poles and twenty-five lengths of cable had been stolen.[75] Soon after repairs were made, there was more sabotage in the same area.[76]

The minister of interior wrote to Governor-General Ratib Pasha and Amir ʿAwn al-Rafiq Pasha, questioning why they had failed to protect telegraph workers and secure completed sections of the telegraph in the Hijaz. He demanded that local authorities investigate these incidents and prosecute the culprits to stop similar acts in the future.[77] Ratib Pasha responded on his own and ʿAwn al-Rafiq Pasha's behalf, expressing frustration over the minister's complaints. He and ʿAwn al-Rafiq Pasha had been nothing but "zealous" in their support, he wrote, claiming that the amir had gone above and beyond the call of duty in spending his own money on the line.[78]

In a later telegram to the office of the grand vizier, Ratib Pasha went on the attack. With the Medina–Mecca line at a standstill, he took the opportunity to criticize all of those who had been responsible for the Hijaz plan. He spoke of the Bedouins' "height of ignorance" and expressed surprise at Istanbul's decision to award some tribesmen with wages, governmental positions, and even medals of honor while the army regiment under his command was woefully starved for funds. Ratib Pasha accused the Ministry of Telegraph and Post of wasting money on highly paid inspectors whom he claimed "wandered" the region without doing anything useful. He especially disliked the "Damascene" Azmzade and İzzet Pasha, accusing them of money mismanagement and unfair complaints against the province.[79] He accused İzzet Pasha of colluding with the Bedouins by rewarding them with high salaries, even though the same tribesmen (allegedly) had interfered with the provincial government as it prepared for the line extension between Mecca and Medina. He sarcastically added that they perhaps would eventually cause the entire project to fail and he would be blamed and "finally sent back to Istanbul."[80] My investigation into the lives and careers of Ratib Pasha and ʿAwn al-Rafiq Pasha reveals their disguised but deep anxiety about Istanbul's direct outreach to the local population.

Like his predecessors, Sharif ʿAwn al-Rafiq Pasha bin Muhammad bin ʿAwn (1882–1905) had served as a vizier on the Ottoman Council of State before becoming amir of Mecca in 1882. He arrived in Mecca on the instructions of Sultan Abdülhamid II to replace Amir ʿAbd al-Mutalib Pasha bin Ghaleb of the Zaid clan (r. 1880–1882), who had been dismissed and placed under house arrest after being accused of courting the British without the sultan's knowledge. He had attempted to balance the increasing power of the Ottoman governor-general, Marshal Osman Nuri Pasha, by asking for the backing of the British consul in Jeddah. Osman Nuri Pasha, a close confidant of the sultan, accused ʿAbd al-Mutalib Pasha of treason, corruption, and oppressive practices against the locals.[81] The sultan was already wary of British designs in the Hijaz; ʿAbd al-Mutalib himself had been a replacement for the previous amir, Sharif Hussein Pasha bin Muhammad bin ʿAwn (r. 1877–1880), because of the latter's suspicious correspondence with the British.[82]

No one could have predicted that ʿAwn al-Rafiq Pasha would partner with an Ottoman officer from Istanbul, not with a foreign entity, as a means of asserting his power in the Hijaz. Soon after his appointment he consolidated his hold over the Hijaz by successfully orchestrating the replacement of Marshal Osman Nuri Pasha with a weak and more malleable substitute. In 1893 the amir of Mecca forged a notorious partnership with Governor-General Ahmed Ratib Pasha.[83] He also used his position to increase his wealth, which came from both official and suspect sources, to such an extent that he could bribe any official who might check his power, including the Ottoman governor.[84] With five Ottoman garrisons under his command, Ratib Pasha's job was to guard Ottoman imperial interests in the Hijaz while maintaining a delicate balance of power with ʿAwn al-Rafiq Pasha. Both understood that a direct connection between

Mecca and Istanbul would be a danger to their shared hold on power in the Hijaz, and they went to great lengths to maintain this hold, which had a large impact on the Hijaz telegraph line project.[85]

In the early 1890s, it appeared that the amir of Mecca was trying to assert his local authority by imposing his own arbitrary laws[86] and controlling the caravan transportation business. The result was a monopoly on the hajj caravan business, including the surcharge fees collected from unsuspecting pilgrims for disembarking from their ships. The logical recourse for foreign consulates would have been to complain to the Ottoman representative in the province, Ratib Pasha. However, according to British vice-consul Muhammad Hussein, the governor-general received a cut of the profits from these shakedowns and was not about to entertain any complaints that might harm the amir's dealings.[87]

With a series of frank reports, Muhammad Hussein has given historians unprecedented access to events in the Hijaz in the 1890s. The vice-consul was under a great deal of pressure from Hijazi authorities and even his superiors to temper his reporting. His accounts of the back stories and the chains of events leading to Bedouin attacks challenged the wisdom that these attacks were simply unprovoked aggression motivated by greed. Hussein was taking a large personal risk by insisting on reporting the abuses he knew were occurring. His predecessor, Dr. ʿAbd al-Razzaq, had paid with his life for his scathing reports on the treatment of pilgrims at the hands of the amir and his men.[88]

Ratib Pasha and ʿAwn al-Rafiq Pasha's corrupt dealings were also documented by Süleyman Kani İrtem, the governor of Istanbul between 1917 and 1918. In his memoirs, İrtem recalled that through dubious means both supplemented their salaries and amassed fortunes on the backs of local Bedouins and unsuspecting pilgrims. He described the province during this period as a place with no "semblance of fairness" where locals were systematically oppressed without recourse to justice and pilgrims were regularly blackmailed. In colorful language, İrtem detailed the alliance of corruption between the governor-general and the amir, which led to the weakening of the Ottoman government's position in the Hijaz.[89] Indeed, the misappropriation of funds and the systematic corruption described by İrtem was detrimental to the progress of the telegraph line beyond Medina.[90] Evidence of Ratib Pasha's corrupt handling of public moneys can be detected throughout his career, during which his untrustworthiness came to the fore in a number of incidents involving the grand vizier, Said Pasha; the director of the Imperial Ottoman Bank,

Gaston Auboyneau; and even the governor (*muḥāfiẓ*) of Medina,[91] causing major budgetary shortages that ultimately had to be shouldered by neighboring provinces.[92] For example, subsidies sent to the Hijaz to be distributed to the Bedouin tribes as *atiye* were withheld or diverted to the coffers of the amir and the governor-general. This provoked the tribes to attack what they saw as government interests, including the telegraph line, in protest and as a way to take what they believed was rightfully theirs.[93]

Conclusion

Construction of the Damascus–Medina line started successfully, but it was not long before complications and delays stemming from an inadequate budget began to crop up. In particular, increasing financial difficulties exposed the gulf between strategy and execution. Moreover, questions of funding were addressed on an ad hoc basis. Despite these challenges, Istanbul was determined to make the project a success, especially because it was the training ground for the bigger and more complex Hijaz Railway.

However, in August 1901, almost seven months after the line had reached the outskirts of Medina, the project was at a standstill. Azmzade advised the Ministry of Telegraph and Post on redressing the grievances of local Bedouins so that construction could recommence. He recommended short- and long-term financial rewards for friendly tribes as an incentive to cooperate and monthly payments to ten Bedouin chiefs, not as forms of *atiye* (which usually went through the amir of Mecca) but as regular salaries paid to them as imperial administrators in posts from Maʿan in Syria to Medaʾin Saleh, a town on the Syrian-Hijazi border, in compensation for providing transportation of construction material and protecting workers along the telegraph line. A monthly subsidy also would be paid to the tribes for their service, which Azmzade asked to be retroactive to June of 1901. He also recommended that the same friendly tribes be hired to transport and accompany hajj pilgrims, which was certainly lucrative. Azmzade's goal was to reward tribes that cooperated with Istanbul and isolate those that had not shown goodwill toward the state's project. The importance of these measures was emphasized at the end of Azmzade's request letter, where he declared that this sum of money and its timely arrival were critical to the success of the project and should be considered a budgetary priority.[94]

Azmzade's recommendations were also intended to undermine the power of the amir of Mecca, who was being "selective" in distributing *atiye* payments and was instigating work disruptions on the line. As a solution, an alternative source of income for local Bedouins would come directly from Istanbul. Additionally, Azmzade hoped to break the amir's monopoly on the caravan business by choosing tribes to hire for protection of hajj caravans based on the telegraph council's recommendations, not, as was traditional, by the amir.[95] This way, strategy and execution would theoretically be controlled by Istanbul. Unfortunately, opposition from the Meccan powers would prove insurmountable as Istanbul pushed toward asserting its will in the face of pressures from within and without.

CONCLUSION

The Blinding Teleology of Failure

With the blessings from the spiritual guidance of the noblest Prophet [*Bi-madad ruḥāniyat haḍrat al-rasūl al-akram*] and in the shadow of his majesty our greatest king [*bi-ẓil jalālat malikunā al-aʿẓam*], the distribution of the columns between Biyar Nasif and Medina was completed. The work in this seventy-five kilometer stretch was completed in three days and the [telegraph] lines were connected with Medina. Thus, this new year started with prayers for the long life and lasting might and power of our greatest benefactor [*al-daʿwa al-khayriyya bi-ṭūl baqāʾ wa dawām shawkat wa iqtiḍār haḍrat waliyyu niʿmatunā al-aʿẓam*]. My entourage, government employees, soldiers, and the people of Medina joined me in performing this duty—the greatest of blessings and the most perfect peace be upon its owner [the Prophet Muhammad, ʿalā ṣāḥibiha afḍal al-ṣalāt wa atam al-taslīm].

Sadik al-Mouayad Azmzade, Medina, January 10, 1901

THE OTTOMAN GOVERNMENT in Istanbul did adopt some of Azmzade's recommendations for getting the telegraph line back on track, even announcing the hiring of tribesmen to protect it. However, a year after the announcement of reaching Medina, no further progress had been made.[1] The obstacles seemed insurmountable, and the provincial powers were unwilling to provide the resources or the security measures that Istanbul requested. To add to the troubles, Istanbul began to turn its attention and resources to the Hijaz Railway which meant diverting the attention of Yıldız Palace away from the problems of the telegraph on its final stretch and toward the much more publically touted railway.[2] Under these discouraging conditions, in January of 1902 Azmzade was unceremoniously reassigned to the railway project as an assistant to one of the directors, Kazım Pasha.[3]

A few days after Azmzade's reassignment, there was a new incident report, this time concerning the theft of ninety poles and isolators and several cable lengths between Biyar Nasif and Medina,[4] triggering yet another round of finger pointing between the Telegraph Commission and Governor-General Ahmed Ratib Pasha.[5] Over the following two years, the Arabian frontiers seemed to descend into chaos as reports of Bedouin attacks against telegraph lines and caravans and counterattacks by the local authorities against Bedouins continued to escalate. Various ministries repeatedly demanded the cooperation of the provincial authorities in securing the area and providing the construction team with tactical support. Again and again, the authorities came back demanding additional funds from Istanbul.[6] Governor-General Ratib Pasha remained in power and managed to obstruct the line extension until the end of his term in 1908. It was then that he got his wish of going back to his beloved Istanbul when he was arrested in Jeddah on charges of corruption and sent back to the capital to be tried. Hijazi townsmen and tribesmen alike reportedly celebrated his arrest and departure in the streets, but by then it was too late for the telegraph line.[7]

Thus, even though Yıldız Palace attempted to build a partnership with the local population as part of its plan to maintain the empire's sovereignty in the face of encroaching European colonialism, the provincial power block created obstacles at every turn. Similar to the contradictory approaches adopted by the imperial and provincial governments toward the Sanusi Order and its followers in Cyrenaica, the imperial strategy of partnership building with the Bedouins of the Arabian frontier in service of Istanbul's strategic objectives was sabotaged at the provincial level to serve the personal interests of the governor-general of the Hijaz and the amir of Mecca. The long arm of the Ottoman state could reach only so far, and external obstacles, domestic and foreign, proved outside the control of the imperial government and its allies. The result was that ultimately neither the telegraph line nor the railway ever reached Mecca, their ultimate destination.

I have chosen to end with the conclusion of this story because it highlights that a historical narrative that focuses on the final result as one of failure often masks many more informative stories of participation, innovation, and interim successes along the way. In the process, all that precedes the final outcome is often buried under the heavy narrative of what never materializes. Lost are the Ottoman Empire's participation in the scramble for Africa, and its efforts to achieve self-reliance and combat European global hegemony, along with twenty years of innovative international diplomacy and negotiation. We limit our questions to those that explain the final outcome—the end of the empire. Despite the failure of the line to reach Mecca, it is important not to lose sight of the major achievement of connecting Istanbul to the empire's far southern reaches. The words of Sultan Abdülhamid II in 1905 sum up the importance of acknowledging the reinvigorated spirit of the Ottoman Empire during this period, imperfect as it may have been and despite all of the internal and external pressures on Istanbul:

> The Hijaz line has proven that our country has not lost its ability to develop, and that we can block Britain's repeated attempts at sabotaging any project we undertake in the service of our country and our people. God willing, the railway line will soon be completed and we will not have to rely on the Suez Canal anymore, and Istanbul will be tied to the two holy cities Mecca and Medina.[8]

Of course, the sultan was putting a positive spin on a program he strongly believed in, but his words are still instructive. The Ottoman Empire was indeed still independent, innovative, and capable of resisting Great Power hegemony. Therefore, despite what we might dismiss as the failure of the original plan in the Hijaz, my hope is that this book has demonstrated the importance of not allowing the teleology of failure in the last decades of the nineteenth century blind us to the alternative paths that Ottoman strategists in post-1878 Istanbul tried to follow and the value that they placed on resisting European colonial hegemony.

Even though the Ottoman Empire's efforts to claim the eastern Sahara as a colony did not bear fruit, I argue that this period of reinvigoration and competitiveness is vital to our understanding of the Hamidian period. Shifting the focus from east–west relations across Europe to north–south relations across the Sahara opens up a new way to examine the Ottoman imperial government's envisioned objectives during the height of colonial competitive expansionism in Africa. By recasting the empire in the last two decades of the nineteenth century as a competitive imperial power on the global stage, we can examine the impact of "new imperialism" on its policies on both international and domestic fronts.

Shifting the analytical paradigm away from metropole versus frontiers has also unshackled us from traditional assumptions of an essentially conflictual relationship between Istanbul and the frontiers' inhabitants, allowing us to investigate the formerly overlooked strategic partnership between Istanbul and the Sanusi Order and its followers, which lasted well into the early twentieth century. Instead of seeing a threat to Ottoman sovereignty in the Grand Sanusi, I have shown that in fact the Grand Sanusi's vast reach and his appeal to the local Bedouin population and the Central Sudanic Kingdoms gave Istanbul an opportunity to strengthen its north–south trans-Saharan relations at a critical time in the run-up to the scramble for Africa. Although the bond with the Mediterranean coast of central North Africa and the Central Sudanic Kingdoms had existed for centuries, establishing a strong relationship with the Sanusi Order in the eastern Sahara strengthened Istanbul's negotiating position on the international stage.

As a participant in the Conference of Berlin of 1884–1885 and a signatory to the General Act of Berlin, Istanbul took the calculated risk of recognizing French and British influence in formerly Ottoman North Africa, but it also embarked on an ambitious plan to assert its legal "right" to the eastern Sahara. Using the legal terms of the Act of Berlin, it negotiated the empire's title to a territory stretching from the Libyan coast to the Lake Chad basin with its European counterparts. Concurrently, taking advantage of a history of mutual recognition and cooperation, Istanbul identified the Sanusi leader as the perfect strategic partner for establishing facts on the ground by proxy. However, as early as 1887 French, British, and Italian designs on the Sahara were well known to Ottoman negotiators. As new international agreements were signed without the empire's consent—a clear violation of the terms of the General Act of Berlin—Istanbul's diplomatic protests grew louder and more incessant.

Such protests fell on increasingly deaf European ears, culminating in the Great Powers' claiming parts of the eastern Sahara. The 1890s witnessed the gradual fall of the Muslim Central African Kingdoms to European military might, exposing a fundamental characteristic of international law: it was never intended to protect the rights of weak parties, which ultimately spelled disaster for the empire's negotiating strategy. By 1895 it had become clear that the European powers were systematically excluding the Ottoman Empire from new negotiations and international agreements, dismissing Istanbul's protests and by extension its legal interpretations of the terms of the General Act of Berlin.

When diplomatic channels failed, Istanbul cemented its partnership with the Sanusi Order in support of Sanusi-led military resistance to European colonial expansion in central Africa. However, even though Ottoman tactical and military assistance in the eastern Sahara continued, by the end of the century Istanbul had all but abandoned its expansionist experiment and was shifting its efforts toward defensive consolidation of its frontiers-cum-borderlands in the Libyan provinces as well as in the Hijaz. The failure of the Ottoman expansionist experiment in central Africa meant a drastic shift in how Istanbul dealt with the threat of European colonialism along its vulnerable frontiers on both sides of the Red Sea.

As the Damascus–Medina telegraph line demonstrates, a transimperial approach must be taken in studying imperial strategy in a centralized intercontinental empire such as the Ottoman Empire. This is especially true for the Hamidian period, when the empire's strategists were part of a relatively small circle that oversaw geopolitical interests across the empire. It stands to reason, then, that their experiences in one part of the empire had a direct impact on their decisions and policies in another. In this case, the deteriorating relationship between the Ottoman and other European empires in Africa manifested in the Ottoman government's considerations in the planning and execution of the Damascus–Medina telegraph line. Its experiences along the empire's African frontiers had a direct impact on its policies along the Arabian frontiers.

Only by knowing the pressure the empire was facing in Africa at the time, and appreciating the Great Powers' betrayal of the principles of international law, can we fully understand the logic behind Ottoman rejection of French and British offers of partnership and the significance of Istanbul's decision to independently undertake a massive infrastructure project such as the Hijaz telegraph line. Only by divorcing ourselves from the limited boundaries of the postimperial nation-states' versions of history and the artificial limitations of twentieth-century area studies and instead viewing state policies through a transimperial lens can we begin to understand the history of the Ottoman Empire on its own late nineteenth-century terms.

Above all, this book has challenged the notion that the Ottoman Empire was irrelevant on the international stage after the Congress of Berlin in 1878. It has demonstrated that the Ottoman government was not a silent observer struggling to survive bankruptcy, political instability, and foreign pressure. On the contrary, at the turn of the century Ottoman interimperial foreign policy was far from mute, and thus it deserves much more scholarly attention than it has received so far. The last two decades of the nineteenth century in fact witnessed an expansionist empire determined to reinvent itself as a global power to be reckoned with. My hope is that I have brought to light the importance of studying Ottoman international relations strategies in particular, and have convincingly advocated for the inclusion of the Ottoman Empire in studies of late nineteenth-century colonialism in general. This book has focused on Ottoman involvement in the scramble for Africa and its impact on the empire's policies along its southern frontiers-cum-borderlands on two continents and over a period of twenty years ending in 1902. However, there is much more about Ottoman imperial strategy in Africa (and the Balkans, the Mediterranean, the eastern frontiers, and elsewhere) that is yet to be explored. Azmzade's next assignment is a case in point.

We left Azmzade after his reassignment to the Hijaz Railway project. Even though British consul William Richards reported that Azmzade privately received much flak for failing to extend the telegraph line further than Medina,[9] publicly his new position was painted in a very different light: as a reward for good service he was being recalled from the harsh desert frontier to the Syrian provincial capital and his hometown, Damascus.[10]

In 1902, however, Azmzade reportedly departed from Damascus, in what seemed like an abrupt ending to his assignment on the Hijaz Railway, to take up a "special assignment" in Benghazi.[11] In fact there is no evidence that I was able to locate in the Ottoman Archives that places Azmzade in Benghazi that summer or anytime after that before his death in 1911. In reality his negotiation skills were needed elsewhere. Soon after arriving in Damascus, he was recalled to Istanbul, his actual primary residence, and within a few months of the announcement of his trip to Benghazi he indeed embarked on another mission to Africa. Instead of Benghazi, however, his destination was much further afield, to the long lost Ottoman province of Ethiopia. Like the Ottoman Empire, the Ethiopian Empire had been locked in a struggle against European colonialism, and it, too, had signed agreements with the European powers that should have guaranteed its territorial rights. In another diplomatic "farce," however, the Amharic version of a key agreement between the king of Italy and the Ethiopian emperor omitted a clause stating that Italy had a protectorate right over Ethiopia. When he recognized the omission, Emperor Menelik II (r. 1889–1913) rejected the agreement. In response, the Italians invaded Ethiopia but, in a surprising turn of events, suffered a humiliating defeat.[12] This military victory raised the Ethiopian Empire's international profile and attracted the attention of another empire facing a European colonial threat, the Ottoman Empire. Azmzade headed to the new Ethiopian imperial capital, Addis Ababa, on a special mission to negotiate an alliance with Menelik II. Thanks to the south–south coalition that would develop between Istanbul and Addis Ababa over the following decade, Istanbul would remain in the game of fin de siècle competitive imperialism for few years longer.[13]

NOTES

Preface

1. Because we have examples of Sadik al-Mouayad Azmzade's own signature in both Ottoman-Turkish and French documents in the Bulgarian Historical Archives, I have decided to follow his spelling and the form of signature he used in his official correspondence (see Bulgarian National Archives [hereafter BHA], F176K/op14/ae925). Therefore, it is not Sadiq or Sadık but Sadik; not al-Mu'ayyad or el-Müeyyed but al-Mouayad; not al-ʿAzm but Azmzade. In catalogues in Turkish archives and libraries, the name is usually rendered "Sadık el-Müeyyed" or "Sadık el-Müeyyed Azmzade," which is how it appears in the endnotes and the bibliography for ease in locating the records. The choice to transliterate Azmzade's name in modern Turkish would have been a wise alternative because he operated in an imperial Turkish speaking environment and in an Osmanlıca writing environment, especially in the contexts of his life that this book deals with.

2. On the 1860 massacre and its implications, see Leila Tarazi Fawaz, *An Occasion for War: Civil Conflict in Lebanon and Damascus in 1860* (Berkeley: University of California Press, 1994).

3. Linda Schatkowski-Schilcher, *Families in Politics: Damascene Factions and Estates of the 18th and 19th Centuries* (Stuttgart: Franz Steiner, 1985), 140–144; Philip Khoury, *Urban Notables and Arab Nationalism: The Politics of Damascus, 1860–1920* (Cambridge: Cambridge University Press, 1983), 1–46.

4. Many of the technological projects undertaken during the reign of Sultan Abdülhamid II (1876–1906), including the famous Ottoman naval cruiser and the covered bazaar in Damascus, were referred to as "Hamidian"—for example, Souq al-Hamidiyya (Hamidian Bazaar). The Hijaz Railway, initially called the Hamidiye Hicaz Demiryolu (Hamidian Hijaz Railway), was no exception. After Abdülhamid II was deposed, the railway was renamed the Hicaz Demiryolu (Hijaz Railway). Similarly, scholars of the Ottoman Empire refer both to the period of Abdülhamid II's rule and to the set of reforms he enacted as "Hamidian." I employ the same terminology.

5. Sadik al-Mouayad Azmzade—to whom I also refer as Sadik Pasha and Azmzade—is sometimes called Sadiq al-Mu'ayyad al-ʿAzm by Arabists. This is a simplified transliteration of the Arabic Ṣādiq al-Mu'ayyad al-ʿAẓm. Azmzade's grandchildren include Sadiq al-ʿAzm, the Syrian philosopher who inherited his name, and, on the Turkish side of the family, his great-grandnephew İklil Azmzade. Both provided much

personal information in interviews I conducted in Damascus and Istanbul in the fall of 2008 and the winter of 2009, some of which appear in this book. I have pieced together the details of Azmzade's life from the Ottoman Archives. For more information on him and family, see Schatkowski-Schilcher, *Families in Politics*, 140–144; Nuri al-Jarrah, "Introduction," in Sadiq al-Mu'ayyad al-ʿAzm, *Rihlat al-Habasha: Min al-Istana ila Addis Ababa*, ed. Nuri al-Jarrah (Beirut: Al-Mu'asasa al-ʿArabiyya li-l-Dirasat wa-l-Nashr and Dar al-Swaydi li-l-Nashr wa-l-Tawziʿ, 2002).

6. For examples of the emerging literature that examines the Ottoman Empire's negotiating power on the international stage, see John Willis, *Unmaking North and South: Cartographies of the Yemen Past, 1857–1934* (New York: Columbia University Press, 2012), 73–103; Aimee M. Genell, "Empire by Law: Ottoman Sovereignty and the British Occupation of Egypt" (PhD diss., Columbia University, 2013).

Introduction

Epigraph: Sadık el-Müeyyed Azmzade, *Afrika Sahra-yı Kebiri'nde Seyahat* (Istanbul: Ahmed İhsan ve Şürekası, 1899), 1. Azmzade's original travelogue was given to Sultan Abdülhamid II as a gift. It is housed at the Nadir Eserler Library at Istanbul University. T4526.

1. The reign of Sultan Abdülaziz (1861–1876) ended in a coup d'état. The reign of his successor, Sultan Murad V, lasted for only a few months until he was deposed allegedly because of alcoholism and mental illness. See James Gelvin, *The Modern Middle East: A History*, 3rd ed. (New York: Oxford University Press, 2011), 151.

2. On the Russo-Ottoman War and the Congress of Berlin, see Matthew S. Anderson, *The Eastern Question, 1774–1923: A Study in International Relations* (London: Macmillan, 1996); A. L. MacFie, *The Eastern Question: 1774–1923*, rev. ed. (Harlow, UK: Addison Wesley Longman, 1996), 34–45.

3. The Ottoman parliament was prorogued on February 14, 1878, during the war with Russia. See Erik Jan Zürcher, *Turkey: A Modern History*, 2nd ed. (London: I. B. Tauris, 2004), 74–76.

4. Ezel Kural Shaw, "Integrity and Integration: Assumptions and Expectations behind Nineteenth Century Decision Making," in *Decision Making and Change in the Ottoman Empire*, ed. Caesar E. Farah (Kirksville, MO: Thomas Jefferson University Press, 1993), 40.

5. Mustafa Aksakal, *The Ottoman Road to War in 1914: The Ottoman Empire and the First World War* (Cambridge: Cambridge University Press, 2008), 4–5.

6. See Christine Philliou, *Biography of an Empire: Governing Ottomans in an Age of Revolution* (Berkeley: University of California Press, 2011); John S. Koliopoulos and Thanos M. Veremis, *Modern Greece: A History since 1821* (Chichester, UK: Wiley Blackwell, 2010).

7. See Jennifer E. Sessions, *By Sword and Plow: France and the Conquest of Algeria* (Ithaca, NY: Cornell University Press, 2011).

8. Aksakal, *Ottoman Road to War*, 5. On Ottoman-British competition in Arabia, see Frederick F. Anscombe, *The Ottoman Gulf: The Creation of Kuwait, Saudi Arabia,*

and Qatar (New York: Columbia University Press, 1997); Gökhan Çetinsaya, "The Otto-man View of British Presence in Iraq and the Gulf: The Era of Abdulhamid II," *Middle Eastern Studies* 39 (2003): 194–203; R. J. Gavin, *Aden under British Rule: 1839–1967* (Lon-don: C. Hurst, 1975); Ş. Tufan Buzpınar, "Vying for Power and Influence in the Hijaz: Ottoman Rule, the Last Emirate of Abdulmuttalib and the British (1880–1882)," *Muslim World* 95 (2005): 1–22; Ş. Tufan Buzpınar, "The Hijaz, Abdülhamid II and Amir Hussein's Secret Dealings with the British, 1877–80," *Middle Eastern Studies* 31 (1995): 99–123.

9. A. S. Kanya-Forstner, "French Expansion in Africa: The Mythical Theory," in *Studies in the Theory of Imperialism*, ed. Roger Owen and Bob Sutcliff (London: Long-man, 1972), 279.

10. Heinz Gollwitzer, *Europe in the Age of Imperialism, 1881–1914* (Norwich, UK: Harcourt, Brace & World, 1969), 12.

11. Ibid.

12. Winfried Baumgart, *Imperialism: The Idea and Reality of British and French Co-lonial Expansion, 1880–1914* (Oxford: Oxford University Press, 1982), 8.

13. Eric Hobsbawm, *The Age of Empire, 1875–1914* (New York: Pantheon, 1987).

14. The empire was fully aware of its weaker position vis-à-vis other empires, but it continuously presented itself as one deserving of sovereignty as an independent empire nonetheless. On the empire rhetoric and images of legitimacy, see Maurus Reinkowski, "Hapless Imperialists and Resentful Nationalists: Trajectories of Radicalization in the Late Ottoman Empire," in *Helpless Imperialists: Imperial Failure, Fear, and Radicaliza-tion*, ed. Maurus Reinkowski and Gregor Thum (Göttingen: Vandenhoeck & Ruprecht, 2014), 59–60; Selim Deringil, *The Well-Protected Domains: Ideology and the Legitimation of Power in the Ottoman Empire, 1876–1909* (London: I. B. Tauris, 1998); Selim Deringil, "The Invention of Tradition as Public Image in the Late Ottoman Empire, 1808–1908," *Comparative Studies in Society and History* 35 (1993): 3–29.

15. I use "Yıldız Palace" throughout the book as "White House" is used in the media—to represent the White House administration.

16. Mary Dewhurst Lewis, *Divided Rule: Sovereignty and Empire in French Tunisia, 1881–1938* (Berkeley: University of California Press, 2013), 15.

17. Ronald Robinson, "The Case for Economic Aid," in *Developing the Third World: The Experience of the Nineteen-Sixties*, ed. Ronald Robinson (London: Cambridge Uni-versity Press, 1971), 262.

18. Ibid.

19. Marc Ferro, *Colonization: A Global History* (London: Routledge, 1997), 11.

20. Henk L. Wesseling, *The European Colonial Empires, 1815–1919*, trans. Diane Webb (Harlow, UK: Pearson, 2004), 134.

21. Ibid.

22. It is telling that this number seems not to include Ottoman imperial rule in North Africa. In other words, either Ottoman rule was counted as "local rule" and thus part of free Africa, or it was simply ignored. See Douglas Northrop, *An Imperial World: Empires and Colonies since 1750* (Upper Saddle River, NJ: Pearson, 2013), 73.

23. Ibid.

24. Wesseling, *European Colonial Empires*, 148.

25. Ibid., 123.

26. A. G. Hopkins, "The Victorians and Africa: A Reconsideration of the Occupation of Egypt, 1882," *Journal of African History* 27 (1986): 363–391; C. W. Newbury and A. S. Kanya-Forstner, "French Policy and the Origins of the Scramble for West Africa," *Journal of African History* 10 (1969): 253–276.

27. Vladimir Lenin posits the years between 1880 and 1900 as the period when imperialism reached its apex with the joining of Germany and France in the colonial territorial grab leading to the next stage for capitalism. See Vladimir Lenin, "The Division of the World among the Great Powers," in *Imperialism: The Highest Stage of Capitalism: A Popular Outline*, rev. trans. (London: Lawrence & Wishart, 1948), 93–103. Eric Hobsbawm also described the period between 1880 and World War I as the "most spectacular expression of the growing division of the globe into strong and weak, the 'advanced' and 'backward,'" in *Age of Empire, 1875–1914*, 59.

28. Robert O. Collins, *The Partition of Africa: Illusion or Necessity* (New York: Wiley, 1969), 234.

29. In some historical works, the administrative and official reception area of the Yıldız Palace compound is referred to by its Ottoman Turkish name, "Mabeyn" (short for "Mabeyn-i Hümayun"). On the intrigues of the Mabeyn, see Ibrahim al-Muwaylihi, *Spies, Scandals, and Sultans: Istanbul in the Twilight of the Ottoman Empire*, trans. Roger Allen (Lanham, MD: Rowman & Littlefield, 2008). For examples of the influential role that the Mabeyn employees played in Hamidian diplomacy, see Jens Hanssen, "Malhamé–Malfamé," *International Journal of Middle East Studies* 43 (2011): 25–48. For the wider bureaucratic structure of the Yıldız Palace, see François Georgeon, "Yıldız, le palais d'Abdülhamid," in *Abdulhamid II: Le sultan calife* (Paris: Librairie Arthème Fayard, 2003), 127–146.

30. On the financial challenges facing Abdülhamid II's administration and the progress made in the first thirty years after his ascension to the throne, see Engin Akarlı, "Economic Policy and Budgets in Ottoman Turkey, 1876–1909," *Middle Eastern Studies* 28 (1992): 443–476.

31. On the refugees in the Ottoman Empire in the late nineteenth century, see James Meyers, "Immigration, Return, and the Politics of Citizenship: Russian Muslims in the Ottoman Empire, 1860–1914," *International Journal of Middle East Studies* 39 (2007): 15–32; Kemal Karpat, "The Hijra from Russia and the Balkans: The Process of Self-Definition in the Late Ottoman State," in *Muslim Travellers: Pilgrimage, Migration, and the Religious Imagination*, ed. Dale Eickelman and James Piscatori (Berkeley: University of California Press, 1990), 131–152. For the history of one of the largest waves of refugees to the Ottoman Empire during the Balkan wars and World War I, see Ryan Gingeras, *Sorrowful Shores: Violence, Ethnicity, and the End of the Ottoman Empire, 1912–1923* (Oxford: Oxford University Press, 2011).

32. Historian Engin Akarlı was one of the first scholars to offer a radical reassessment of the Hamidian era reforms in his dissertation, "The Problems of External Pressures, Power Struggles, and Budgetary Deficits in Ottoman Politics under

Abdülhamid II (1876–1909): Origins and Solutions" (PhD diss., Princeton University, 1976). Even though Akarlı never converted his dissertation into a monograph, he developed his argument further over the next few decades, most significantly in a seminal article "The Tangled Ends of an Empire: Ottoman Encounters with the West and Problems of Westernization—An Overview," *Comparative Studies of South Asia, Africa, and the Middle East* 26 (2006): 353–366.

33. See Donald Quataert, "Ottoman Reform and Agriculture in Anatolia, 1876–1908" (PhD diss., University of California, Los Angeles, 1973); Carter Findley, *Bureaucratic Reform in the Ottoman Empire: The Sublime Porte, 1789–1922* (Princeton, NJ: Princeton University Press, 1980).

34. On Abdülhamid II's use of Islamic symbolism for political ends, see Deringil, *Well-Protected Domains*; Deringil, "Invention of Tradition," 3–29. On the pan-Islamic ideology promoted by Abdülhamid II, see Kemal Karpat, *The Politicization of Islam: Reconstructing Identity, State, Faith, and Community in the Late Ottoman State* (Oxford: Oxford University Press, 2001).

35. See Selçuk Akşin Somel, *The Modernization of Public Education in the Ottoman Empire, 1839–1908: Islamization, Autocracy, and Discipline* (Leiden: Brill, 2001), 199.

36. Deringil, "Invention of Tradition," 29; Engin Akarlı, "Tangled Ends of an Empire," in *Modernity and Culture from the Mediterranean to the Indian Ocean*, ed. Leila Fawaz and C. A. Bayly (New York: Columbia University Press, 2002), 271.

37. Reşad Pasha's *Muhtasar Osmanlı Tarihi* as quoted in George Walter Gawrych, *The Crescent and the Eagle: Ottoman Rule, Islam and the Albanians, 1874–1913* (London: I. B. Tauris, 2006), 79.

38. M. Şükrü Hanioğlu, *A Brief History of the Late Ottoman Empire* (Princeton, NJ: Princeton University Press, 2008), 215. A noted exception focusing on the first decade of Hamidian rule is F. A. K. Yasamee, *Ottoman Diplomacy: Abdulhamid II and the Great Powers, 1878–1888* (Istanbul: ISIS, 1996).

39. Frederick Cooper, *Colonialism in Question: Theory, Knowledge, History* (Berkeley: University of California Press, 2005), 23; Daniel Goffman and Christopher Stroop, "Empire as Composite: The Ottoman Polity and the Typology of Dominion," in *Imperialisms: Historical and Literary Investigations, 1500–1900*, ed. Balachandra Rajan and Elizabeth Sauer (New York: Palgrave Macmillan, 2004), 129–145.

40. Durba Ghosh and Dane Kennedy, "Introduction," in *Decentering Empire: Britain, India and the Transcolonial World*, ed. Durba Ghosh and Dane Kennedy (Hyderabad, India: Orient Longman, 2006), 7.

41. Antoinette Burton, *Empire in Question: Reading, Writing and Teaching British Imperialism* (Durham, NC: Duke University Press, 2011), 282.

42. Lewis, *Divided Rule*, 16.

43. John Lowe, *The Great Powers: Imperialism and the German Problem, 1865–1925* (New York: Routledge, 1994), 74–85.

44. For the diplomatic history of the Congress of Berlin from an Ottoman perspective, see Roderic H. Davison, *Nineteenth Century Ottoman Diplomacy and Reforms* (Istanbul: ISIS, 1999), 175–206.

45. Suraiya Faroqhi, *Approaching Ottoman History: An Introduction to the Sources* (Cambridge: Cambridge University Press, 1999), 49–53.

46. Abdurrahman Çaycı, *al-Sira' al-Turki-al-Faransi fi al-Sahara' al-Kubra*, trans. (Turkish to Arabic) 'Ali A'zazi (Tripoli: Markaz Dirasat Jihad al-Libiyyin Did al-Ghazw al-Itali, 1982); Ahmet Kavas, *Osmanlı-Afrika İlişkileri* (Istanbul: Tasam Yayınları, 2006); Ahmet Kavas, *Geçmişten Günümüze Afrika* (Istanbul: Kitabevi, 2005); Muhammed Tandoğan, *Afrika'da Sömürgecilik ve Osmanlı Siyaseti (1800–1922)* (Ankara: Türk Tarih Kurumu Yayınları, 2013). Michel Le Gall also used some Ottoman records in his research on Ottoman-Libyan relationships in "The Ottoman Government and the Sanusiyya: A Reappraisal," *International Journal of Middle East Studies* 21 (1989): 91–106.

47. Jeffrey C. Stone, "Imperialism, Colonialism, and Cartography," *Transactions of the Institute of British Geographers*, n.s., 13 (1988): 57–58; Wesseling, *European Colonial Empires*, 122.

48. *Lisan al-Hal*, a popular daily newspaper in Beirut, provided full coverage of the conference from 1884 onward and devoted several columns to its outcome. This was a reflection of the reading public's interests in colonialism in Africa. *Lisan al-Hal*, February 28, 1885, 2.

49. John M. MacKenzie, *Law, History, Colonialism: The Reach of Empire*, ed. Catharine Coleborne and Diane Kirkby (Manchester: Manchester University Press, 2001), vii–viii.

50. J. Westlake, "John Westlake on the Title to Sovereignty," in *Imperialism*, ed. P. D. Curtin (London: Macmillan, 1971), 47, quoted in Peter Fitzpatrick, "Terminal Legality: Imperialism and the (de)Composition of Law," in *Law, History, Colonialism: The Reach of Empire*, ed. Catharine Coleborne and Diane Kirkby (Manchester: Manchester University Press, 2001), 17.

51. On James Lorimer's legal opinions in international law, see James Lorimer, *The Institutes of the Law of Nations* (London: Blackwood, 1883); see also Aimee M. Genell, "Empire by Law: Ottoman Sovereignty and the British Occupation of Egypt" (PhD diss., Columbia University, 2013), 7–11.

52. Here I am referencing Dipesh Chakrabarty, *Provincializing Europe: Postcolonial Thought and Historical Difference* (Princeton, NJ: Princeton University Press, 2007).

53. Fitzpatrick, "Terminal Legality," 17.

54. For examples of the emerging literature that examines the Ottoman Empire's negotiating power on the international stage, see John Willis, *Unmaking North and South: Cartographies of the Yemen Past, 1857–1934* (New York: Columbia University Press, 2012), 73–103; and Genell, "Empire by Law."

55. Isabel V. Hull, *A Scrap of Paper: Breaking and Making International Law during the Great War* (Ithaca, NY: Cornell University Press, 2014), 18.

56. On the impact of the Conference of Berlin on the creation and deployment of international law as legal justification for colonialism in Africa, see Anthony Anghie, *Imperialism, Sovereignty, and the Making of International Law* (Cambridge: Cambridge University Press, 2004), 32–114.

57. I was inspired by the work of Turan Kayaoğlu, who traced the influence of Ottoman international agreements at the 1856 Conference of Paris on domestic policies, particularly the introduction of the Ottoman Land Law of 1860. See Turan Kayaoğlu, *Legal Imperialism: Sovereignty and Extraterritoriality in Japan, the Ottoman Empire and China* (New York: Cambridge University Press, 2010), 104–148. I am especially indebted in my thinking about the Ottoman Empire's role in international agreements and the reflection of international law on Istanbul's international diplomacy to Surya Sharma, *Territorial Acquisition, Disputes, and International Law* (The Hague: Kluwer Law International, 1997); and Godfrey N. Uzoigwe, "Spheres of Influence, Effective Occupation and the Doctrine of Hinterland in the Partition of Africa," *Journal of African Studies* 3 (1976): 183–203.

58. D. M. Schreuder, *The Scramble for Africa, 1877–1895: The Politics of Partition Reappraised* (Cambridge: Cambridge University Press, 1980), 6.

59. David Ludden, "The Process of Empire: Frontiers and Borderlands," in *Tributary Empires in Global History*, ed. Peter Fibiger Bang and C. A. Bayly (London: Palgrave Macmillan, 2011), 133.

60. Ibid., 136.

61. Pekka Hämäläinen and Samuel Truett, "On Borderlands," *Journal of American History* 98 (2011): 343.

62. Ibid., 344.

63. Xiuyu Wang, *China's Last Imperial Frontier: Late Qing Expansion in Sichuan's Tibetan Borderlands* (Plymouth, UK: Lexington, 2011), 242.

64. Ludden, "Process of Empire," 136.

65. Hämäläinen and Truett, "On Borderlands," 344.

66. Here I borrow the definition of frontiers and borderlands from Fabricio Prado, "The Fringes of Empires: Recent Scholarship on Colonial Frontiers and Borderlands in Latin America," *History Compass* 10 (2012): 319.

67. The Ottoman imperial efforts along the frontiers have been the subject of historical study for well over two decades now. For some of the more recent studies on specific aspects of the Hamidian state's relationship with its frontiers, see Nadir Özbek, "Policing the Countryside: Gendarmes of the Late 19th-Century Ottoman Empire (1876–1908)," *International Journal of Middle East Studies* 40 (2008): 47–67; Yasemin Avcı, "The Application of *Tanzimat* in the Desert: The Bedouins and the Creation of a New Town in Southern Palestine (1860–1914)," *Middle Eastern Studies* 45 (2009): 969–983. A. C. S. Peacock, ed., *The Frontiers of the Ottoman World* (Oxford: Oxford University Press, 2009) is a major contribution to the study of frontiers across the Ottoman Empire, particularly in the late nineteenth century; on the relationship between the Ottoman state and its nomadic populations before Abdülhamid II's reign, see Reşat Kasaba, *A Movable Empire: Ottoman Nomads, Migrants, and Refugees* (Seattle: University of Washington Press, 2009). Norman Lewis's *Nomads and Settlers in Syria and Jordan, 1800–1980* (Cambridge: Cambridge University Press, 1987) is a classic text on Bedouins in the Ottoman period. The latest research on the eastern Ottoman frontiers in the nineteenth century includes

Janet Klein, *Kurdish Militias in the Ottoman Tribal Zone* (Stanford, CA: Stanford University Press, 2011); and Sabri Ateş, *The Ottoman-Iranian Borderlands: Making a Boundary, 1843–1914* (New York: Cambridge University Press, 2013).

68. Eugene L. Rogan, *Frontiers of the State in the Late Ottoman Empire: Transjordan, 1850–1921* (Cambridge: Cambridge University Press, 1999), 6.

69. Eugene L. Rogan, "The Aşiret Mektebi: Abdülhamid II's School for Tribes (1892–1907)," *International Journal of Middle East Studies* 28 (1996): 83.

70. Ibid.

71. Isa Blumi, *Rethinking the Late Ottoman Empire: A Comparative Social and Political History of Albania and the Yemen, 1878–1918* (Istanbul: ISIS, 2003), 49.

72. Thomas Kühn, *Empire, Islam, and Politics of Difference: Ottoman Rule in Yemen, 1849–1919* (Leiden: Brill, 2011), 4–8.

73. This is not to be confused with Partha Chatterjee's "rule of colonial difference," which Kühn hints at. The difference between Chatterjee's "rule of colonial difference" and Kühn's "politics of difference" lies at the heart of Kühn's argument. Chatterjee posits a perceived essential, nonchanging difference based on theories of racial difference between the ruler and the ruled in the case of India. In the case of Yemen, the difference emphasized by the Ottoman ruler was not racial or legal or unchangeable; it was cultural and changeable. See Partha Chatterjee, *The Nation and Its Fragments: Colonial and Postcolonial Histories* (Princeton, NJ: Princeton University Press, 1993), 14–34. See also Thomas Kühn, "Shaping and Reshaping Colonial Ottomanism: Contesting Boundaries of Difference and Integration in Ottoman Yemen, 1872–1919," *Comparative Studies of South Asia, Africa and the Middle East* 27 (2007): 315–331; Thomas Kühn, "Ordering Urban Space in Ottoman Yemen 1872–1914," in *The Empire in the City: Arab Provincial Capitals in the Late Ottoman Empire*, ed. Jens Hanssen, Thomas Philipp, and Stefan Weber (Beirut: Ergon Verlag Würzburg in Kommission, 2002), 329–367.

74. Dina Rizk Khoury and Dane Kennedy, "Comparing Empires: The Ottoman Domains and the British Raj in the Long Nineteenth Century," *Comparative Studies of South Asia, Africa, and the Middle East* 27 (2007): 241.

75. Kühn, *Empire, Islam, and Politics of Difference*, 13.

76. Ibid., 244–245.

77. See Thomas Kühn, "An Imperial Borderland as Colony: Knowledge Production and the Elaboration of Difference in Ottoman Yemen, 1872–1918," *MIT Electronic Journal of Middle East Studies* 3 (2003): 5–17.

78. Jane Burbank and Frederick Cooper, *Empires in World History: Power and the Politics of Difference* (Princeton, NJ: Princeton University Press, 2010), 12.

79. See Doreen Massey's *For Space* (London: Sage, 2005) and its adoption by David Lambert and Alan Lester in "Imperial Spaces, Imperial Subjects," in *Colonial Lives across the British Empire: Imperial Careering in the Long Nineteenth Century*, ed. David Lambert and Alan Lester (Cambridge: Cambridge University Press, 2006), 14.

80. There are several examples of the transimperial approach in other imperial histories, particularly that of the British Empire. For example, see Thomas Metcalf, *Imperial Connections: India in the Indian Ocean Arena, 1860–1920* (Berkeley: University of

California Press, 2007); David Lambert and Alan Lester, eds. *Colonial Lives across the British Empire: Imperial Careering in the Long Nineteenth Century* (Cambridge: Cambridge University Press, 2006). Isa Blumi takes a multi-sited comparative approach in his research. See Isa Blumi, "The Frontier as a Measure of Modern Power: Local Limits to Empire in Yemen, 1872–1914," in *The Frontiers of the Ottoman World*, ed. A. C. S. Peacock (Oxford: Oxford University Press, 2010), 289–304.

Chapter 1
Epigraph: Sadık el-Müeyyed Azmzade, *Afrika Sahra-yı Kebiri'nde Seyahat, Bir Osmanlı Zabitinin Büyük Sahra'da Seyahati*, translated from Ottoman Turkish to Turkish and introduced by İdris Bostan (Istanbul: Çamlıca, 2008), 158.

1. James McDougall, "Frontiers, Borderlands, and Saharan/World History," in *Saharan Frontiers: Space and Mobility in Northwest Africa*, ed. James McDougall and Judith Scheele (Bloomington: Indiana University Press, 2012), 81. A number of historians have been working to transcend divides between the writing of the history of Africa and the Middle East, the Red Sea, and the Indian Ocean. See, for example, Amal Ghazal, "Transcending Area Studies: Piecing Together the Cross-Regional Networks of Ibadi Islam," *Comparative Studies of South Asia, Africa, and the Middle East* 34 (2014): 582–589; Amal Ghazal, "An Ottoman Pasha and the End of Empire: Sulayman al-Baruni and the Networks of Islamic Reform," in *Global Muslims in the Age of Steam and Print*, ed. James Gelvin and Nile Green (Berkeley: University of California Press, 2014), 40–58; Matthew Ellis, "Between Empire and Nation: The Emergence of Egypt's Libyan Borderland, 1841–1911" (PhD diss., Princeton University, 2011); Jonathan Miran, "Mapping Space and Mobility in the Red Sea Region, c. 1500–1950," *History Compass* 12 (2014): 197–216.

2. See Eve Troutt Powell, *A Different Shade of Colonialism: Egypt, Great Britain, and the Mastery of Sudan* (Berkeley: University of California Press, 2003), 31.

3. A note on the use of the term "Libya." Of course, Libya as a kingdom and later the Arab Republic of Libya did not exist until the twentieth century, and its boundaries were mostly determined by Italian colonial rule. However, for ease of reference, the three administrative regions (Fezzan, Tripolitania, and Cyrenaica) are occasionally referred to collectively as Ottoman Libya.

4. Alan G. Jamieson, *Lords of the Sea: A History of the Barbary Corsairs* (London: Reaktion, 2012), 34–51.

5. Djerba is an island off the coast of Tunisia, close to the Libyan-Tunisian border.

6. Jamieson, *Lords of the Sea*, 34–51.

7. In 2013 the shrine was attacked by extremists as part of a bombing campaign targeting Sufi shrines across Libya. See "Libya'da Osmanlı Türbesine Saldırı," *NTVMSNBC*, November 28, 2013, http://NTVMSNBC.com/id/25482517 (accessed August 17, 2015).

8. David Abulafia, *The Great Sea: A Human History of the Mediterranean* (Oxford: Oxford University Press, 2011), 414; Ahmed Akgündüz and Said Öztürk, *Ottoman History: Misperceptions and Truths* (Rotterdam: Islamic University of Rotterdam Press, 2011), 185.

9. For a military history of the Ottoman-Hapsburg battles for the Mediterranean, see Andrew C. Hess, *The Forgotten Frontier: History of the Sixteenth-Century Ibero-African Frontier* (Chicago: University of Chicago Press, 1978). On the Battle of Lepanto and its long-term ramifications in the Mediterranean, see Fernand Braudel, *The Mediterranean and the Mediterranean World in the Age of Philip II*, trans. Sian Reynolds (New York: Harper Colophon, 1973), 2:1088–1142. For an economic and diplomatic history of Ottoman involvement in the eastern Mediterranean—the Levant, the Aegean Sea, and the Adriatic Sea—during the same period, see Palmira Brummett, *Ottoman Seapower and Levantine Diplomacy in the Age of Discovery* (Albany: State University of New York Press, 1994).

10. According to Sir James W. Redhouse, in *Turkish and English Lexicon*, dey is a corruption of *dayı* initially used to refer solely to the chief of the Janissaries of Algiers; it was later applied by Europeans to the ruling pashas in Algiers. See James W. Redhouse, *Redhouse Turkish and English Lexicon* (Istanbul: Çağrı Yayınları, 1890), 887. In this context, it began to be adopted as the title of the head of a North African regency (*paşalık* in Ottoman-Turkish).

11. John Wright, *A History of Libya* (New York: Columbia University Press, 2010), 74–79; Yılmaz Öztuna, *Devletler ve Hanedanlar* (Ankara: Kültür Bakanlığı, 2005), 3:240.

12. M. Houtsma, *First Encyclopedia of Islam* (Leiden: Brill, 1913–1936), 4:749; David Lea and Annamarie Rowe, eds., *A Political Chronology of Africa* (London: Europa, 2001), 238.

13. Ali Abdullatif Ahmida, *The Making of Modern Libya: State Formation, Colonization, and Resistance, 1830–1932* (Albany: State University of New York Press, 1994), 23.

14. Ludovico Micara, "The Ottoman Tripoli: A Mediterranean Median," in *The City in the Islamic World*, ed. Salma Khadra Jayyusi, Renata Holod, Attilio Petruccioli, and Andre Raymond (Leiden: Brill, 2008), 1:394.

15. al-Tahir Ahmad al-Zawi, *Wulat Tarablus min Bidayat al-Fath al-ʿArabi ila Nihayat al-ʿAhd al-Turki* (Beirut: Dar al-Fath li-l-Tibaʿa wa-l-Nashr, 1970), 115.

16. Wright, *History of Libya*, 80–81. The battles between the Karamanlı forces and the Americans are credited with the establishment of the American Navy. For more on this short war, see Gregory Fremont-Barnes, *The Wars of the Barbary Pirates: To the Shores of Tripoli: The Rise of the US Navy and Marines* (Oxford: Osprey, 2006); A. B. C. Whipple, *To the Shores of Tripoli: The Birth of the US Navy and Marines* (Annapolis, MD: Naval Institute Press, 2001); Joshua London, *Victory in Tripoli: How America's War with the Barbary Pirates Established the US Navy and Built a Nation* (Hoboken, NJ: Wiley, 2005).

17. This area was recently thrust back into the news because it is the main theater of operations for the Boko Haram militia. On Boko Haram in Borno, see J. Peter Pham, *Boko Haram's Evolving Threat* (Washington, DC: Africa Center for Strategic Studies, 2012); Andrew Walker, *What Is Boko Haram?* (Washington, DC: US Institute of Peace, 2012).

18. William Keith Hallam, "The Chad Basin," *Nigeria Magazine* (1966): 261.

19. Jean-Claude Zeltner, *Pages d'histoire du Kanem: Pays tchadien* (Paris: Harmattan, 1980), 200. On the Kanemi rule in Kanem-Borno in the nineteenth century, see

Jean-Claude Zeltner, *Histoire des Arabes sur les rives du lac Tchad* (Paris: Karthala, 2002), 37–81.

20. *Mai* is the Kanuri and Kanembu word for king.

21. Andres J. Bjørkelo, *State and Society in the Three Central Sudanic Kingdoms: Kanem-Bornu, Bagirmi, and Wadai* (Bergen, Norway: Hovedoppgave i Historie Høsten, University of Bergen, 1976), 15. On the arrival of the al-Kanemi Dynasty in Borno and the events leading to the demise of the Kanuri Dynasty, see William Keith Hallam, "An Introduction to the History of Bornu," *Nigerian Field* (1977): 147–164; Louis Brenner, *The Shehus of Kukawa: A History of the al-Kanemi Dynasty of Bornu* (Oxford: Clarendon, 1973).

22. Bjørkelo, *State and Society*, 19.

23. Saʿid ʿAbd al-Rahman al-Hindiri, *al-ʿAlaqat al-Libiyya al-Tchadiyya, 1843–1975* (Tripoli: Markaz Dirasat Jihad al-Libiyyin Did al-Ghazw al-Itali, 1983), 19.

24. On the demise of the Barbary corsairs, see Daniel Panzac, *Barbary Corsairs: The End of a Legend, 1800–1820* (Leiden: Brill, 2005). It would be very difficult to overstate the scale of the slave trade and the economic reliance of settlements in the Sahara and Libyan port cities on it. For more on the slave trade and the involvement of the Sanusi Order in the facilitation of trade routes from sub-Saharan Africa to Benghazi, see Robert O. Collins, "The African Slave Trade to Asia and the Indian Ocean Islands," *African and Asian Studies* 5 (2006): 325–346; Dennis Cordell, *Dar al-Kuti and the Last Years of the Trans-Saharan Slave Trade* (Madison: University of Wisconsin Press, 1985); John Wright, *Libya, Chad and the Central Sahara* (Totowa, NJ: Barnes & Noble Books, 1989), 59–64. For more on the political and economic ties between the kingdoms of the Chad Lake basin and Ottoman Libya before the nineteenth century, see B. G. Martin, "Kanem, Bornu, and the Fazzan: Notes on the Political History of a Trade Route," *Journal of African History* 10 (1969): 15–27.

25. Brenner, *Shehus of Kukawa*, 83.

26. Muhammad Rajeb al-Zaʾidi, *Qbaʾil al-ʿArab fi Libya*, pt. 1 (Benghazi: Dar al-Kitab al-Libi, 1968), 57–64.

27. Dennis Cordell, "The Awlad Sulayman of Libya and Chad: Power and Adaptation in the Sahara and Sahel," *Canadian Journal of African Studies* 19 (1985): 324–325.

28. Wright, *Libya, Chad and the Central Sahara*, 71–74.

29. Cordell, "Awlad Sulayman of Libya and Chad," 321.

30. Ahmida, *Making of Modern Libya*, 30.

31. On the economic and social conditions under the rule of the Karamanlı Dynasty, see K. S. McLachlan, "Tripoli and Tripolitania: Conflict and Cohesion during the Period of the Barbary Corsairs (1551–1850)," *Transactions of the Institute of British Geographers* 3 (1978): 285–294. On the collapse of the Karamanlı Dynasty, see L. J. Hume, "Preparations for Civil War in Tripoli in the 1820s: Ali Karamanli, Hassuna D'Ghies and Jeremy Bentham," *Journal of African History* 21 (1980): 311–322; ʿUmar ʿAli bin Ismaʿil, *Inhiyar Hukm al-Usra al-Qaramanliyya fi Libya, 1795–1835* (Tripoli: Maktabat al-Farajani, 1966).

32. Wright, *Libya, Chad and the Central Sahara*, 81–83.

33. M. Şükrü Hanioğlu, *A Brief History of the Late Ottoman Empire* (Princeton, NJ: Princeton University Press, 2008), 9, 66–67.

34. Cyrenaica, the ancient Roman province (Barqa' in Arabic), is often referred to in the sources as Benghazi—its largest city. *Trablusgarb* (*Tarablus al-Gharb* in Arabic), literally Tripoli of the West, is used to differentiate it from the city of Tripoli in the province of Damascus (*Tarablusşam* in Ottoman-Turkish), which lies in the north of modern-day Lebanon along the eastern Mediterranean coast.

35. On the drawing of intra- and interimperial boundaries during this period, see Ellis, "Between Empire and Nation."

36. For a brief summary of the Tanzimat program, see Hanioğlu, *Brief History*, 72–108.

37. Lisa Anderson, "Nineteenth-Century Reform in Ottoman Libya," *International Journal of Middle East Studies* 16 (1984): 325.

38. Magali Morsy, *North Africa 1800–1900: A Survey from the Nile Valley to the Atlantic* (London: Longman, 1984), 269.

39. Anderson, "Nineteenth-Century Reform in Ottoman Libya," 328. For a detailed study of the evolution of the state in Libya up to 1980, see Lisa Anderson, *The State and Social Transformation in Tunisia and Libya, 1830–1980* (Princeton, NJ: Princeton University Press, 1986).

40. al-Hindiri, *al-'Alaqat al-Libiyya al-Tchadiyya*, 18, 19. On the historic ties between Tripolitania and the Kingdoms of Central Sudan, see Muftah Yunus Rabasi, *al-'Alaqat Bayn Bilad al-Maghreb wa Dawlat al-Kanem wa-l-Borno (7–10 AH/13–16 AD)* (Benghazi: Seventh of October University, 2008), 130–187.

41. Zeltner, *Pages d'histoire du Kanem*, 224–251; Wright, *Libya, Chad and the Central Sahara*, 74–78; Cordell, "Awlad Sulayman of Libya and Chad," 337–338.

42. Wright, *Libya, Chad and the Central Sahara*, 71.

43. Ahmida, *Making of Modern Libya*, 22–25.

44. Arabic *zāwiya*, plural *zawāyā*; Ottoman-Turkish *zaviye*, plural *zaviyeler*; Turkish *tekke*, plural *tekkeler*. I use the Arabic form throughout the book because the language of instruction and communication and the cultural milieu of the Sanusi Order was Arabic. I stay away from the English Sufi "lodge" because it implies a structure where Sufi religious rituals were performed, a place for quiet meditation, or a place for shelter. All of these were offered in a Sanusi *zāwiya*, but were only a part of its services.

45. Ahmed Hilmi Şehbenderzade, *Asr-ı Hamidi'de Alem-i İslam ve Senusiler* (Istanbul: İkdam Matbaası, 1907); republished as Ahmed Hilmi Şehbenderzade, *Senusiler ve Sultan Abdülhamid*, ed. and trans. (Ottoman-Turkish to Turkish) İsmail Cömert (Istanbul: SES Yayınları, 1992), 20.

46. Şehbenderzade, *Senusiler ve Sultan Abdülhamid*, 20.

47. E. E. Evans-Pritchard, *The Sanusi of Cyrenaica* (Oxford: Clarendon, 1949), 88.

48. Ahmida, *Making of Modern Libya*, 32.

49. See Evans-Pritchard, *Sanusi of Cyrenaica*; E. E. Evans-Pritchard, "Italy and the Sanusiya Order in Cyrenaica," *Bulletin of the School of Oriental and African Studies* 11 (1946): 843–853; E. E. Evans-Pritchard, "The Distribution of the Sanusi Lodges," *Africa: Journal of the International African Institute* 15 (1945): 183–187; E. E. Evans-Pritchard, "Italy and the Bedouin in Cyrenaica," *African Affairs* 45 (1946): 12–21.

50. Kunt S. Vikør has published several articles on the Sanusi Order, the most important work to date being *Sufi and Scholar on the Desert Edge: Muhammad b. Ali al-Sanusi and His Brotherhood* (London: Hurst, 1995). Anthropologist Emrys L. Peters has written extensively on the Bedouins in the Libyan Desert, with the most important for this book being *The Bedouin of Cyrenaica: Studies in Personal and Corporate Power*, ed. Jack Goody and Emanuel Marx (New York: Cambridge University Press, 1990). I rely heavily on both.

51. Ahmad Sidqi al-Dajani, *al-Haraka al-Sanusiyya: Nash'atuha wa Numuwwuha fi al-Qarn al-Tasi' 'Ashar* (Cairo, 1967).

52. A. S. al-Hourier, "Social and Economic Transformations in the Libyan Hinterland during the Second Half of the Nineteenth Century: The Rule of the Sayyid Ahmad al-Sharif al-Sanusi" (PhD diss., University of California, Los Angeles, 1981), xii.

53. Here I am referring specifically to 'Ali Muhammad Muhammad al-Sallabi, *Tarikh al-Haraka al-Sanusiyya fi Ifriqya, al-Qism al-Awwal: al-Imam Muhmammad Bin 'Ali al-Sanusi wa Nahjoh fi al-Ta'sis al-Ta'limi wa-l-Haraki wa-l-Tarbawi wa-l-Da'awi wa-l-Siyasi* (Beirut: Dar al-Ma'rifa li-l-Tab' wa-l-Nashr, 2005).

54. In Arabic sources, the Sanusi Order is usually referred to as *al-Ṭarīqa al-Sanūsiyya* or *al-Ḥaraka al-Sanūsiyya*, with each reference having a different connotation. The first one privileges the order's Sufi/ritualistic/philosophical practices; the second, *ḥaraka* (movement), privileges its political/military/religious/social activist aspects. I use the more "neutral" *Sanusi Order* and, rarely, *Sanusiyya* throughout the book.

55. Dennis Cordell, "Eastern Libya, Wadai and the Sanusiya: A Tariqa and a Trade Route," *Journal of African History* 18 (1977): 28; Wright, *Libya, Chad and the Central Sahara*, 81.

56. According to Nicola A. Ziadeh in *Sanusiyah: A Study of a Revivalist Movement in Islam* (Leiden: Brill, 1968), a variety of dates are given by different historians, making this date an approximation. Ziadeh estimates his birth to be sometime between 1791 and 1806, in the latter of which he had much more confidence. However, the date given and used most often is the one used by the future king of Libya, the grandson of the Grand Sanusi, in an introduction to one of the Grand Sanusi's published works. Earlier Ottoman sources, such as Şehbenderzade, put his date of birth at 1792; see Şehbenderzade, *Asr-ı Hamidi'de Alem-i İslam ve Senusiler*, 37.

57. Ziadeh, *Sanusiyah*, 35–36.

58. Wright, *Libya, Chad and the Central Sahara*, 81.

59. The Arabic *hajj* simply means "pilgrimage," but in English texts is mostly used in reference to the Muslim pilgrimage to Mecca.

60. Sayyid Ahmad bin Idris al-Fasi was the fourth head of the Moroccan Khadiriyya Sufi Order, a sub-branch of the Shadhiliyya Order. Evans-Pritchard, *Sanusi of Cyrenaica*, 12.

61. Cordell, "Eastern Libya, Wadai and the Sanusiya," 24–25.

62. Morsy, *North Africa 1800–1900*, 273; Evans-Pritchard, *Sanusi of Cyrenaica*, 13.

63. el-Müeyyed Azmzade, *Afrika Sahra-yı Kebiri'nde Seyahat, Bir Osmanlı Zabitinin Büyük Sahra'da Seyahati*, 112–114.

64. Vikør, *Sufi and Scholar on the Desert Edge*, 124–131.

65. el-Müeyyed Azmzade, *Afrika Sahra-yı Kebiri'nde Seyahat, Bir Osmanlı Zabitinin Büyük Sahra'da Seyahati*, 112–114.

66. Ibid., 28.

67. al-Dajani, *al-Haraka al-Sanusiyya*, 78–79.

68. On King Idris, see E. A. V. De Candole, *The Life and Times of King Idris of Libya* (privately published by Mohamed Ben Ghalbon, 1990).

69. Cecil Godfrey Wood was born in Damascus in 1851 and entered the British Foreign Service as a clerk at the British legation in Tangiers in 1875. He moved to Morocco in 1880. In 1882, he was promoted to British consul in Benghazi and then transferred to Jeddah in 1888. In 1892, he was promoted to consul-general in Tabriz and from there moved to Balboa, Spain, in 1902. An entry for Cecil Wood appears in *Who's Who, 1906* (London: A & C Black, 1906), 1846.

70. National Archives, formerly British National Archives (hereafter BNA), "Memorandum Regarding Sidi Mohammad el Mehedy Essenoossy and the Senoossia Confraternity," April 1889, FO 78/4218-2, 181.

71. Ibid.

72. Ibid.

73. Louis Rinn, *Marabouts et Khouan: Étude sur l'Islam en Algerie* (Algiers, 1884). For more on Rinn's opinion of the impact of Sufi orders on French colonial administration, see George Trumbull IV, *An Empire of Facts: Colonial Power, Cultural Knowledge and Islam in Algeria, 1870–1914* (Cambridge: Cambridge University Press, 2009), 11–48.

74. Gustav Nachtigal, *Sahara and Sudan*, vol. 1, *Tripoli, Fezzan and Tibesti or Tu*, trans. Allan and Humphrey Fisher (London: C. Hurst, 1974), 176.

75. Wright, *Libya, Chad and the Central Sahara*, 84. See also Henri Duveyrier, *Exploration du Sahara*, 2 vols. (Paris, 1864). A good example of the essentialist descriptions of the Sanusi Order is the eleven-part *Handbook on Cyrenaica*, authored by a group of British military officers in the mid-1940s (the exact date is unknown). In particular, booklets by Brigadier D. C. Cumming do not mince words when talking about the mind of "the Arab" and the "primitive" nature of Sanusi Islam. See D. C. Cumming, *Handbook on Cyrenaica*, pts. 5 and 6 (London: Printing and Stationery Services, M.E.F., n.d.).

76. Benjamin Claude Brower, *A Desert Named Peace: The Violence of France's Empire in the Algerian Sahara, 1844–1902* (New York: Columbia University Press, 2009), 230.

77. For more on the "Black legend of the Sanusiyya," see Jean-Louis Triaud, ed., *La légende noire de la Sanusiyya: Une confrérie musulmane saharienne sous le regard français, 1840–1930*, 2 vols. (Paris: Éditions de la Maison de Science de l'Homme; Aix-en-Provence: Institut de Recherches et d'Études sur le Monde Arabe et Musulmane, 1995).

78. Evans-Pritchard, *Sanusi of Cyrenaica*, 8.

79. al-Zawi, *Wulat Tarablus*, 244; al-Hourier, "Social and Economic Transformations in the Libyan Hinterland," 48.

80. al-Dajani, *al-Haraka al-Sanusiyya*, 274.

81. Anderson, "Nineteenth-Century Reform in Ottoman Libya," 332; BNA, May 21, 1889, FO 195/1653, 356.

82. BNA, May 21, 1889, FO 195/1653, 356. Donald Andreas Cameron replaced Cecil Wood in Benghazi in 1888. Born in 1856, he started his career in the Foreign Service in 1879 as an interpreter in Istanbul. He was assigned as a British consul in Suakin in 1885 and then in Benghazi in 1888. He was promoted to consul-general for Port Said in 1905 and then for Alexandria in 1909. He retired in 1919. In 1898 Cameron published *The History of Egypt in the 19th Century*. See *Who's Who, 1924* (London: A & C Black, 1924), 446.

83. al-Dajani, *al-Haraka al-Sanusiyya*, 276.

84. Vikør provides evidence that even the initial suspicious meeting and eventual "charming" of the Ottoman governor was most probably a legend. See Vikør, *Sufi and Scholar on the Desert Edge*, 143–145.

85. Ibid., 149.

86. Selim Deringil, *The Well-Protected Domains: Ideology and the Legitimation of Power in the Ottoman Empire, 1876–1909* (London: I. B. Tauris, 1998), 94–101.

87. On the social and political impact of missionary schools in the Ottoman Empire, see Ussama Makdisi, *Artillery of Heaven: American Missionaries and the Failed Conversion of the Middle East* (Ithaca, NY: Cornell University Press, 2008); Deringil, *Well-Protected Domains*, 112–134; Fatma Müge Göçek, "Ethnic Segmentation, Western Education, and Political Outcomes: Nineteenth-Century Ottoman Society," *Poetics Today* 14 (1993): 524.

88. For more on the lives, education, and career paths of Ottoman Syrian bureaucrats, see Corinne Lee Blake, "Training Arab-Ottoman Bureaucrats: Syrian Graduates of the Mülkiye Mektebi, 1890–1920" (PhD diss., Princeton University, 1991). An empire-wide education system had been designed initially in 1839, but did not gain legal legitimacy until 1869. For the main provisions of the Regulations for General Education (Maarif-i Umumiye Nizamnamesi), see Andreas M. Kazamias, *Education and the Quest for Modernity in Turkey* (Chicago: University of Chicago Press, 1966), 63.

89. Blake, "Training Arab-Ottoman Bureaucrats," 64.

90. On the adoption of Hanafism as the official Ottoman state *madhhab*, see Rudolph Peters, "What Does It Mean to Be an Official Madhhab? Hanafism and the Ottoman Empire," in *The Islamic School of Law: Evolution, Devolution, and Progress*, ed. Peri J. Bearman, Rudolph Peters, and Frank E. Vogel (Cambridge, MA: Harvard University Press, 2005), 147–158.

91. Randi Deguilhem, "A Revolution in Learning? The Islamic Contribution to the Ottoman State Schools: Examples from the Syrian Provinces," in *Proceedings of the International Congress on Learning and Education in the Ottoman World*, ed. Ali Çaksu (Istanbul: IRCICA, 2001), 285; Benjamin C. Fortna, *Imperial Classroom: Islam, the State, and Education in the Late Ottoman Empire* (Oxford: Oxford University Press, 2002), 25–27; see also Martin Strohmeier, "Muslim Education in the Vilayet of Beirut, 1880–1918," in *Decision Making and Change in the Ottoman Empire*, ed. Caesar E. Farah (Kirksville, MO: Thomas Jefferson University Press, 1993), 215–241.

92. Engin Akarlı, "Tangled Ends of an Empire," in *Modernity and Culture from the Mediterranean to the Indian Ocean*, ed. Leila Fawaz and C. A. Bayly, 261–284 (New York: Columbia University Press, 2002), 271–273.

93. Selçuk Akşin Somel, *The Modernization of Public Education in the Ottoman Empire, 1839–1908: Islamization, Autocracy, and Discipline* (Leiden: Brill, 2001), 190.

94. Anderson, "Nineteenth-Century Reform in Ottoman Libya," 332.

95. al-Hourier, "Social and Economic Transformations in the Libyan Hinterland," 94–95.

96. On the diverse Sufi orders of the Ottoman Empire, including North Africa, see Julia Ann Clancy-Smith, *Rebel and Saint: Muslim Notables, Populist Protest, Colonial Encounters (Algeria and Tunisia, 1800–1904)* (Berkeley: University of California Press, 1994); Dina Le Gall provides a comprehensive look at one of the most powerful Sufi orders in the Ottoman Empire in *A Culture of Sufism—Naqshbandis in the Ottoman World, 1450–1700* (Albany: State University of New York Press, 2005). On Tanzimat-era changes in the relationship of the Ottoman state to the Sufi orders in the center of the Empire, see E. Melek Cevahiroğlu, "The Sufi Order in a Modernizing Empire: 1808–1876," *Tarih* 1 (2009): 70–93.

97. BNA, May 12, 1889, FO 195/1653-4, 337. It is important not to confuse the uncomplicated practices associated with being a member of the order with the simplicity of the *tarikat* philosophy. Needless to say, the Sanusi *tarikat* was a sophisticated combination of Islamic orthodoxy and Sufi philosophical thought, which I do not delve into at all in this book. For a concise introduction to the basic tenants of the order, see W. M. Watt, *Islamic Creeds: A Selection* (Edinburgh: Edinburgh University Press, 1994), 90–97.

98. A. Adu Boahen, *Britain, the Sahara, and the Western Sudan, 1788–1861* (Oxford: Oxford University Press, 1964), 111.

99. James Wright, *The Trans-Saharan Slave Trade* (London: Routledge, 2007), 112–113.

100. For more details on the relationship between the establishment and spread of the Sanusi Order and the opening up of trade routes, see Cordell, "Eastern Libya, Wadai and the Sanusiya," 21–36.

101. The *zawāyā* in North Africa, particularly the ones housing a Sufi saint or his tomb, were considered neutral zones, with a sacred armistice imposed because of the Sufi saint's presence. See Clancy-Smith, *Rebel and Saint*, 37.

102. Evans-Pritchard, *Sanusi of Cyrenaica*, 71–72.

103. Kunt Vikør, "Mystics in the Desert," in *The Middle East: Unity and Diversity: Papers from the Second Nordic Conference on Middle Eastern Studies*, ed. K. Vikør and H. Palva (Copenhagen: Nordic Institute of Asian Studies Press, 1993), 141.

104. Vikør, *Sufi and Scholar on the Desert Edge*, 150–151.

Chapter 2

Epigraph: Sadık el-Müeyyed Azmzade, *Afrika Sahra-yı Kebiri'nde Seyahat, Bir Osmanlı Zabitinin Büyük Sahra'da Seyahati*, translated from Ottoman Turkish to Turkish and introduced by İdris Bostan (Istanbul: Çamlıca, 2008), 123.

1. For a detailed recounting of the 1877–1878 Russo-Ottoman War, see Quintin Barry, *War in the East: A Military History of the Russo-Turkish War, 1877–78* (Solihull, UK: Helion, 2012).

2. On the early days of Russian intervention in ethnic and religious rebellions in the Ottoman Empire, see Christine Philliou, *Biography of an Empire: Governing Ottomans*

in the Age of Revolution (Berkeley: University of California Press, 2011). For examples of French and British intervention during earlier rebellions in the Ottoman Empire, see Ussama Makdisi, *The Culture of Sectarianism: Community, History, and Violence in Nineteenth-Century Ottoman Lebanon* (Berkeley: University of California Press, 2000).

3. Peter Sluglett and M. Hakan Yavuz, "Introduction: Laying the Foundation for Future Instability," in *War and Diplomacy: The Russo-Turkish War of 1877-78 and the Treaty of Berlin,* ed. Peter Sluglett and M. Hakan Yavuz (Salt Lake City: University of Utah Press, 2011), 1–2; Selim Deringil, "The Ottoman Response to the Egyptian Crisis of 1881–82," *Middle Eastern Studies* 24 (1988): 3. For a more traditional narrative of the Congress of Berlin, see W. N. Medlicott, *The Congress of Berlin: A Diplomatic History of the Near Eastern Settlement, 1878–1880* (London: Methuen, 1938).

4. Mary Dewhurst Lewis, *Divided Rule: Sovereignty and Empire in French Tunisia, 1881–1938* (Berkeley: University of California Press, 2013), 102.

5. Selim Sabit, *Muhtasar-ı Coğrafya Risalesi, Subyan Mektblerine Muhasasdır,* 3rd ed. (Damascus: Waqf Majlis al-Maʿarif ʿala al-Maktaba al-ʿUmumiyya bi-Dimashq, LaTürkü Matbaası, 1880), 37. For more on the expansion of the Ottoman Empire in the sixteenth century, see Asma Moalla, *The Regency of Tunis and the Ottoman Porte, 1777–1814: Army and Government of a North-African Ottoman Eyalet at the End of the Eighteenth Century* (London: RoutledgeCurzon, 2004).

6. In May of 1881, it was reported that the Ottoman government had sent lengthy protests over France's violent invasion of Tunisia; see *Lisan al-Hal,* May 3, 1881, 1. For more on the early years of French planning and execution of the invasion of Tunisia, see François Broche, *L'expédition de Tunisie, 1881* (Paris: Presses de la Cité, 1996). On Tunisian-Algerian cross-border military and political resistance, see Julia Ann Clancy-Smith, *Rebel and Saint: Muslim Notables, Populist Protest, Colonial Encounters (Algeria and Tunisia, 1800–1904)* (Berkeley: University of California Press, 1994), 125–167. The agreement with the British to allow French domination of Tunisia had been drawn up much earlier, in 1878, during the Congress of Berlin. During conference negotiations, the French agreed to the British occupation of Ottoman Cyprus in return for Britain's guarantee that it would not object to French claims to Tunisia in the near future. See Julia Clancy-Smith and Charles D. Smith, *The Modern Middle East and North Africa: A History in Documents* (Oxford: Oxford University Press, 2014), 37.

7. After the Provincial Law of 1864, *mutasarrifiyya* connoted a certain level of autonomy for an administrative zone, often under pressure from the European powers. Most famous are the cases of Ottoman Mount Lebanon, Cyprus, and Jerusalem, but other regions were given this designation without the threat of European interference, allowing Istanbul a direct hand in the internal affairs of the *mutasarrifiyya,* as in the case of Cyrenaica. For more on the *mutasarrifiyya* of Jerusalem and Mount Lebanon, see David Kushner, "The Mutasarrıflık of Jerusalem at the End of the Hamidian Period," in *Eighth International Congress of the Economic and Social History of Turkey Papers,* ed. Nurcan Abacı (Morrisville, NC: Lulu Press, 2006), 121–125; Carol Hakim, *Origins of the Lebanese National Idea: 1840–1920* (Berkeley: University of California Press, 2013), 99–194.

8. *Ferik* (*farīq* in Arabic) is the rank of divisional general in the Ottoman military. See *Redhouse Sözlüğü Türkçe/Osmalıca-İngilizce*, 7th ed. (Istanbul: SEV Matbaacılık ve Yayınlılık A.Ş., 1999). It is equivalent to the modern Turkey *korgeneral* according to the *Türk Dil Kurumu*, http://www.tdk.gov.tr.

9. On the role that Zeki Pasha played as the Ottoman military commander in this crisis, see Kemal Karpat, *Islam: Reconstructing Identity, State, Faith, and Community in the Late Ottoman State* (Oxford: Oxford University Press, 2001), 259–261. He was referred to as "commander in chief" in Michel Le Gall, "Pashas, Bedouins and Notables: Ottoman Administration in Tripoli and Benghazi, 1881–1902" (PhD diss., Princeton University, 1986), 26.

10. *Lisan al-Hal*, August 18, 1881, 2.

11. Başbakanlık Osmanli Arşivleri (hereafter BOA), March 21, 1882, Y.PRK.SRN-1/47.

12. Ibid.

13. Sabit, *Muhtasar-ı Coğrafya*, 35.

14. On the international and domestic factors behind Britain's decision to invade Egypt, see John Gallagher and Ronald Robinson, *Africa and the Victorians: The Official Mind of Imperialism* (London: Macmillan, 1965), 76–121.

15. Comprehensive studies of the social and political factors leading to the 'Urabi Revolt can be found in Alexander Schölch, *Egypt for the Egyptians! The Socio-Political Crisis in Egypt, 1878–1882* (Oxford: Oxford University Press, 1981); Juan Cole, *Colonialism and Revolution in the Middle East: Social and Cultural Origins of Egypt's 'Urabi Movement* (Princeton, NJ: Princeton University Press, 1993).

16. Sabit, *Muhtasar-ı Coğrafya*, 37.

17. Yılmaz Öztuna, *Devletler ve Hanedanlar: Türkiye (1074–1990)* (Ankara: Kültür Bakanlığı Yayınları, 1989), 2:1009.

18. For the full text of the Act of Berlin, see Arthur Berriedale Keith, *The Belgian Congo and the Act of Berlin* (Oxford: Oxford University Press, 1919), 302–316.

19. Friedrich Kratochwil, "Of Systems, Boundaries, and Territoriality: An Inquiry into the Formation of the State System," *World Politics* 39 (1986): 39.

20. S. Akweenda, *International Law and the Protection of Namibia's Territorial Integrity: Boundaries and Territorial Claims* (The Hague: Kluwer Law International, 1997), 21.

21. For more on the sphere of influence and hinterland doctrines as well as effective occupation in the colonization of Africa starting with the Act of Berlin, see Godfrey N. Uzoigwe, "Spheres of Influence, Effective Occupation and the Doctrine of Hinterland in the Partition of Africa," *Journal of African Studies* 3 (1976): 183–203; Godfrey N. Uzoigwe, "The Scramble for Territory," *UNESCO Courier* (1984), http://bi.galegroup.com.proxy .library.cornell.edu/essentials/article/GALE%7CA3247483?u=nysl_sc_cornl (accessed August 17, 2015).

22. Peter Fitzpatrick, "Terminal Legality: Imperialism and the (de)Composition of Law," in *Law, History, Colonialism, the Reach of Empire*, ed. Catharine Coleborne and Diane Kirkby (Manchester: Manchester University Press, 2001), 18.

23. Joshua Castellino, Steven Allen, and Jeremie Gilbert, *Title to Territory in International Law: A Temporal Analysis* (Aldershot, UK: Dartmouth, 2003), 46.

24. Surya Sharma, *Territorial Acquisition, Disputes, and International Law* (The Hague: Kluwer Law International, 1997), 65.

25. Ibid., 66.

26. Ibid.

27. BOA, November 30, 1890, HR.SYS-1601/22.

28. On rule by proxy, see Moses E. Ochonu, *Colonialism by Proxy: Hausa Imperial Agents and Middle Belt Consciousness in Nigeria* (Bloomington: Indiana University Press, 2014). For an analysis of direct and indirect colonial rule and its modern legacy, see Mahmoud Mamdani, *Citizen and Subject: Contemporary Africa and the Legacy of Late Colonialism* (Princeton, NJ: Princeton University Press, 1997).

29. Ahmida describes the system of Sanusi *zawāya* and the various functions they performed as a "Sanusi state" and charts the Sanusi state's hierarchic structure. See Ali Abdullatif Ahmida, *The Making of Modern Libya: State Formation, Colonization, and Resistance, 1830–1932* (Albany: State University of New York Press, 1994), 99.

30. BOA, December 3, 1887, Y.MTV-29/15.

31. Dana Sajdi skillfully summarizes the long-standing debate over decentralization and its relationship to the so-called decline of the Ottoman Empire, with special emphasis on the Ottoman treasury's ability to collect taxes. See Dana Sajdi, "Decline, Its Discontent and Ottoman Cultural History: By Way of Introduction," in *Ottoman Tulips, Ottoman Coffee: Leisure and Lifestyle in the Eighteenth Century*, ed. Dana Sajdi (London: I. B. Tauris, 2007), 1–40.

32. See, for example, Eugene Rogan and Yoav Alon, historians of Ottoman Jordan, who take the state taxation schemes as one of the main measures of centralization on the edge of the Syrian Desert, an area with many socioeconomic similarities to the Libyan Desert. See Eugene L. Rogan, *Frontiers of the State in the Late Ottoman Empire: Transjordan, 1850–1921* (New York: Columbia University Press, 1999); Yoav Alon, *The Making of Jordan: Tribes, Colonialism, and the Modern State* (London: I. B. Tauris, 2007).

33. E. E. Evans-Pritchard, *The Sanusi of Cyrenaica* (Oxford: Clarendon, 1949), 70.

34. *Khalīfa* (Turkish *halife*; Arabic plural *khulafāʾ*) in this context meant a sheikh of a *zāwiya* who functioned as the local deputy of the Sanusi; it is not to be confused with the Anglicized *caliph*, which usually referred exclusively to the successors of the Prophet Muhammad or the head of a caliphate.

35. A. S. al-Hourier, "Social and Economic Transformations in the Libyan Hinterland during the Second Half of the Nineteenth Century: The Rule of the Sayyid Ahmad al-Sharif al-Sanusi" (PhD diss., University of California, Los Angeles, 1981), 52.

36. In Turkish *vakıf* (singular); in Ottoman-Turkish *evkaf* (plural); in modern Turkish *vakıflar* (plural); in Arabic *waqf* (singular) and *awqāf* (plural).

37. Even though the word *firman* exists in English, it carries with it an orientalist connotation that is not useful or accurate. I use the simple *decree*, which means the same thing without the orientalist baggage.

38. Ahmad Sidqi al-Dajani, *al-Haraka al-Sanusiyya: Nashʾatuha wa Numuwwuha fi al-Qarn al-Tasiʿ ʿAshar* (Cairo, 1967), 105.

39. al-Hourier, "Social and Economic Transformations in the Libyan Hinterland," 148.

40. el-Müeyyed Azmzade, *Afrika Sahra-yı Kebiri'nde Seyahat, Bir Osmanlı Zabitinin Büyük Sahra'da Seyahati,* 100–101.

41. al-Hourier, "Social and Economic Transformations in the Libyan Hinterland," 147.

42. Ibid., 148.

43. Ibid.

44. Ibid.

45. For more on the relationship between the palace and the various late nineteenth-century influential leaders in Islamic thought, see Caroline Finkel, *Osman's Dream: The History of the Ottoman Empire* (New York: Basic Books, 2006), 495–496; Thomas Eich, "Abu al-Huda al-Sayyadi—Still Such a Polarizing Figure," *Arabica* 55 (2008): 433–444; B. Abu-Manneh, "Sultan Abdulhamid II and Shaikh Abdulhuda Al-Sayyadi," *Middle Eastern Studies* 15 (1979): 131–153; Kemal Karpat, *The Politicization of Islam: Reconstructing Identity, State, Faith, and Community in the Late Ottoman State* (Oxford: Oxford University Press, 2001), 185–197; Nikki R. Keddi, "The Pan-Islamic Appeal: Afghani and Abdülhamid II," *Middle Eastern Studies* 3 (1966): 46–67.

46. Le Gall, "Pashas, Bedouins and Notables," 181–284.

47. Michel Le Gall, "The Ottoman Government and the Sanusiyya: A Reappraisal," *International Journal of Middle Eastern Studies* 21 (1989): 96–99.

48. Ibid., 98.

49. Evans-Pritchard, *Sanusi of Cyrenaica,* 91.

50. Le Gall, "The Ottoman Government and the Sanusiyya," 97.

51. el-Müeyyed Azmzade, *Afrika Sahra-yı Kebiri'nde Seyahat, Bir Osmanlı Zabitinin Büyük Sahra'da Seyahati,* 100–101.

52. BNA, May 21, 1889, FO 195/1653-4, 356.

53. BOA, January 4, 1906, MV-112/69.

54. Meclis-i Vükela was the executive branch of the post-Tanzimat Ottoman government. Its members were appointed ministers, the grand vizier, and *şeyhülislam* (the empire's head of religious affairs). The term is also sometimes translated as "the cabinet" as in *Redhouse Sözlüğü Türkçe/Osmalıca-İngilizce* or "Chamber of State Agents" in Ami Ayalon, *Language and Change in the Arab Middle East: The Evolution of Modern Arab Political Discourse* (Oxford: Oxford University Press, 1987), 72.

55. BOA, January 4, 1906, MV-112/69; Nicola Ziadeh references Muhammad ʿUthman al-Hashaʾishi in a manuscript titled *Mufarrij al-Karb ʿAn Tarablus al-Gharb,* in which al-Hashaʾishsi states that the privileges extended well beyond the death of the Grand Sanusi: "Respect the Sayyid al-Mahdi's agents and observe strictly all privileges granted to the Sanusis in previous *firmans.*" Nicola A. Ziadeh, *Sanusiyah: A Study of a Revivalist Movement in Islam* (Leiden: Brill, 1968), 64.

56. At the time of the first mission, he was an Ottoman army officer of the *binbaşı* rank and thus was referred to as a *bey,* not yet a *paşa* (pasha). Honorary titles are very important in researching the lives and careers of late Ottoman government employees because they were mostly referred to only by their first name and then *bey, paşa, ağa, efendi, usta,* and the like. All titles were indications of rank and position in society. More important, they are often a key to knowing whether references in a document refer to the relevant individual or someone else with the same name.

57. ʿAli Muhammad Muhammad al-Sallabi mistakenly dates Azmzade's mission as circa 1889, which conflicts with the date of the report I found in the Ottoman Archives (BOA). See ʿAli Muhammad Muhammad al-Sallabi, *Tarikh al-Haraka al-Sanusiyya fi Ifriqya, al-Qism al-Awwal: al-Imam Muhmammad Bin ʿAli al-Sanusi wa Nahjoh fi al-Taʾsis al-Taʿlimi wa-l-Haraki wa-l-Tarbawi wa-l-Daʿawi wa-l-Siyasi* (Beirut: Dar al-Maʿrifa li-l-Tabʿ wa-l-Nashr, 2005), 193.

58. Ibid., 169.

59. ʿUmar al-Madani, *Bunat al-Majd al-ʿArabi fi Ifriqya: Muhammad al-Khamis, Idris al-Sanusi, Al-Habib Burayqa, Jamal ʿAbd al-Nasser* (Amman: Dar al-Muttahida li-l-Nashr, 1997), 100.

60. BOA, December 3, 1887, Y.MTV-29/15.

61. al-Madani, *Bunat al-Majd al-ʿArabi fi Ifriqya*, 102. On the life and work of Muhammad al-Mahdi al-Sanusi, see ʿAli Muhammad Muhammad al-Sallabi, *al-Thimar al-Dhakiyya li-l-Haraka al-Sanusiyya fi Libya: Sirat al-Zaʿimayn Muhammad al-Mahdi al-Sanusi wa Ahmad al-Sharif*, pt. 2 (Cairo: Dar al-Tawziʿ wa-l-Nashr al-Islamiyya, 2005); E. A. V. De Candole, *The Life and Times of King Idris of Libya* (privately published by Mohamed Ben Ghalbon, 1990).

62. Magali Morsy, *North Africa 1800–1900: A Survey from the Nile Valley to the Atlantic* (London: Longman, 1984), 279.

63. BNA, May 4, 1889, FO 195/1653-4, 320.

64. BOA, December 3, 1887, Y.MTV-29/15.

65. Evans-Pritchard, *Sanusi of Cyrenaica*, 24–25.

66. el-Müeyyed Azmzade, *Afrika Sahra-yı Kebiri'nde Seyahat, Bir Osmanlı Zabitinin Büyük Sahra'da Seyahati*, 112–114.

67. BNA, April 30, 1889, FO 78/4218-1, 169.

68. Ibid.

69. BOA, December 3, 1887, Y.MTV-29/15.

70. BNA, 1886–1887, FO 78/4218-2, 181.

71. BNA, May 13, 1889, FO 195/1653-4, 339.

72. Ibid.

73. Ibid.

74. Maurus Reinkowski and Gregor Thum offer an insightful analysis of the "helplessness" imperialists felt in their colonies, creating fear of the local unknown and an obsession with collecting as much information as possible. Perhaps nowhere is this more obvious than in Britain's late nineteenth-century fixation with information that would help them predict any pan-Islamic threat. See Maurus Reinkowski and Gregor Thum, "Introduction," in *Helpless Imperialists: Imperial Failure, Fear and Radicalization*, ed. Maurus Reinkowski and Gregor Thum (Göttingen: Vandenhoeck & Ruprecht, 2014), 7–20. See also Azmi Özcan, *Pan-Islamism: Indian Muslims, the Ottomans and Britain (1877–1924)* (Leiden: Brill, 1997); John Ferris, "'The Internationalism of Islam': The British Perception of a Muslim Menace, 1840–1951," *Intelligence and National Security* 24 (2009): 57–77. Edward Said offers a critique of colonialism and the misleading stereotypes of late nineteenth-century orientalism that might explain Wood's mistaken assumptions. See Edward Said, *Orientalism* (New York: Random House, 1978).

Chapter 3

Epigraph: Sadık el-Müeyyed Azmzade, *Afrika Sahra-yı Kebiri'nde Seyahat, Bir Osmanlı Zabitinin Büyük Sahra'da Seyahati*, translated from Ottoman Turkish to Turkish and introduced by İdris Bostan (Istanbul: Çamlıca, 2008), 107.

1. The followers of Muhammad Ahmad al-Mahdi (aka al-Mahdi) (1844–1885) and his successors were referred to as dervishes in British and Ottoman sources. I use this term to refer to the Mahdist army. Other names include *Anṣār* al-Mahdi and *Shī'at* al-Mahdi.

2. For a comprehensive study of the Mahdist state, see Lidwien Kapteijns, *Mahdist Faith and Sudanic Tradition: The History of the Masalit Sultanate, 1870–1930* (London: Kegan Paul, 1985); P. M. Holt, *The Mahdist State in the Sudan, 1881–1898: A Study in Its Origins, Development and Overthrow* (Oxford: Clarendon, 1970).

3. To avoid confusion, I refer to the Sudanese Mahdi as al-Mahdi and to Muhammad al-Mahdi al-Sanusi by his full name or as al-Mahdi al-Sanusi.

4. Ahmad Sidqi al-Dajani, *al-Haraka al-Sanusiyya: Nash'atuha wa Numuwwuha fi al-Qarn al-Tasi' 'Ashar* (Cairo, 1967), 182–186.

5. BNA, "Memorandum Regarding Sidi Mohammad el Mehedy Essenoossy and the Senoossia Confraternity," April 1889, FO 78/4218-2, 181.

6. BNA, March 18, 1889, FO 195/1653-2, 227.

7. BNA, April 27, 1889, FO 195/1653-3, 304.

8. al-Dajani, *al-Haraka al-Sanusiyya*, 186.

9. John Voll, "The Sudanese Mahdi: Frontier Fundamentalist," *International Journal of Middle East Studies* 10 (1979): 158–160. For an analysis of the sociopolitical dimensions of the khedivate Egyptian colonial experiment in the Sudan, see Eve Troutt Powell, *A Different Shade of Colonialism: Egypt, Great Britain, and the Mastery of the Sudan* (Berkeley: University of California Press, 2002).

10. al-Dajani, *al-Haraka al-Sanusiyya*, 187; Şehbenderzade wrote that al-Mahdi al-Sanusi rejected the offer of the Sudanese "pretender to mahdısım [*mütemehdi*]" because he essentially rejected Muhammad Ahmad al-Mahdi's claim to Mahdism (*mehdilik*). Ahmed Hilmi Şehbenderzade, *Asr-ı Hamidi'de Alem-i İslam ve Senusiler* (Istanbul: İkdam Matbaası, 1907), 84–85.

11. Here al-Mahdi al-Sanusi is referring to the companion of the Prophet and the fourth Rightfully Guided Caliph, 'Uthman bin 'Affan (d. AD 656).

12. 'Ali Muhammad Muhammad al-Sallabi, *al-Thimar al-Dhakiyya li-l-Haraka al-Sanusiyya fi Libya: Sirat al-Za'imayn Muhammad al-Mahdi al-Sanusi wa Ahmad al-Sharif*, pt. 2 (Cairo: Dar al-Tawzi' wa-l-Nashr al-Islamiyya, 2005), 226.

13. Jean-Claude Zeltner, *Les pays du Tchad dans la tourmente, 1880–1903* (Paris: Harmattan, 1985), 95.

14. BOA, February 10, 1888, Y.PRK.UM-11/31.

15. François Georgeon, *Abdulhamid II: Le sultan calife* (Paris: Librairie Arthème Fayard, 2003), 230–231.

16. In his travelogue of Ethiopia, al-Mahdi comes up frequently. See Sadiq al-Mu'ayyad al-'Azm, *Rihlat al-Habasha: Min al-Istana ila Addis Ababa*, ed. Nuri al-Jarrah (Beirut: Al-Mu'asasa al-'Arabiyya li-l-Dirasat wa-l-Nashr, 2001).

17. BNA, December 22, 1888, FO 195/1610-2.

18. Lidwien Kapteijns and Jay Spaulding, *After the Millennium: Diplomatic Correspondence from Wadai and Dar Fur on the Eve of the Colonial Conquest, 1885–1916* (East Lansing: Michigan State University Press, 1988), 47. For the most comprehensive account of Rabih Fadl Allah's expansionist efforts in central Africa, see W. K. R. Hallam, *The Life and Times of Rabih Fadl Allah* (Devon, UK: Arthur H. Stockwell, 1977).

19. On the relationship between the Central Sudanic Kingdoms and the Mahdist state before and after the death of Muhammad Ahmad al-Mahdi, see Lidwien Kapteijns, "Mahdist Faith and the Legitimating of Popular Revolt in Western Sudan," *Africa: Journal of the International African Institute* 55 (1985): 390–399.

20. BNA, May 4, 1889, FO 195/1653, 321.

21. After being appointed to replace Yusuf Ibrahim of Darfur, ʿUthman Adam fought three battles before killing Yusuf and taking his post as governor-general of Darfur. See Kapteijns and Spaulding, *After the Millennium*, 47–48.

22. BNA, May 4, 1889, FO 195/1653, 330. It would not be out of the question for a Sufi leader's word to hold sway, even against powerful warlords, because he was often considered to be holy and had what is known as *baraka*, a kind of supernatural power attained through Sufi practice and becoming closer to the divine. Belief in the holiness of some of the Sufi sheikhs, such as the Grand Sanusi and his son, transcended political affiliation and the town-desert divide. See Julia Ann Clancy-Smith, *Rebel and Saint: Muslim Notables, Populist Protest, Colonial Encounters (Algeria and Tunisia, 1800–1904)* (Berkeley: University of California Press, 1994), 34–35.

23. Kapteijns and Spaulding, *After the Millennium*, 109.

24. Louis Brenner, *The Shehus of Kukawa: A History of the al-Kanemi Dynasty of Bornu* (Oxford: Clarendon, 1973), 117–130. See also Jean-Claude Zeltner, "Rabeh sur le Moyen-Chari (1889–1991)," *Les pays du Tchad*, 112–121. For more on the important role that Rabih would play in the history of the Lake Chad basin, see Ahmet Kavas, *Osmanlı-Afrika İlişkileri* (Istanbul: Tasam Yayınları, 2006), 129–144; Kyari Mohammed, *Bornu in the Rabih Years, 1893–1901: The Rise and Crash of a Predatory State* (Maiduguri, Nigeria: University of Maidurguri, 2006).

25. el-Müeyyed Azmzade, *Afrika Sahra-yı Kebiri'nde Seyahat, Bir Osmanlı Zabitinin Büyük Sahra'da Seyahati*, 163.

26. BNA, May 4, 1889, FO 195/1653-4, 320.

27. BNA, April 27, 1889, FO 195/1653-3, 304; May 21, 1889, FO 195/1653-4, 356.

28. Lisa Anderson, *The State and Social Transformation in Tunisia and Libya, 1830–1980* (Princeton, NJ: Princeton University Press, 1986), 110, 114.

29. BOA, July 4, 1887, Y.A.HUS-204/31; February 10, 1888, Y.PRK.UM-11/31.

30. Kemal Karpat, *The Politicization of Islam: Reconstructing Identity, State, Faith, and Community in the Late Ottoman State* (Oxford: Oxford University Press, 2001), 264.

31. Anderson, *State and Social Transformation*, 110.

32. Karpat, *Politicization of Islam*, 264.

33. Zeltner, *Les pays du Tchad*, 95.

34. BNA, December 14, 1889, FO 195/1653, 441.

35. BNA, May 13, 1889, FO 195/1653-4, 347.

36. Sultan Abdülhamid II, *Siyasi Hatıratım* (1987), cited in Karpat, *Politicization of Islam*, 264.

37. Germany was a party to some of these negotiations, attempting to secure a possession in Adamawa that would become official through the Anglo-German Treaty of 1893 and the Franco-German Agreement of 1894. On negotiations over the Lake Chad region between France, Britain, and Germany at the beginning of the last decade of the nineteenth century, see Olayemi Akinwumi, *The Colonial Contest for the Nigerian Region, 1884–1900: A History of German Participation* (Hamburg: LIT, 2002).

38. Yılmaz Öztuna, *Develetler ve Hanedanlar: Türkiye (1074–1990)* (Ankara: Kültür Bakanlığı Yayınları, 1989), 2:1076.

39. BOA, August 12, 1890, HR.SYS-1601/16.

40. BNA, November 15, 1890, FO 195/1677.

41. BOA, November 7, 1890, HR.SYS-1601/20.

42. BOA, November 30, 1890, HR.SYS-1601/22.

43. BNA, November 27, 1890, FO 195/1677.

44. BOA, December 31, 1891, İ.DH-1257/98689.

45. For a comprehensive history of Ottoman-French negotiations and conflict over Tunisia and the drawing of the Ottoman-Tunisian border, see Abdurrahman Çaycı, *La question tunisienne et la politique ottomane (1881–1913)* (Ankara: Société Turque d'Histoire, 1992).

46. BOA, January 5, 1891, HR.SYS-1601/23.

47. On the Ottoman-French competition in central Africa after the British-French 1890 agreement, see Abdurrahman Çaycı, *al-Sira' al-Turki-al-Faransi fi al-Sahara' al-Kubra*, trans. (Turkish to Arabic) Ali A'zazi (Tripoli: Markaz Dirasat Jihad al-Libiyyin Did al-Ghazw al-Itali, 1982), 134–140.

48. The Arabic *jihad* means "to strive or to struggle for a noble cause." Here it is used in the same way it is used in the Western press nowadays, as equivalent to the English "crusade." Rudolph Peters, *Jihad in Classical and Modern Islam: A Reader*, 2nd ed. (Princeton, NJ: Markus Wiener, 2008), 1.

49. BOA, August 18, 1892, Y.A.HUS-263/90.

50. BOA, August 23, 1892, Y.PRK.UM-25/13; August 26, 1892, Y.A.HUS-264/15.

51. BOA, July 1, 1894, HR.SYS-63/16; July 23, 1894, Y.A.HUS-303/88.

52. For a nuanced reassessment of the Hamidian government's censorship strategy, see Ebru Boyar, "The Press and the Palace: The Two-Way Relationship between Abdülhamid II and the Press, 1876–1908," *Bulletin of the School of Oriental and African Studies* 69 (2006): 417–432.

53. BOA, September 18, 1888, Y.EE-38/39.

54. Ibid. On the link between methods used by proselytizing Muslim organizations like the Muslim Brotherhood and the activities of Christian missionaries, see Beth Baron, *The Orphan Scandal: Christian Missionaries and the Rise of the Muslim Brotherhood* (Stanford, CA: Stanford University Press, 2014).

55. BNA, June 10, 1894, FO 195/1829-3.

56. Ahmed Muhtar Pasha was an Ottoman special commissioner in Egypt between 1885 and 1908. Special commissioners represented Istanbul in some autonomous provinces, such as Egypt. The Principality of Bulgaria after the Congress of Berlin, for example, had a special commissioner stationed in Sofia. In fact, Azmzade himself occupied this post between 1904 and 1908. Ahmed Muhtar Pasha earned the honorific *gazi* (veteran or war hero) after the Russo-Ottoman War of 1877–1878, when he served as the supreme military commander of the eastern Anatolian front. His role was of such delicate importance that newspapers in Ottoman cities devoted several columns to the pomp and circumstance afforded him on his arrival in Alexandria to take up his post. See Maurus Reinkowski, "Hapless Imperialists and Resentful Nationalists: Trajectories of Radicalization in the Late Ottoman Empire," in *Helpless Imperialists: Imperial Failure, Fear and Radicalization*, ed. Maurus Reinkowski and Gregor Thum (Göttingen: Vandenhoeck & Ruprecht, 2014), 62–63. For more on the role of Ahmed Muhtar Pasha in the Ottoman reconquest of Yemen, see Thomas Kühn, *Empire, Islam and Politics of Difference: Ottoman Rule in Yemen, 1849–1919* (Leiden: Brill, 2011), 32–51. For a description of his arrival in Alexandria, see *Lisan al-Hal*, December 30, 1885, 2.

57. İdris Bostan, "The Ottoman Empire and the Congo: The Crisis of 1893–95," in *Studies on Ottoman Diplomatic History*, pt. 5, ed. Selim Deringil and Sinan Kuneralp (Istanbul: ISIS, 1990), 103–106.

58. BNA, April 20, 1894, FO 195/1829.

59. BNA, "A Telegraph from Belgium to Lord Kimberley," May 25, 1894, FO 195/1829-2.

60. In his article on Ottoman interests in the Congo basin, İdris Bostan argues that these areas rebelled against their occupation by Khedive Ismail. This led to the necessity of British forces reoccupying the same area, thus placing the entire region, including the Sultanate of Wadai, within the British sphere of influence. See Bostan, "The Ottoman Empire and the Congo," 108–109. However, in his 2008 dissertation, Avishai Ben-Dror proposes that the British came to take control of Egyptian possessions in the south. He describes the British as forcing out the Egyptians during the former's takeover of the area, which they claimed as a British protectorate. This took place in 1885, almost a decade before the Belgian-English agreement and, more important, immediately on the heels of the General Act of Berlin. See Avishai Ben-Dror, "The Egyptian Hikimdariya of Harar and Its Hinterland—Historical Aspects, 1875–1887" (PhD diss., Tel Aviv University, 2008).

61. Rüstem Pasha was the former governor-general of Mount Lebanon (1873–1883). Born in Florence in 1810, he moved to Istanbul at a very young age after becoming the protégé of the Ottoman ambassador to Rome. He went on to serve as the Ottoman plenipotentiary in Florence and Rome and as ambassador in Saint Petersburg. He had a noted animosity toward to the French because of his experience as the governor of Mount Lebanon which he brought to his assignment as ambassador to London. See Engin Akarlı, *The Long Peace: Ottoman Lebanon, 1861–1920* (London: Centre for Lebanese Studies / I. B. Tauris, 1993), 22–49, 195. Akarlı mistakenly dates Rüstem Pasha's death in 1885, which was in fact the year of his assignment as ambassador to London. According to the Turkish Embassy and his *New York Times* obituary, he died in 1895, having served as an ambassador since 1885. See http://london.emb.mfa.gov.tr/MissionChiefHistory

.aspx, and "Death of Rustem Pasha, the Turkish Ambassador to Britain for Ten Years," *New York Times*, November 20, 1895.

62. BNA, June 14, 1894, FO 195/1829-3.

63. BNA, November 10, 1890, FO 195/1829-3. The Ottomans initially took some comfort in their close and powerful ally, Germany, which was also strongly opposed to the Anglo-Belgian deal. However, as Bostan shows, after a few changes were made in the agreement to address German concerns, the Ottoman government could no longer count on German support. Yet again, the empire found itself abandoned by its European allies. See Bostan, "The Ottoman Empire and the Congo," 119. International treaties between the Congo Free State and foreign entities were concluded with the approval of King Leopold II of Belgium. For more on the agreement, see "Convention between Belgium and the Congo Free State," "Official Documents," supplement, *American Journal of International Law* 3 (1909): 61–62; see also M. P. Hornik, "The Anglo-Belgian Agreement of 12 May 1894," *English Historical Review* 57 (1942): 229.

64. John Wodehouse, first Earl of Kimberley, was the secretary of state for India from 1882 to 1886 and the secretary of state for foreign affairs from 1894 to 1895. He died in 1902. See "Death of Lord Kimberley," *New York Times*, April 9, 1902.

65. BNA, June 17, 1894, FO 195/1829-3.

66. BNA, June 4, 1894, FO 195/1829-3.

67. BOA, July 18, 1894, HR.SYS-1601/58.

68. On Gustav Nachtigal's influence on European perceptions of the Sanusi Order, see Chapter 2.

69. BOA, July 2, 1894, HR.SYS-1601/57.

70. Kassala was one of nine *sancaks* of the province of (Egyptian) Sudan. The other eight were Khartoum, Blue Nile, Kordofan, Darfur, Upper Nile, Bahr al-Ghazal, Nubia, and Equatoria. See Öztuna, *Develetler ve Hanedanlar*, 1094.

71. BOA, September 14, 1894, HR.SYS-1603/10. The original details of the Italian-British Agreement of 1891 are preserved in BNA, "Protocols between the Governments of Her Britannic Majesty and His Majesty the King of Italy, for the Demarcation of Their Respective Sphere of Influence in East Africa," March 24, 1891, FO 195/1829-3.

72. BOA, September 21, 1894, Y.A.HUS-308/7.

73. BOA, May 23, 1894, Y.PRK.ASK-98/54.

74. The city of Massawa came under Ottoman rule in the sixteenth century and was at one time the capital of the province of Ethiopia. In 1813, Mehmed Ali Pasha of Egypt occupied the city, holding it until 1840, when it was returned to the Ottomans. Istanbul, unable to maintain effective control over this important Red Sea port city, leased it to the khedive of Egypt in 1846. It remained under Egyptian rule, and Ottoman sovereignty, until Italy occupied it in 1885. This episode of territorial losses on the Red Sea is an understudied aspect of Ottoman history during the age of imperial competition. See Jonathan Miran, *Red Sea Citizens: Cosmopolitan Society and Cultural Change in Massawa* (Bloomington: Indiana University Press, 2009), 4.

75. BOA, August 15, 1894, Y.PRK.AZJ-29/64. Mehmed Kamil Pasha, also known as Kıbrıslı Mehmed Kamil Pasha, served as grand vizier between 1885 and 1891.

76. Khedive Ismail had conquered this area south of Khartoum in the name of Sultan Abdülaziz, but no substantial Ottoman presence was subsequently established. The area discussed in the British-Belgian agreement was considered part of Egyptian Sudan and an extended region of the Egyptian hinterland. See Bostan, "The Ottoman Empire and the Congo," 103–106. For more on Khedive Ismail's military expansion into East Africa south of Egypt, see John P. Dunn, *Khedive Ismail's Army* (London: Routledge, 2005).

77. BOA, August 15, 1894, Y.PRK.AZJ-29/64.

78. BOA, September 25, 1894, HR.SYS-1603/11.

79. BOA, September 30, 1894, Y.A.HUS-309/111.

80. BOA, October 30, 1894, Y.A.HUS-311/91.

81. BNA, October 17, 1894, FO 195/1829-4.

82. Born in 1850, Mahmud Nedim entered the Foreign Service in 1874 and became secretary of the Ottoman legation in Belgrade in 1886. In 1891 he was appointed ambassador to Rome and in 1896 ambassador to Vienna, where he had an important role in negotiations with Theodor Herzl on behalf of the Ottoman government. See Theodor Herzl, *The Complete Diaries of Theodor Herzl*, ed. Raphael Patai, trans. Harry Zohn (New York: Herzl Press, 1960), 5:1788.

83. I learned of Baron Blanc's title from "Protocol between Italy and Colombia for the Arbitration of the Cerruti Claim," "Official Documents," supplement, *American Journal of International Law* 6 (1912): 240–242.

84. BOA, December 29, 1894, HR.SYS-1603/18.

Chapter 4

Epigraph: Sadık el-Müeyyed Azmzade, *Afrika Sahra-yı Kebiri'nde Seyahat, Bir Osmanlı Zabitinin Büyük Sahra'da Seyahati*, translated from Ottoman Turkish to Turkish and introduced by İdris Bostan (Istanbul: Çamlıca, 2008), 158.

1. See Jeremy Salt, "Britain, the Armenian Question, and the Cause of Ottoman Reform: 1894–96," *Middle Eastern Studies* 26 (1900): 308–328.

2. Pınar Şenışık, *The Transformation of Ottoman Crete: Revolts, Politics and Identity in the Late Nineteenth Century* (London: I. B. Tauris, 2011), 148–149.

3. Elektra Kostopoulou, "Armed Negotiations: The Institutionalization of the Late Ottoman Locality," *Comparative Studies of South Asia, Africa, and the Middle East* 33 (2013): 302–303. For a detailed account of the empire's diplomatic efforts to hold onto Ottoman Crete, and the eventual handing over of its effective rule to the Kingdom of Greece, see Şenışık, *Transformation of Ottoman Crete*, 137–230.

4. Justin Charles Alvarez replaced Donald Cameron in 1890. He was married to a Greek-Ottoman subject from Istanbul and became a dragoman in training in 1877, then vice-consul and interpreter in Istanbul in 1885. After leaving Benghazi, he became a judicial reforms commissioner in Crete in 1896 and then consul-general for Spain in Benghazi. He retired and moved to Malta in 1913. See *Who's Who, 1918* (London: A & C Black, 1918), 88. For more on the fascinating world of dragomans and British diplomats, see G. R. Berridge, *British Diplomacy in Turkey, 1583 to Present: A Study in the Evolution of the Resident Embassy* (Leiden: Martinus Nijhoff, 2009).

5. BNA, November 1, 1894, FO 195/1839-2.

6. The manuscript of the book written and illustrated by Sadik al-Mouayad Azmzade as a young first lieutenant (*mülazım evvel*) was titled "Fen-i Fotoğraf" (The science of photography) and is preserved in the Nadır Eserler Library at Istanbul University. A contemporary of Azmzade, a captain (*yuzbaşı*) in the Fifth Science Department (Photography section) of the Military Department by the name of Hasan Hussain, wrote a strikingly similar book titled *Fotoğrafçılık* (Photography). The manuscript of this book is also preserved in the Nadır Eserler Library. For more on the history of photography in the late Ottoman Empire, see Engin Özendes, *Photography in the Ottoman Empire, 1839–1923* (Istanbul: YEM Yayın, 2013).

7. İdris Bostan, "Introduction," in Sadık el-Müeyyed Azmzade, *Afrika Sahra-yı Kebiri'nde Seyahat, Bir Osmanlı Zabitinin Büyük Sahra'da Seyahati*, trans. İdris Bostan (Istanbul: Çamlıca, 2008), xxiii; Sadık el-Müeyyid, "Bir Osmanlı Zabitinin Afrika Sahra-yı Kebirinde Seyahati ve Şeyh Sunusi ile Mülakatı," *Servet-i Fünun* 354 (December 23, 1897): 252–253; Sadık el-Müeyyid, "Bir Osmanlı Zabitinin Afrika Sahra-yı Kebirinde Seyahati ve Şeyh Sunusi ile Mülakatı," *Servet-i Fünun* 362 (February 17, 1898): 372–374; Sadık el-Müeyyid, "Bir Osmanlı Zabitinin Afrika Sahra-i Kebirinde Seyahati ve Şeyh Sunusi ile Mülakatı," *Servet-i Fünun* 364 (March 3, 1898): 406–407.

8. BOA, January 13, 1896, Y.PRK.MYD-17/36; January 14, 1896, Y.EE-9/13.

9. BOA, January 24, 1908, İ.DH-1462/1325-z-14.

10. BNA, "Memorandum on the Tripoli-Tunis Frontier Question," July 16, 1894, FO 195/1829.

11. el-Müeyyed Azmzade, *Afrika Sahra-yı Kebiri'nde Seyahat, Bir Osmanlı Zabitinin Büyük Sahra'da Seyahati*, 154.

12. BOA, January 13, 1896, Y.PRK.MYD-17/36; January 14, 1896, Y.EE-9/13.

13. BNA, April 4, 1894, FO 195/1839-1; May 14, 1894, FO 195/1839-1.

14. BOA, January 13, 1896, Y.PRK.MYD-17/36; January 14, 1896, Y.EE-9/13; February 27, 1896, Y.PRK.MYD-21/106.

15. Ibid.

16. BOA, n.d., Y.PRK.BŞK-81/35; December 12, 1895, Y.PRK.UM-34/31. Azmzade used the old terminology to refer to Meclis-i Vükela, which by that time had replaced the older Meclis-i Şura but effectively maintained the same function. Meclis-i Şura was a term given to the sultan's advisory council. Meclis-i Vükela was a post-Tanzimat body made up of ministers, the grand vizier, and Şeyhülislam, which essentially fulfilled the same function of ruling on issues of transimperial significance.

17. See Engin Akarlı, *The Long Peace: Ottoman Lebanon, 1861–1920* (London: Centre for Lebanese Studies / I. B. Tauris, 1993); Ussama Makdisi, *The Culture of Sectarianism: Community, History, and Violence in Nineteenth-Century Ottoman Lebanon* (Berkeley: University of California Press, 2000); Caesar E. Farah, *The Politics of Interventionism in Ottoman Lebanon, 1830–1862* (New York: I. B. Tauris, 2000).

18. BOA, May 27, 1895, Y.A.HUS-329/25.

19. BOA, December 12, 1895, Y.PRK.UM-34/21; September 22, 1895, İ.HUS-42/1313-R-25; September 22, 1895, İ.HUS-42/1313-R-26.

20. For more on the symbolic meaning of the various orders of medals and their significance in a post–Abdülmecid I world, see Edhem Eldem, *Pride and Privilege: A History of Ottoman Orders, Medals, and Decorations* (Istanbul: Osmanlı Bankası Arşiv ve Araştırma Merkezi, 2004).

21. BOA, December 22, 1895, Y.PRK.UM-34/27.

22. Unfortunately, most of the issues published before 1897 are not well preserved and are unavailable for public viewing at Beyazıt Kütüphanesi in Istanbul at the time of my research.

23. *İkdam* (Istanbul), January 21, 1897, 1.

24. *İkdam* (Istanbul), October 8, 1898, 1.

25. "Sikak Hadidiyya Jadida," *Lisan al-Hal*, February 25, 1899, 4.

26. BOA, n.d., Y.PRK.BŞK-81/35; December 12, 1895, Y.PRK.UM-34/31.

27. Muhammad al-Ashhab also speculates that the Ottoman government's movements in Jaghbub gave the Sanusi Order enough cause for concern to eventually close down the Jaghbub *zāwiya*. See Muhammad al-Tayyib bin Idris al-Ashhab, *al-Mahdi al-Sanusi* (Tripoli: Bilniyu Maji Press, 1952), 66.

28. BNA, August 3, 1896, FO 195/1936-1. Nicola Ziadeh, in *Barqat al-Dawla al-ʿArabiyya al-Thamina* (Beirut: Dar al-ʿIlm li-l-Malayin, 1950), also discusses the practical reasons for al-Mahdi al-Sanusi's move further south into the Sudan. Ziadeh, quoted in al-Ashhab, *al-Mahdi al-Sanusi*, 42–43.

29. Royal Geographical Society, "Delimitation of British and French Spheres in Central Africa," *Geographical Journal* 13 (1899): 524–525.

30. BNA, September 17, 1896, FO 195/1936-1.

31. BNA, October 8, 1896, FO 195/1936-2.

32. BOA, November 26, 1899, Y.PRK.AZJ-39/78. Zinder, northwest of Borno, was a mere twenty-day journey, according to Azmzade (el-Müeyyed Azmzade, *Afrika Sahra-yı Kebiri'nde Seyahat, Bir Osmanlı Zabitinin Büyük Sahra'da Seyahati*, 162). Ghat, close to the Algerian-Libyan border, was the southernmost city having an official Ottoman presence. For the history of Ghat as a trading post along the western trans-Saharan caravan route during the nineteenth century, see Najmi Rajab Diyaf, *Madinat Ghat wa Tijarat al-Qawafil al-Sahrawiyya Khilal al-Qarn al-Tasiʿ ʿAshar al-Miladi* (Benghazi: Markaz Jihad al-Libiyin li-l-Dirasat al-Tarikhiyya, 1999).

33. *Lisan al-Hal*, January 21, 1899, 1–2; February 17, 1899, 1; March 25, 1899, 1; March 26, 1899, 1.

34. On the events leading up to the Fashoda Crisis, from French, British, Egyptian, Mahdist, and Ethiopian perspectives, see David Levering Lewis, *The Race to Fashoda: European Colonialism and African Resistance in the Scramble for Africa* (New York: Weidenfeld & Nicolson, 1987).

35. Royal Geographical Society, "Delimitation of British and French Spheres," 524–525.

36. Ibid., 527.

37. One more Ottoman try to negotiate directly with the French over the definition of *hinterland* took place between 1901 and 1902, but to no avail. For more on Ottoman

diplomatic efforts after the 1899 London Declaration, see Abdurrahman Çaycı, *al-Sira*'
al-Turki-al-Faransi fi al-Sahara' al-Kubra, trans. (Turkish to Arabic) Ali A'zazi (Tripoli:
Markaz Dirasat Jihad al-Libiyyin Did al-Ghazw al-Itali, 1982), 154–198.

38. BNA, February 19, 1899, FO 195/2054-1.

39. BOA, November 28, 1899, Y.PRK.MŞ-7/10.

40. 'Abd al-Hamid al-Thani Khan [Sultan Abdülhamid II], *Mudhakarati al-Siyasiyya (1891–1908)*, trans. (Ottoman-Turkish to Arabic) unknown (Beirut: Mu'asasat al-
Risala, 1979), 147.

41. BNA, June 9, 1901, FO 195/2094-9.

42. BNA, April 24, 1899, FO 195/2054; June 4, 1899, FO 195/2054; June 29, 1899,
FO 195/2054; October 7, 1899, FO 195/2054. For more on the turbulent relationship
between the Sanusi Order and 'Ali Dinar of Darfur during the early years of the Sa-
nusi-French conflict, see Jay Spaulding and Lidwien Kapteijns, *An Islamic Alliance:
'Ali Dinar and the Sanusiyya, 1906–1916* (Evanston, IL: Northwestern University Press,
1994), 3–19.

43. BNA, April 24, 1899, FO 195/2054; June 4, 1899, FO 195/2054; June 29, 1899, FO
195/2054; October 7, 1899, FO 195/2054.

44. BNA, September 1900, FO 195/2093.

45. BNA, June 9, 1901, FO 195/2094.

46. BNA, November 11, 1900, FO 195/2093.

47. BNA, December 4, 1901, FO 195/2094-11; February 24, 1902, FO 195/2123-1.

48. BOA, February 23, 1911, DH.SYS-36/6-7; March 11, 1911, DH.H-39/4; September 19, 1911, DH.SYS-1/1; August 22, 1912, A.MTZ.TG.HB-9B/62; November 25, 1914,
DH.KMS 23/55; May 5, 1915, A.AMD-1245/37; April 2, 1922, DH.KMS-56-2/35. For more
on Ahmad al-Sharif al-Sanusi's role from 1902 onward, see A. S. al-Hourier, "Social
and Economic Transformations in the Libyan Hinterland during the Second Half of
the Nineteenth Century: The Rule of the Sayyid Ahmad al-Sharif al-Sanusi" (PhD diss.,
University of California, Los Angeles, 1981). See also Claudia Anna Gazzini, "Jihad in
Exile: Ahmad al-Sharif al-Sanusi, 1918–1933" (master's thesis, Princeton University,
2004).

49. BOA, September 3, 1899, DH.MKT-2242/16.

50. BOA, July 15, 1901, ŞD-1135/6.

51. BOA, August 8, 1902, DH.MKT-555/27.

52. BNA, April 23, 1904, FO 195/2160-1.

53. BNA, June 19, 1904, FO 195/2160-2.

54. BOA, October 25, 1902, DH.MKT-603/33; February 2, 1903, DH.MKT-646/22.

55. BNA, October 10, 1904, FO 195/2160-4.

56. BOA, June 29, 1893, Y.PRK.A-8/57.

57. BOA, December 6, 1896, Y.PRK.MK-7/51.

58. Ibid.

59. BOA, June 12, 1896, Y.PRK.PT-10/67.

60. BOA, January 24, 1899, DH.MKT-2162/95; February 23, 1899, DH.MKT-2169/54.

Chapter 5

Epigraph: Sadık el-Müeyyed Azmzade, *Afrika Sahra-yı Kebiri'nde Seyahat, Bir Osmanlı Zabitinin Büyük Sahra'da Seyahati*, translated from Ottoman Turkish to Turkish and introduced by İdris Bostan (Istanbul: Çamlıca, 2008), 76–77.

1. William Ochsenwald, *The Hijaz Railroad* (Charlottesville: University Press of Virginia, 1980), 23.

2. Halil İnalcık, "Decision Making in the Ottoman Empire," in *Decision Making and Change in the Ottoman Empire*, ed. Caesar E. Farah (Kirksville, MO: Thomas Jefferson University Press, 1993), 11.

3. According to a 1900 Ottoman intermediary school geography textbook, the political boundaries of Hicaz Vilayeti were the province of Syria, the subprovince of Jerusalem, ʿAqaba in the north, the Red Sea to the west, Nejd to the east, and the province of Yemen to the south. Its population was "mostly Muslim inhabitants who along with the Bedouins" totaled an estimated 2,500,000 people. Note the distinction the author made between the "inhabitants" and the "Bedouins." Ali Tevfik, *Memalik-i Osmaniye Coğrafyası* (Istanbul: Kasbar Matbaası, 1900), 407.

4. For more on the province of Ethiopia, see Cengiz Orhanlu, *Habeş Eyaleti, Osmanlı İmparatorluğu'nun Güney Siyaseti* (Istanbul: İstanbul Üniversitesi Edebiyat Fakültesi Yayınları, Edebiyat Fakültesi Matbaası, 1974).

5. Yılmaz Öztuna, *Develetler ve Hanedanlar: Türkiye (1074–1990)* (Ankara: Kültür Bakanlığı Yayınları, 1989), 2:1069.

6. Arabic *sharīf*, plural *ashrāf*; Turkish *şerif*. This is a person of noble heritage, acknowledged as a direct descendant of the family of the Prophet Muhammad. In Mecca, the *ashrāf* were mostly the descendants of Hasan, the son of Fatima and Ali. See David Hogarth, *Hejaz before World War I: A Handbook*, 2nd ed. (London: Falcon-Oleander, 1978), 42.

7. Faʾiq Bakr al-Sawwaf, *al-ʿAlaqat Bayn al-Dawla al-ʿUthmaniyya wa Iqlim al-Hijaz fi Fatrat ma Bayn 1293–1334 H (1876–1915 M)* (Mecca: Abdul Aziz University, 1978), 53–54. For more on the unique relationship between Mehmed Ali Pasha and Istanbul in the first half of the nineteenth century, see Khaled Fahmy, *All the Pasha's Men: Mehmed Ali, His Army and the Making of Modern Egypt* (Cambridge: Cambridge University Press, 1997), 38–75.

8. Öztuna, *Develetler ve Hanedanlar*, 430–431.

9. On the various responsibilities of the Şura-yı Devlet and how it changed during the second half of the nineteenth century, see Öztuna, *Develetler ve Hanedanlar*, 1054; Stanford Shaw and Ezel Shaw, *History of the Ottoman Empire and Modern Turkey*, vol. 2, *Reform, Revolution, and Republic: The Rise of Modern Turkey, 1808–1975* (Cambridge: Cambridge University Press, 1977), 216–218.

10. Hogarth, *Hejaz before World War I*, 48.

11. al-Sawwaf, *al-ʿAlaqat Bayn al-Dawla al-ʿUthmaniyya wa Iqlim al-Hijaz*, 46.

12. William Ochsenwald, "The Financing of the Hijaz Railroad," *Die Welt des Islams* 14 (1973): 129–149; William Ochsenwald, "A Modern Waqf: The Hijaz Railroad, 1900–48," *Arabian Studies* 3 (1976): 1–12. For more on the political economy of the Hijaz

Railway in the Syrian hinterland, see Linda Schatkowski-Schilcher, "Railways in the Political Economy of Southern Syria 1890–1925," in *The Syrian Land: Processes of Integration and Fragmentation: Bilad al-Sham from the 18th to the 20th Century*, ed. Thomas Philipp and Birgit Schaebler (Stuttgart: Franz Steiner, 1998), 97–112. On the political capital of the Hijaz Railway, see Jacob M. Landau, *The Hejaz Railway and the Muslim Pilgrimage: A Case of Ottoman Political Propaganda* (Detroit: Wayne State University Press, 1971).

13. Ufuk Gülsöy, *Hicaz Demiryolu* (Istanbul: Eren, 1994).

14. See Murat Özyüksel, *Hicaz Demiryolu* (Istanbul: Tarih Vakfı Yurt Yayınları, 2000). On the Hijaz Railway branch to Haifa, see Recep Kürekli, "Hicaz Demiryolu'nun Akdeniz'e Açılası ile Yaşayan Sosyo-Ekonomik Dönüşüm: Hayfa Kazası Örneği," special issue, *History Studies: International Journal of History* (2010): 245–269.

15. Two unpublished dissertations that relied on Syrian and Egyptian archives, by Ahmad al-Marwani and ʿIzza Aqbiq, stand out. See Ahmad Raʾfat al-Marwani, "al-Khat al-Hadidi al-Hijazi" (PhD diss., University of Damascus, 1959); ʿIzza ʿAli Aqbiq, "Dukhul al-Sikak al-Hadidiyya ila Bilad al-Sham Awakhir al-Hukm al-ʿUthmani wa Atharuha al-Siyasiyya wa-l-ʿAskariyya w-al-Ijtimaʿiyya w-al-Iqtisadiyya, 1891–1918" (master's thesis, University of Damascus, 2006). Johnny Mansour focuses on the Darʿa–Haifa branch of the Hijaz Railway. See Johnny Mansour, *al-Khat al-Hadidi al-Hijazi: Tarikh wa Tatawor Qitar Darʿa–Haifa* (Jerusalem: Muʾasasat al-Dirasat al-Maqdisiyya, 2008).

16. I am inspired here by Burbank and Cooper's advice on considering the late imperial period on its own terms, avoiding the limitations of national boundaries and the teleological understanding of history as empires that necessarily led to nation-states. Jane Burbank and Frederick Cooper, *Empires in World History: Power and the Politics of Difference* (Princeton, NJ: Princeton University Press, 2010), 7–11.

17. Yakup Bektaş, "The Sultan's Messenger: Cultural Constructions of Ottoman Telegraphy, 1847–1880," *Technology and Culture* 41 (2000): 669.

18. Kenneth Silverman, *Lightning Man: The Accursed Life of Samuel F. B. Morse* (New York: Knopf, 2003), 278, 295–296; see also Yakub Bektaş, "Displaying the American Genius: The Electromagnetic Telegraph in the Wider World," *British Journal of the History of Science* 34 (2001): 199–232.

19. P. M. Kennedy, "Imperial Cable Communication and Strategy, 1870–1914," *English Historical Review* 86 (1971): 730.

20. This is according to Telecom Egypt, http://www.telecomegypt.com.eg/english/te_history.asp (accessed September 20, 2010).

21. For more on the early years of the telegraph in the Ottoman Empire, see Bektaş "Sultan's Messenger," 669–696.

22. Ibid., 669.

23. Kennedy, "Imperial Cable Communication," 731.

24. Tom Standage, *The Victorian Internet: The Remarkable Story of the Telegraph and the Nineteenth Century On-Line Pioneers* (New York: Walker, 1998), 69.

25. Ibid., 78–89. For a detailed history of the laying of the transatlantic cable, see John Steele Gordon, *A Thread across the Ocean: The Heroic Story of the Transatlantic Cable* (New York: Walker, 2002).

26. In 1869 Pender founded the Falmouth, Gibraltar and Malta Cable Company and the British Indian Submarine Telegraph Company, which respectively connected the Anglo-Mediterranean cable (linking Malta to Alexandria using a cable manufactured by one of Pender's subsidiaries) to Britain and India. The London–Bombay telegraph line was completed in 1870, and in 1872 the two companies merged with the Marseilles, Algiers and Malta Telegraph Company to form the Eastern Telegraph Company, with Pender at its helm. See www.atlantic-cable.com.

27. BOA, July 22, 1880, ŞD-2254/15.

28. Ibid.

29. The special Council of Telegraph and Post is not to be confused with the Ministry of Post and Telegraph (Telgraf ve Posta Nezareti). The council was a special board of experts and bureaucrats assembled for the Hijaz telegraph extension project.

30. BOA, July 22, 1880, ŞD-2254/15.

31. Christina Harris, "The Persian Gulf Submarine Telegraph of 1864," *Geographical Journal* 135 (1969): 184.

32. Kennedy, "Imperial Cable Communication," 731.

33. BOA, July 22, 1880, ŞD-2254/15.

34. The Ottoman Empire's treasury declared bankruptcy in 1876.

35. The British government was determined to be the dominant force in international telecommunications as a way to maintain a military advantage over its European counterparts. It understood that control of communication was as vital as a strong naval fleet. See Pascal Griset and Daniel R. Headrick, "Submarine Telegraph Cables: Business and Politics, 1838–1939," *Business History Review* 75 (2001): 543–578.

36. BOA, July 22, 1880, ŞD-2254/15.

37. The complexity of the codes is evident in the yearly telegraph guides issued to telegraph offices. Some of the guides used in the Damascus office are preserved at the Institut Français du Proche-Orient (IFPO): *Telgraf Rehebleri* (Istanbul: Posta ve Telgraf ve Telefon Nezareti, 1912).

38. On the problems caused by the conflict between the Ottoman government and the local tribes in Iraq, see Soli Shahvar, "Concession Hunting in the Age of Reform: British Companies and the Search for Government Guarantees; Telegraph Concessions through Ottoman Territories, 1855–58," *Middle Eastern Studies* 38 (2002): 169–193; Soli Shahvar, "Tribes and Telegraphs in Lower Iraq: The Muntafiq and the Baghdad–Basrah Telegraph Line of 1863–65," *Middle Eastern Studies* 39 (2003): 89–116.

39. BOA, July 22, 1880, ŞD-2254/15.

40. Ibid.

41. For a day-by-day account of events in 1881–1882 leading to the British invasion, see William Wright, *A Tidy Little War: The British Invasion of Egypt, 1882* (Stroud, UK: Spellmount, 2009).

42. ʿAbd al-Hamid al-Thani Khan [Sultan Abdülhamid II], *Mudhakarati al-Siyasiyya (1891–1908)*, trans. (Ottoman-Turkish to Arabic) unknown (Beirut: Muʾasasat al-Risala, 1979), 111.

43. Juan Cole, *Colonialism and Revolution in the Middle East: Social and Cultural Origins of Egypt's ʿUrabi Movement* (Princeton, NJ: Princeton University Press, 1992), 112.

44. For more on the development of Sudanese infrastructure during the rule of Khedive Ismail, see Ghada H. Talhami, *Suakin and Massawa under Egyptian Rule, 1865–1885* (Washington, DC: University Press of America, 1979), 97–124.

45. BOA, May 1, 1882, İ.DH-853/68401.

46. BOA, October 30, 1882, Y.A.RES-17/59.

47. Standage, *Victorian Internet*, 92–93.

48. BOA, October 31, 1882, Y.A.HUS-171/112. According to On Barak, the unreliability extended to the overland route between Cairo and Istanbul as well, prompting many in Cairo to use the postal service as a backup for important messages. See On Barak, *On Time: Technology and Temporality in Modern Egypt* (Berkeley: University of California Press, 2013).

49. BOA, October 8, 1883, Y.A.RES-21/46. Émile Bey did not follow orders to immediately relocate because he wanted additional compensation, given the importance of the mission and the length of time he would have to spend away from his home in Syria. Once these compensations were provided, he and two assistants moved to Cairo to assume their new responsibilities. This turned out not to be a temporary assignment, and three years later Émile Bey and his Syrian assistants had to be financially enticed yet again to remain in Cairo, indicating the necessity of their presence in Egypt. BOA, April 4, 1886, I.ŞD-80/4747.

50. Talhami, *Suakin and Massawa under Egyptian Rule*, 195–216.

51. Kennedy, "Imperial Cable Communication," 741.

52. Muzeyrib (al-Muzairib) is a city about 90 kilometers south of Damascus along the hajj caravan route. It is part of Darʿa Province in present-day Syria.

53. For more on the early days of telegraphy in the Syrian provinces, see Uğur Akbulut, "Suriye'ye İlk Telgraf Hatlarının Çekilmesi," special issue, *History Studies: International Journal of History* (2010): 1–11.

54. BOA, October 16, 1886, DH.MKT-1372/64.

55. BOA, December 14, 1886, DH.MKT-1384/107.

56. BOA, October 16, 1887, MV-25/27; November 17, 1887, DH.MKT-1464/61.

57. BOA, June 27, 1889, DH.MKT-1632/11. Diversion of Jeddah–Suakin traffic to the Syrian network, coupled with the exponential increase in demand for the telegraph in general led to an expansion of the Syrian network and increased staffing of telegraph offices in Beirut and Damascus. For example, the Beirut office, which had been under the directorship of the Damascus office, was made an independent branch with its own director. BOA, January 29, 1889, DH.MKT-1588/96.

58. BOA, May 13, 1896, ŞD-2667/41; May 16, 1896, İ.PTII-8/1313-Z-3; November 7, 1895, İ.PT-5/1313-ca-3. The ripple effect could be felt as far as Kayseri, a nodal point for messages coming from the Arab provinces. In 1893 the Ottoman government approved construction of an additional telegraph line in Kayseri to handle the increase in messages. BOA, June 21, 1893, İ.PT-2/1310-Z-2.

59. In 1893, a decade after the line went into operation, urgent repairs were finally approved by the Ministry of Telegraph and Post, the Office of the Grand Vizier, and the Ministry of Interior. BOA, January 31, 1893, DH.MKT-6/60; May 15, 1893, İ.PT-2/1310-l-5; May 27, 1893, DH.MKT-48/25.

60. The *Elektra* was built in 1884, owned by the Lloyd Austria Company, and registered in Trieste, a port city in the Austro-Hungarian Empire. *Lloyd's Register of Ships, 1900–1* (London: Ross, 1901).

61. BOA, August 13, 1897, Ş.D-2665/58. The location of the submarine cable continued to be problematic until 1907, when an order endorsed by the Council of Ministers and the Sublime Porte was sent out to move it away from Jeddah harbor. Breakage became an increased risk particularly because of increased ship traffic delivering equipment and material for the construction of the last phase of the Hijaz Railway. BOA, April 4, 1907, İ.PT-23/1325-S-3.

62. BOA, January 31, 1893, DH.MKT-6/60.

63. BOA, September 9, 1888, Y.A.HUS-217/13.

64. For more on the second period of Ottoman rule in Yemen, starting in 1872, and the special status of Yemen as a southern borderland of the empire during a time of colonial competition in the Red Sea, see Caesar E. Farah, *The Sultan's Yemen: Nineteenth-Century Challenges to Ottoman Rule* (London: I. B. Tauris, 2002); see also Thomas Kühn, *Empire, Islam, and Politics of Difference: Ottoman Rule in Yemen, 1849–1919* (Leiden: Brill, 2011).

65. BOA, September 16, 1888, Y.A.HUS-217/28; September 15, 1888, İ.DH-1099/86125.

66. Claudio Canaparo, "Marconi and Other Artifices: Long-Range Technology and the Conquest of the Desert," in *Images of Power: Iconography, Culture and the State in Latin America*, ed. Jens Andermann and William Rowe (New York: Berghahn, 2005), 243–244.

67. Of course, in eastern Anatolia the Armenian question was becoming more important, and Istanbul was aware of the danger of foreign intervention after the 1878 Congress of Berlin. For more on this issue and its impact on Ottoman diplomacy, see Fuat Dundar, "First Period: The Congress of Berlin and the Emergence of the Armenian Question, 1878," in *Crime of Numbers: The Role of Statistics in the Armenian Question (1878–1914)* (New Brunswick, NJ: Transaction, 2010), 11–30.

68. BOA, September 9, 1888, Y.A.HUS-217/13.

69. Griset and Headrick, "Submarine Telegraph Cables," 549–562.

70. Robert M. Pike and Dwayne R. Winseck, *Communication and Empire: Media, Markets, and Globalization, 1860–1930* (Durham, NC: Duke University Press, 2007), 108.

71. Ibid., 93. Ariane Knuesel similarly argues that Europeans in China before 1900 used "informal imperialism" to support a strong local government that would protect their commercial interests. See Ariane Knuesel, "British Diplomacy and the Telegraph in Nineteenth-Century China," *Diplomacy and Statecraft* 18 (2007): 526. For a detailed analysis of British techno-imperialism and the Ottoman Empire, see Mostafa Minawi, "Techno-Imperialism, Telegraphs, and Territoriality in Ottoman Africa and Arabia during the Age of High Imperialism," *Journal of Balkan and Near Eastern Studies* 18 (2016).

72. Khan, *Mudhakarati al-Siyasiyya*, 126–127.

Chapter 6

Epigraph: Sadık el-Müeyyed Azmzade, *Afrika Sahra-yı Kebiri'nde Seyahat, Bir Osmanlı Zabitinin Büyük Sahra'da Seyahati*, translated from Ottoman Turkish to Turkish and introduced by İdris Bostan (Istanbul: Çamlıca, 2008), 112–124.

1. Carter Findley points to *Arap* as a racist term: "The common Turkish use of the term Arab for blacks is, however, a clear illustration of the ethnic animosity." The term had become so exclusively derogatory that *Beyaz Arap* (literally, "white Arab") became necessary to refer to Arab-Ottomans without racial derision. Carter Findley, *Ottoman Civil Officialdom: A Social History* (Princeton, NJ: Princeton University Press, 1989), 235.

2. At the end of Abdülhamid II's rule, İzzet Pasha was accused of corruption and embezzlement and fled to Cairo, where he lived until his death. For more on this influential character and his position in the Arab power block in Istanbul, see Caesar E. Farah, "Arab Supporters of Sultan Abdulamid II: Izzet al-Abid," *Archivum Ottomanicum* 15 (1997): 189–219.

3. *İkdam* (Istanbul), May 17, 1900, 1.

4. Alexander Schölch, "Jerusalem in the 19th Century," in *Jerusalem in History*, ed. K. J. Asali (Brooklyn: Olive Branch, 2000), 237.

5. BOA, December 20, 1896, İ.HUS-51/1314-b-54; December 20, 1896, Y.A.HUS-363/76.

6. BOA, December 30, 1896, MV-90/67; December 31, 1896, Y.A.HUS-363/147.

7. BOA, December 6, 1905, DH.MKT-1028/66.

8. BOA, January 28, 1897, Y.A.RES-84/79.

9. Ibid.

10. Ibid.

11. For more on the Hijazi powers' impact on Ottoman efforts, see Mostafa Minawi, "Beyond Rhetoric: Reassessing Bedouin-Ottoman Relations along the Route of the Hijaz Telegraph Line at the End of the Nineteenth Century," *Journal of Economic and Social History of the Orient* 58 (2015): 75–104.

12. BOA, January 28, 1897, Y.A.RES-84/79. Based on estimates of total Ottoman expenditures in fiscal year 1897–1898, the cost of building the telegraph amounted to 35 percent of the total annual imperial budget. See Engin Akarlı, "Economic Policy and Budgets in Ottoman Turkey, 1876–1909," *Middle Eastern Studies* 28 (1992): 465.

13. BOA, February 17, 1898, İ.PT-8/1315-N-4.

14. Hussein Hilmi Pasha (1855–1923), from Midilli, held a number of senior positions, including the governorships of Adana (1897) and Yemen (1898–1902) and an inspector-generalship of Macedonia (1902–1908). He also served as a minister of interior (1908–1909), grand vizier (1909–1910), minister of justice (1912), and ambassador to Vienna (1912–1919). See Thomas Kühn, *Empire, Islam, and Politics of Difference: Ottoman Rule in Yemen, 1849–1919* (Leiden: Brill, 2011), 20n28.

15. BOA, September 13, 1897, Y.MTV-194/29.

16. BOA, January 28, 1897, Y.A.RES-84/79. The Ministry of Interior continued to express doubts about budget estimates, planning, and security. More than two years

later, interior ministers were still warning about the financial problems that awaited. A memo to the grand vizier's office stated that because Damascus was not able to fulfill its promised contribution of wooden poles, there was very little chance that Istanbul would be able to cover the construction costs. With no other solution found, the cost would have to come from the public purse of the provinces of Izmir, Syria, and Aleppo. BOA, April 1, 1899, DH.MKT-2156/31.

17. BOA, January 28, 1897, Y.A.RES-84/79.

18. BOA, February 14, 1897, Y.A.HUS-366/70. *Surra-yı Hümayun* was the annual delegation, sent by the sultan and guarded by soldiers, to deliver the *Muhammal*, an annual gift from the sultan to Mecca that was met with a great deal of pomp and circumstance at every station along its route. Egypt and Morocco sent similar gifts as a sign of their status in the Muslim world.

19. BOA, July 31, 1898, İ.HUS-66/1316-RA-45; September 8, 1898, DH.MKT-2103/2; September 8, 1898, DH.MKT-2103/18.

20. 'Abd al-Hamid al-Thani Khan [Sultan Abdülhamid II], *Mudhakarati al-Siya-siyya (1891–1908)*, trans. (Ottoman-Turkish to Arabic) unknown (Beirut: Mu'asasat al-Risala, 1979), 126–127.

21. BOA, October 29, 1898, DH.MKT-2125/1.

22. BOA, April 9, 1900, Y.MTV-201/29; BNA, April 6, 1900, FO 195/2075, 324.

23. *İkdam* (Istanbul), June 30, 1900, 1.

24. BNA, May 3, 1900, FO 195/2075, 338; May 7, 1900, FO 195/2075, 100; *İkdam* (Istanbul), April 23, 1900, 1; *Suriye* (Damascus), May 3, 1900, 1.

25. İzzet Efendi was the minister of telegraph and post between 1880 and 1888. See Roderic H. Davison, *Essays in Ottoman and Turkish History, 1775–1923: The Impact of the West* (Austin: University of Texas Press, 1999), 133–156.

26. BOA, August 8, 1900, İ.PT-11/1318-R-6. On the impact of the telegraph line extension, on the administration of southern Syria, see Eugene L. Rogan, "Instant Communication: The Impact of the Telegraph in Ottoman Syria," in *The Syrian Land: Process of Integration and Fragmentation: Bilad al-Sham from the 18th to the 20th Century*, ed. Thomas Philipp and Birgit Schaebler (Stuttgart: Franz Steiner, 1998), 113–128.

27. *İkdam* (Istanbul), July 1, 1900, 3.

28. BOA, July 24, 1900, DH.MKT-2378/104.

29. BOA, August 24, 1900, DH.MKT-2394/30.

30. BOA, November 10, 1903, DH.MKT-792/12.

31. BOA, July 31, 1900, Ş.D-1133/28.

32. BNA, April 30, 1900, FO 195/2075, 330.

33. BOA, July 26, 1901, İ.AS-37/1319-R-3.

34. *Suriye* (Damascus), July 12, 1900, 1; *İkdam* (Istanbul), August 1, 1900, 2; August 8, 1900, 3.

35. BOA, July 31, 1900, Y.MTV-205/15; *Suriye* (Damascus), August 2, 1900, 1. Eugene Rogan discusses the Ottoman government's expansion into the Karak district during this period, finding that the government was successful in securing the lines from Bedouin attacks by paying tribal chiefs to ensure their protection. See Eugene L. Rogan,

Frontiers of the State in the Late Ottoman Empire: Transjordan, 1850–1921 (New York: Columbia University Press, 1999), 63–65.

36. *Suriye* (Damascus), August 9, 1900, 1.

37. BNA, July 31, 1900, FO 195/2075, 438; July 31, 1900, FO 78/5071, 373.

38. BNA, September 3, 1900, FO 195/2075, 454.

39. Stefan Weber, *Damascus: Ottoman Modernity and Urban Transformation, 1808–1918*, vol. 1, *Proceedings of the Danish Institute in Damascus V* (Aarhus: Aarhus University Press, 2009), 91.

40. *İkdam* (Istanbul), September 6, 1900, 2; *Suriye* (Damascus), August 23, 1900, 1.

41. Klaus Kreiser, "Public Monuments in Turkey and Egypt, 1840–1916," in *Muqarnas: An Annual on the Visual Culture of the Islamic World*, ed. Gülru Necipoğlu (Leiden: Brill, 1997), 14:111. For more on this column, including a number of other monuments in cities along the Hamidian line, see Zeynep Çelik, *Empire, Architecture, and the City: French-Ottoman Encounters, 1830–1914* (Seattle: University of Washington Press, 2008), 137–142.

42. BOA, October 14, 1900, DH.MKT-2414/73; November 8, 1900, İ.PT-12/1318-B-7; November 22, 1900, DH.MKT-2430/118; December 6, 1900, DH.MKT-2435/5.

43. BOA, November 22, 1900, İ.HUS-85/1318-B-85.

44. BOA, June 25, 1901, İ.AS-36/1319-RA-6. The Fifth Regiment was formed during the Russian-Ottoman War of 1877–1878, when one hundred thousand local reserves were called up in Syria. See William Ochsenwald, *The Hijaz Railroad* (Charlottesville: University Press of Virginia, 1980), 14.

45. At this point, even though the annual cost of operation took into consideration the salaries of workers and military guards, it did not consider annual maintenance or payments to local tribes. This meant either that salaries for wardens and guards would sometimes be given to local Bedouin employees and symbolic positions given to chiefs, or that the budget for such costs was ignored. BOA, September 17, 1900, Y.MTV-206/119.

46. François Georgeon, *Abdulhamid II: Le sultan calife* (Paris: Librairie Arthème Fayard, 2003), 150–151; Khan, *Mudhakarati al-Siyasiyya*, 106. For a detailed discussion of the financing of the Hijaz Railway, see Murat Özyüksel, *Hicaz Demiryolu* (Istanbul: Tarih Vakfı Yurt Yayınları, 2000), 81–117.

47. BOA, October 13, 1900, DH.MKT-2414/34; November 14, 1900, İ.PT-12/1318-B-5; August 18, 1900, İ.HUS-83/1318-R-18; August 24, 1900, DH.MKT-2394/77; September 10, 1900, DH.MKT-2400/140; October 13, 1900, Y.MTV-207/88.

48. Beni ʿAtiyya and Huwaytat were large tribal confederations in the vicinity of the Hijaz telegraph line path, close to the border of what are now Saudi Arabia and Jordan.

49. BOA, October 13, 1900, DH.MKT-2414/13.

50. The leader of the Huwaytat owed his status in the region partially to the backing of the Syrian provincial government. Therefore, I speculate that Azmzade might have leveraged his status as an Ottoman representative to bring him back to negotiations. See Ochsenwald, *Hijaz Railroad*, 121.

51. On the transportation of pilgrims during the various Ottoman periods, see F. E. Peters, *The Hajj: The Muslim Pilgrimage to Mecca and the Holy Places* (Princeton, NJ:

Princeton University Press, 1994), 144–171, 282–300; Abdul-Karim Rafeq, "New Light on the Transportation of Damascene Pilgrimage during the Ottoman Period," in *Islamic and Middle Eastern Societies*, ed. R. Olson (Brattleboro, VT: Amana, 1987), 127–136. On the hajj during Ottoman rule in the early modern period, see Suraiya Faroqhi, *Pilgrims and Sultans: The Hajj under the Ottomans* (London: I. B. Tauris, 1994).

52. Ochsenwald has a similar argument about the Hijaz Railway in *The Hijaz Railroad*, 120.

53. Bill Finlayson and Samantha Denis, "Landscape, Archaeology and Heritage," *Levant* 34 (2002): 219–227.

54. Andrew Merrifield, "Place and Space: A Lefebvrian Reconciliation," *Transactions of the Institute of British Geographers*, n.s., 18 (1993): 526.

55. I found Donald Meining's edited volume *The Interpretation of Ordinary Landscapes* (Oxford: Oxford University Press, 1979) to be very helpful in my theorizing of the sociopolitical significance of the physical presence of telegraph structures in the Arabian Desert. I was also influenced in my thinking about reading the local landscape and colonialism by Jennifer Cole's investigation into seemingly invisible signs of the memory of colonialism in Madagascar, which in reality were very visible to the local population. See Jennifer Cole, "Constructing a Betsimisarak Memoryscape," in *Forget Colonialism? Sacrifice and the Art of Memory in Madagascar* (Berkeley: University of California Press, 2001), 274–300.

56. Chris Rumford, "Theorizing Borders," *European Journal of Social Theory* 9 (2006): 166.

57. See Yakup Bektaş, "The Sultan's Messenger: Cultural Constructions of Ottoman Telegraphy, 1847–1880," *Technology and Culture* 41 (2000): 669–696.

58. For more on this episode, see Minawi, "Beyond Rhetoric."

59. I borrow the term from Robert S. G. Fletcher, who deals with similar questions about the relationship between an imperial state and Bedouins in the Middle East. See Robert S. G. Fletcher, *British Imperialism and "The Tribal Question": Desert Administration and Nomadic Societies in the Middle East, 1919–1936* (Oxford: Oxford University Press, 2015).

60. BOA, July 19, 1900, Y.PRK.BŞK-62/60.

61. William Richards was the British consul in Jeddah until 1895, when he was injured in an attempted assassination and his vice-consul ʿAbd al-Razzaq was killed. He was transferred to Damascus and replaced by George Devey. See William Ochsenwald, *Religion, Society and the State in Arabia: The Hijaz under Ottoman Control, 1840–1908* (Columbus: Ohio State University Press, 1984), 197.

62. One lira is one hundred *kuruş*. In Karak anywhere from two to nine lira per family was collected without receipts. BNA, July 31, 1900, FO 195/2075, 432.

63. In January 1901, Azmzade was awarded a *Mecidiye* of the first order for his good service. BOA, January 9, 1901, İ.TAL-237/1318-N23. Individuals awarded an honor of the fourth order include members of the Salt community and a member of the Sanaʿiyya tribe by the name of Butros, for financial assistance and help in transporting wooden poles. BOA, October 31, 1900, DH.MKT-2422/116.

64. *İkdam* (Istanbul), July 24, 1900, 2.

65. BOA, March 31, 1902, DH.MKT-463/23.

66. BNA, September 28, 1900, FO 195/2075, 469.

67. BNA, October 4, 1900, FO 195/2075, 472.

68. See John Dwyer, *To Wire the World: Perry M. Collins and the North Pacific Telegraph Expedition* (Westport, CT: Praeger, 2001).

69. See Hynek Burda, Sabin Begall, Jarsoslav Cerveney, Julia Neef, and Pavel Nemec, "Extremely Low-Frequency Electromagnetic Fields Disrupt Magnetic Alignment of Ruminants," *Proceedings of the National Academy of Sciences* 106 (2009): 5708–5713.

70. BOA, March 31, 1902, DH.MKT-463/23.

71. See Ochsenwald, *Hijaz Railroad*, 26–27.

72. BNA, November 20, 1900, FO 195/2075, 517; *Suriye* (Damascus), November 1, 1900, 1.

73. BNA, January 10, 1901, FO 195/2097.

74. BNA, February 20, 1901, FO 195/2105; April 6, 1901, FO 195/2097; April 6, 1901, FO 618/3.

75. *İkdam* (Istanbul), March 23, 1901, 1.

76. BOA, March 31, 1902, DH.MKT-463/23.

77. BOA, May 28, 1901, DH.MKT-2490/58.

78. BOA, January 30, 1901, Y.PRK.UM-52/103.

79. BOA, December 15, 1901, Y.A.HUS-423/5.

80. Ibid. At the time, Ratib Pasha was building a mansion in Istanbul to return to. Known as Ahmet Ratip Pasha's mansion, it was taken over by the Ottoman Ministry of Education in 1908 and is now the Küçük Çamlica School for Girls. See Aykut Kansu, *The Revolution of 1908 in Turkey* (Leiden: Brill, 1997), 145–146; Diane Barillari and Ezio Godoli, *Istanbul 1900: Art-Nouveau Architecture and Interiors* (Rome: Rizoli International, 1996), 194–195.

81. Ş. Tufan Buzpınar, "Vying for Power and Influence in the Hijaz: Ottoman Rule, the Last Emirate of Abdulmuttalib and the British (1880–1882)," *Muslim World* 95 (2005): 1–13; Georgeon, *Abdulhamid II*, 202–207.

82. For more on the Hussein 'Awn Pasha's term as the amir of Mecca and his dealings with the British leading to his dismissal, see Ş. Tufan Buzpınar, "The Hijaz, Abdülhamid II and Amir Hussein's Secret Dealings with the British, 1877–80," *Middle Eastern Studies* 31 (1995): 99–123.

83. The relationship of Ahmed Ratib Pasha and Amir 'Awn al-Rafiq Pasha and its disastrous impact on the Bedouin population is well documented. See Kemal Karpat, *The Politicization of Islam: Reconstructing Identity, State, Faith, and Community in the Late Ottoman State* (Oxford: Oxford University Press, 2001), 248; Ochsenwald, *Religion, Society and the State in Arabia*, 194, 205; Fa'iq Bakr al-Sawwaf, *al-'Alaqat Bayn al-Dawla al-'Uthmaniyya wa Iqlim al-Hijaz fi Fatrat ma Bayn 1293–1334 H (1876–1915 M)* (Mecca: Abdul Aziz University, 1978), 90. For a damning account of corruption under the rules of Ahmed Ratib and 'Awn al-Rafiq, see the political diary of the former governor of Istanbul, Süleyman Kani İrtem: *Osmanlı Devleti'nin Mısır, Yemen, Hicaz Meselesi*, ed. Osman Selim Kocahanoğlu (Istanbul: Temel Yayınları, 1999), 172–207.

84. Ochsenwald, *Religion, Society and the State in Arabia,* 191.

85. Ibid., 188–189.

86. BNA, February 1, 1899, FO 195/2061, 33.

87. BNA, May 5, 1899, FO 195/2061, 167; February 12, 1905, FO 195/2198, 40–48.

88. Dr. ʿAbd al-Razzaq was an Indian subject of the British Empire initially hired in 1879 to report on and oversee the sanitary conditions of Indian pilgrims in Mecca. He later became the British vice-consul, which allowed him access to Mecca's inner circles of power, and remained in this position until his assassination in 1895. Al-Razzaq was thought to be a spy for the British government, inspiring a plan for a special branch of British intelligence to be staffed by Muslim British subjects, which never came to fruition. See Michael Christopher Low, "Empire and the Hajj: Pilgrims, Plagues, and Pan-Islam under British Surveillance, 1865–1908," *International Journal of Middle East Studies* 40 (2008): 280–285.

89. İrtem, *Osmanlı Devleti'nin Mısır,* 172–202.

90. BOA, December 13, 1901, Y.A.HUS-425/20; February 13, 1901, Y.A.HUS-425/20; William Ochsenwald, "Ottoman Subsidies to the Hijaz (1877–1886)," *International Journal of Middle East Studies* 6 (1975): 300–307.

91. The *muhafiz* (governor) of Medina was a close confidant of the sultan and a balancing power to the governor and the amir's coalition. He stayed in office until two incidents of non-payment of soldiers caused a mutiny in 1904 and 1906. See Ochsenwald, *Religion, Society and the State in Arabia,* 209–211.

92. BOA, March 31, 1902, DH.MKT-463/23.

93. BNA, May 24, 1899, FO 195/2061, 205.

94. BOA, August 19, 1901, İ.PT-13/1319-C-2.

95. The government in Istanbul made public its decision to hire and pay various tribesmen along the route, which was announced in *İkdam* (Istanbul), October 20, 1901, 1.

Conclusion

Epigraph: *Suriye* (Damascus), January 10, 1901, 1.

1. The telegraph line between Mecca and Medina was not progressing, but other work had not stopped. A decision to double the line with a second cable was made late in 1900. That work, along with other maintenance, proceeded as scheduled. On May 29, 1901, William Richards reported that a second cable was being laid between Damascus and the holy cities. See BNA, May 29, 1901, FO 195/2097. On June 15, 1901, Richards reported that the head of the Ministry of Telegraph and Post had decided to replace the old wire between Salt and Damascus, and on July 11, 1901, he reported that work was proceeding rapidly and that the line was now only 247 miles from Medina. See BNA, June 15, 1901, FO 195/2097; July 11, 1901, FO 195/2097.

2. BNA, January 8, 1902, FO 195/2122.

3. Kazım Pasha would replace Ratib Pasha as the governor-general of the province of Hijaz in 1908. See Hasan Kayalı, *Arabs and Young Turks: Ottomanism, Arabism, and Islamism in the Ottoman Empire, 1908–1918* (Berkeley: University of California Press, 1997), 245n17.

4. On February 1, 1902, after a more thorough assessment of the damages, the verdict was much more pessimistic; the columns and lines had been completely destroyed between Medina and Biyar Nasif. See BOA, March 13, 1902, DH.MKT-463/23.

5. BOA, March 31, 1902, DH.MKT-463/23.

6. BNA, January 24, 1902, FO 195/2126 14; BOA, May 5, 1902, DH.MKT-496/45; BOA, March 31, 1902, DH.MKT-463/23; BNA, May 19, 1902, FO 195/2126, 95; BNA, July 31, 1902, FO 195/2126, 174; BOA, March 31, 1902, DH.MKT-463/23; BNA, May 19, 1902, FO 195/2126, 95.

7. Aykut Kansu, *The Revolution of 1908 in Turkey* (Leiden: Brill, 1997), 145, 146.

8. ʿAbd al-Hamid al-Thani Khan [Sultan Abdülhamid II], *Mudhakarati al-Siyasiyya (1891–1908)*, trans. (Ottoman-Turkish to Arabic) unknown (Beirut: Muʾasasat al-Risala, 1979), 106.

9. BNA, January 29, 1902, FO 195/2122.

10. *Suriye* (Damascus), February 12, 1902, 1.

11. *Suriye* (Damascus), November 8, 1902, 1.

12. See Harold G. Marcus, *A History of Ethiopia*, updated ed. (Berkeley: University of California Press, 2002), 91–103.

13. Sadik al-Mouayad Azmzade, "Habeşstan Siyahatnamesi." This is the original copy of Azmzade's travelogue manuscript, a generous gift from the great-grandnephew of Sadik Pasha, Mr. İklil Azmzade.

BIBLIOGRAPHY

Primary Sources

Başbakanlık Osmanli Arşivleri (BOA), Istanbul

A.AMD: Amedi Kalemi
A.MTZ.TG.HB.: Sadaret Eyalet-i Mümtaze Kalemi Belgeleri, Trablusgarb, Haribiye
DH.H: Dahiliye Nezareti Hukuk Kalemi Evrakı
DH.MKT.: Dahiliye Nezareti Mektubi Kalemi
HR.SYS.: Hariciye Nezareti Siyasi Kısım Evrakı
İ.AS.: İrade, Askari
İ.DH.: İrade, Dahiliye
İ.HR.: İrade, Hariciye
İ.HUS.: İrade, Hususi
İ.PT.: İrade, Posta ve Telegraf
İ.ŞD.: İrade, Şura-yı Devlet
İ.TAL.: İrade, Taltif
MV.: Meclis-i Vükela Mazbatları
ŞD.: Şura-yı Devlet Maruzatı
Y.A.HUS.: Yıldız Sadaret Hususi Maruzat Evrakı
Y.A.RES.: Yıldız Sadaret Resmi Maruzat Evrakı
YEE.: Yıldız Esas Evrakı
Y.MTV.: Yıldız Mütenevvi Maruzat Evrakı
Y.PRK.A.: Yıldız Perakende Sadaret Maruzatı
Y.PRK.ASK.: Yıldız Perakende Askeri Maruzat
Y.PRK.AZJ.: Yıldız Perakende Arzuhaller ve Jurnaller
Y.PRK.BŞK.: Yıldız Perakende Mabeyn Başkitabeti Maruzatı
Y.PRK.DH.: Yıldız Perakende Dahiliye Nezareti Maruzatı
Y.PRK.EŞA.: Yıldız Perakende Elçilik ve Şehbenderlik Maruzatı
Y.PRK.HH.: Yıldız Perakende Hazine-i Hassa Nezareti Maruzatı
Y.PRK.HR.: Yıldız Perakende Hariciye Nezareti Maruzatı
Y.PRK.KOM.: Yıldız Perakende Komiyonlar Maruzatı
Y.PRK.M.: Yıldız Perakende Müteferrik Evrak
Y.PRK.MF.: Yıldız Perakende Maarif Nezareti Maruzatı
Y.PRK.MK.: Yıldız Perakende Müfettişlik ve Komiserlikler Tahriratı

Y.PRK.ML.: Yıldız Perakende Maliye Nezareti Maruzatı
Y.PRK.MŞ.: Yıldız Perakende Evrakı Meşahat Dairesi Maruzatı
Y.PRK.MYD.: Yıldız Perakende Yaveran ve Maiyet-i Seniyye Erkan-ı Harbiye Dairesi
Y.PRK.PT.: Yıldız Perakende Posta ve Telegraf Nezareti Maruzatı
Y.PRK.SRN.: Yıldız Perakende Serkurenalık Maruzatı
Y.PRK.ŞD.: Yıldız Perakende Şura-yı Devlet Maruzatı
Y.PRK.TŞF.: Yıldız Perakende Teşrifat-ı Umumiye Dairesi
Y.PRK.UM.: Yıldız Perakende Umum Vilayetler Tahriratı

National Archives (formerly British National Archives) (BNA), London

Records of the Foreign Office

Bulgarian Historical Archives, Sofia

Diplomatic correspondence between the Office of the Ottoman Commissariat and the Principality of Bulgaria

Rare Works Collections, Nadır Eserler Kütüphanesi, İstanbul Üniversitesi

el-Müeyyed (Azmzade), Sadık. "Bir Osmanlı Zabitinin Büyük Sahra'da Seyahati" (manuscript)
———."Fen-i Fotoğraf" (manuscript)
Photo collection (Istanbul, Benghazi, and Hijaz)

Private Collection

al-Mouayad Azmzade, Sadik. "Habeşstan Siyahatnamesi" (manuscript)

Beyazıt Kütüphanesi, Istanbul

Rare newspaper collection
İkdam (Istanbul)
Suriye (Damascus)

İslam Araştırmaları Merkezi (İSAM), Istanbul

Rare journals collection
Servet-i Fünun (Istanbul)

American University of Beirut Library, Beirut

Newspaper collection
Lisan al-Hal (Beirut)

Al-Maktaba al-Zahiriyya, Rare Books, Old City, Damascus

Cemal, Ahmed. Coğrafya-yı Osmani. Istanbul: Mektebi Fünun-ı Harbiye-yi Şahane Matbaası, 1903.

———. *Coğrafya-yı Umumi*. Istanbul: Mektebi Fünun-ı Harbiye-yi Şahane Matbaası, 1891.

Hilmi, İbrahim. *Cep Atlası Umumi*. Istanbul: Kütüphane-yi Askeri, 1906.

Remzi, Muhammed. *Coğrafya-yı Umumi*. Istanbul: Mektebi Fünun-ı Harbiye-yi Şahane Matbaası, 1903.

Sabit, Selim. *Muhtasar-ı Coğrafya Risalesi, Subyan Mektblerine Muhasasdır*. 3rd ed. Damascus: Waqf Majlis al-Maʿarif ʿala al-Maktaba al-ʿUmumiyya bi-Dimashq, LaTürkü Matbaası, 1880.

Tevfik, Ali. *Memalik-i Osmaniye Coğrafyası*. Istanbul: Kasbar Matbaası, 1900.

Yeni Atlas. Translated by Ali Hafız. Paris, 1868.

Library of Congress, Washington, DC

Historical Photograph Collections from the Ottoman Empire

Published and Secondary Sources

Abulafia, David. *The Great Sea: A Human History of the Mediterranean*. Oxford: Oxford University Press, 2011.

Abu-Manneh, B. "Sultan Abdulhamid II and Shaikh Abdulhuda Al-Sayyadi." *Middle Eastern Studies* 15 (1979): 131–153.

Ahmida, Ali Abdullatif. *The Making of Modern Libya: State Formation, Colonization, and Resistance, 1830–1932*. Albany: State University of New York Press, 1994.

Akarlı, Engin. "Economic Policy and Budgets in Ottoman Turkey, 1876–1909." *Middle Eastern Studies* 28 (1992): 443–476.

———. *The Long Peace: Ottoman Lebanon, 1861–1920*. London: Centre for Lebanese Studies / I. B. Tauris, 1993.

———. "The Problems of External Pressures, Power Struggles, and Budgetary Deficits in Ottoman Politics under Abdülhamid II (1876–1909): Origins and Solutions." PhD diss., Princeton University, 1976.

———. "Tangled Ends of an Empire." In *Modernity and Culture from the Mediterranean to the Indian Ocean*, edited by Leila Fawaz and C. A. Bayly, 261–284. New York: Columbia University Press, 2002.

———. "The Tangled Ends of an Empire: Ottoman Encounters with the West and Problems of Westernization—An Overview." *Comparative Studies of South Asia, Africa, and the Middle East* 26 (2006): 353–366.

Akbulut, Uğur. "Suriye'ye İlk Telgraf Hatlarının Çekilmesi." Special issue, *History Studies: International Journal of History* (2010): 1–11. http://www.historystudies.net/Makaleler/1085089875_Uğur%20Akbulut.pdf. Accessed August 17, 2015

Akgündüz, Ahmed, and Said Öztürk. *Ottoman History: Misperceptions and Truths*. Rotterdam: Islamic University of Rotterdam Press, 2011.

Akinwumi, Olayemi. *The Colonial Contest for the Nigerian Region, 1884–1900: A History of German Participation*. Hamburg: LIT, 2002.

Aksakal, Mustafa. *The Ottoman Road to War in 1914: The Ottoman Empire and the First World War*. Cambridge: Cambridge University Press, 2008.

Akweenda, S. *International Law and the Protection of Namibia's Territorial Integrity: Boundaries and Territorial Claims*. The Hague: Kluwer Law International, 1997.

Allen, Roger. *Spies, Scandals, and Sultans: Istanbul in the Twilight of the Ottoman Empire*. Lanham, MD: Rowman & Littlefield, 2008.

Alon, Yoav. *The Making of Jordan: Tribes, Colonialism, and the Modern State*. London: I. B. Tauris, 2007.

Anderson, Lisa. "Nineteenth-Century Reform in Ottoman Libya." *International Journal of Middle East Studies* 16 (1984): 325–348.

——. "Obligation and Accountability: Islamic Politics in North Africa." *Daedalus* 120 (1991): 93–112.

——. *The State and Social Transformation in Tunisia and Libya, 1830–1980*. Princeton, NJ: Princeton University Press, 1986.

Anderson, Matthew S. *The Eastern Question, 1774–1923: A Study in International Relations*. London: Macmillan, 1996.

Anghie, Anthony. *Imperialism, Sovereignty, and the Making of International Law*. Cambridge: Cambridge University Press, 2004.

Anscombe, Frederick F. *The Ottoman Gulf: The Creation of Kuwait, Saudi Arabia, and Qatar*. New York: Columbia University Press, 1997.

Aqbiq, ʿIzza ʿAli. "Dukhul al-Sikak al-Hadidiyya ila Bilad al-Sham Awakhir al-Hukm al-ʿUthmani wa Atharuha al-Siyasiyya wa-l-ʿAskariyya w-al-Ijtimaʿiyya w-al-Iqtisadiyya, 1891–1918." Master's thesis, University of Damascus, 2006.

al-Ashhab, Muhammad al-Tayyib bin Idris. *Al-Mahdi al-Sanusi*. Tripoli: Bilniyu Maji Press, 1952.

Ateş, Sabri. *The Ottoman-Iranian Borderlands: Making a Boundary, 1843–1914*. New York: Cambridge University Press, 2013.

Avcı, Yasemin. "The Application of *Tanzimat* in the Desert: The Bedouins and the Creation of a New Town in Southern Palestine (1860–1914)." *Middle Eastern Studies* 45 (2009): 969–983.

ʿAwad, ʿAbd al-ʿAziz Mohammad. *Al-Idara al-ʿUthmaniyya fi Wilayat Surya, 1864–1914*. Cairo: Dar al-Maʿarif bi-Misr, 1969.

Ayalon, Ami. *Language and Change in the Arab Middle East: The Evolution of Modern Arab Political Discourse*. Oxford: Oxford University Press, 1987.

Aymes, Marc. *Un grand progrès sur le papier: Histoire provinciale des réformes ottomanes à Chypre au XIXᵉ siècle*. Paris: Peeters, 2010.

Barak, On. *On Time: Technology and Temporality in Modern Egypt*. Berkeley: University of California Press, 2013.

Barillari, Diane, and Ezio Godoli. *Istanbul 1900: Art-Nouveau Architecture and Interiors*. Rome: Rizoli International, 1996.

Baron, Beth. *The Orphan Scandal: Christian Missionaries and the Rise of the Muslim Brotherhood*. Stanford, CA: Stanford University Press, 2014.

Barry, Quintin. *War in the East: A Military History of the Russo-Turkish War, 1877–78*. Solihull, UK: Helion, 2012.

Baumgart, Winfried. *Imperialism: The Idea and Reality of British and French Colonial Expansion, 1880–1914.* Oxford: Oxford University Press, 1982.

Bektaş, Yakub. "Displaying the American Genius: The Electromagnetic Telegraph in the Wider World." *British Journal of the History of Science* 34 (2001): 199–232.

Bektaş, Yakup. "The Sultan's Messenger: Cultural Constructions of Ottoman Telegraphy, 1847–1880." *Technology and Culture* 41 (2000): 669–696.

Ben-Dror, Avishai. "The Egyptian Hikimdariya of Harar and Its Hinterland—Historical Aspects, 1875–1887." PhD diss., Tel Aviv University, 2008.

Berridge, G. R. *British Diplomacy in Turkey, 1583 to Present: A Study in the Evolution of the Resident Embassy.* Leiden: Martinus Nijhoff, 2009.

Bin Ismaʿil, ʿUmar ʿAli. *Inhiyar Hukm al-Usra al-Qaramanliyya fi Libya, 1795–1835.* Tripoli: Maktabat al-Farajani, 1966.

Bjørkelo, Andres J. *State and Society in the Three Central Sudanic Kingdoms: Kanem-Bornu, Bagirmi, and Wadai.* Bergen, Norway: Hovedoppgave i Historie Høsten, University of Bergen, 1976.

Blake, Corinne Lee. "Training Arab-Ottoman Bureaucrats: Syrian Graduates of the Mülkiye Mektebi, 1890–1920." PhD diss., Princeton University, 1991.

Blumi, Isa. "The Consequences of Empire in the Balkans and Red Sea: Reading Possibilities in the Transformations of the Modern World." PhD diss., New York University, 2005.

——. "The Frontier as a Measure of Modern Power: Local Limits to Empire in Yemen, 1872–1914." In *The Frontiers of the Ottoman World*, edited by A. C. S. Peacock, 289–304. Oxford: Oxford University Press, 2009.

——. "The Ottoman Empire and Yemeni Politics in the Sancaq of Taʾizz, 1911–1918." In *The Empire in the City: Arab Provincial Capitals in the Late Ottoman Empire*, edited by J. Hanssen, T. Philipp, and S. Weber, 349–367. Beirut: Beiruter Texte and Studien, 2002.

——. *Reinstating the Ottomans: Alternative Balkan Modernities, 1800–1912.* New York: Palgrave Macmillan, 2011.

——. *Rethinking the Late Ottoman Empire: A Comparative Social and Political History of Albania and the Yemen, 1878–1918.* Istanbul: ISIS, 2003.

Boahen, A. Adu. *Britain, the Sahara, and the Western Sudan, 1788–1861.* Oxford: Oxford University Press, 1964.

Bostan, İdris. "The Ottoman Empire and the Congo: The Crisis of 1893–95." In *Studies on Ottoman Diplomatic History*, pt. 5, edited by Selim Deringil and Sinan Kuneralp, 103–119. Istanbul: ISIS, 1990.

Boyar, Ebru. "The Press and the Palace: The Two-Way Relationship between Abdülhamid II and the Press, 1876–1908." *Bulletin of the School of Oriental and African Studies* 69 (2006): 417–432.

Braudel, Fernand. *The Mediterranean and the Mediterranean World in the Age of Philip II.* Vol. 2. Translated by Sian Reynolds. New York: Harper Colophon, 1973.

Brenner, Louis. *The Shehus of Kukawa: A History of the al-Kanemi Dynasty of Bornu.* Oxford: Clarendon, 1973.

Broche, François. *L'expédition de Tunisie, 1881.* Paris: Presses de la Cité, 1996.

Brower, Benjamin Claude. *A Desert Named Peace: The Violence of France's Empire in the Algerian Sahara, 1844–1902*. New York: Columbia University Press, 2009.

Brummett, Palmira. *Ottoman Seapower and Levantine Diplomacy in the Age of Discovery*. Albany: State University of New York Press, 1994.

Burbank, Jane, and Frederick Cooper. *Empires in World History: Power and the Politics of Difference*. Princeton, NJ: Princeton University Press, 2010.

Burda, Hynek, Sabin Begall, Jarsoslav Cerveney, Julia Neef, and Pavel Nemec. "Extremely Low-Frequency Electromagnetic Fields Disrupt Magnetic Alignment of Ruminants." *Proceedings of the National Academy of Sciences* 106 (2009): 5708–5713.

Burton, Antoinette. *Empire in Question: Reading, Writing and Teaching British Imperialism*. Durham, NC: Duke University Press, 2011.

Buzpınar, Ş. Tufan. "The Hijaz, Abdülhamid II and Amir Hussein's Secret Dealings with the British, 1877–80." *Middle Eastern Studies* 31 (1995): 99–123.

———. "Vying for Power and Influence in the Hijaz: Ottoman Rule, the Last Emirate of Abdulmuttalib and the British (1880–1882)." *Muslim World* 95 (2005): 1–22.

Canaparo, Claudio. "Marconi and Other Artifices: Long-Range Technology and the Conquest of the Desert." In *Images of Power: Iconography, Culture and the State in Latin America*, edited by Jens Andermann and William Rowe, 241–251. New York: Berghahn, 2005.

Castellino, Joshua, Steven Allen, and Jeremie Gilbert. *Title to Territory in International Law: A Temporal Analysis*. Aldershot, UK: Dartmouth, 2003.

Cevahiroğlu, E. Melek. "The Sufi Order in a Modernizing Empire: 1808–1876." *Tarih* 1 (2009): 70–93.

Chakrabarty, Dipesh. *Provincializing Europe: Postcolonial Thought and Historical Difference*. Princeton, NJ: Princeton University Press, 2007.

Chamberlain, M. E. *The Scramble for Africa*. 3rd ed. London: Longman Press, 2010.

Chatterjee, Partha. *The Nation and Its Fragments: Colonial and Postcolonial Histories*. Princeton, NJ: Princeton University Press, 1993.

Clancy-Smith, Julia Ann. *Rebel and Saint: Muslim Notables, Populist Protest, Colonial Encounters (Algeria and Tunisia, 1800–1904)*. Berkeley: University of California Press, 1994.

Clancy-Smith, Julia, and Charles D. Smith. *The Modern Middle East and North Africa: A History in Documents*. Oxford: Oxford University Press, 2014.

Cole, Jennifer. *Forget Colonialism? Sacrifice and the Art of Memory in Madagascar*. Berkeley: University of California Press, 2001.

Cole, Juan. *Colonialism and Revolution in the Middle East: Social and Cultural Origins of Egypt's ʿUrabi Movement*. Princeton, NJ: Princeton University Press, 1992.

Collins, Robert O. "The African Slave Trade to Asia and the Indian Ocean Islands." *African and Asian Studies* 5 (2006): 325–346.

———. *The Partition of Africa: Illusion or Necessity*. New York: Wiley, 1969.

Cooper, Frederick. *Colonialism in Question: Theory, Knowledge, History*. Berkeley: University of California Press, 2005.

Cordell, Dennis. "The Awlad Sulayman of Libya and Chad: Power and Adaptation in the Sahara and Sahel." *Canadian Journal of African Studies* 19 (1985): 319–343.

———. *Dar al-Kuti and the Last Years of the Trans-Saharan Slave Trade.* Madison: University of Wisconsin Press, 1985.

———. "Eastern Libya, Wadai and the Sanusiya: A Tariqa and a Trade Route." *Journal of African History* 18 (1977): 21–36.

Cumming, D. C. *Handbook on Cyrenaica.* Pts. 5 and 6. London: Printing and Stationery Services, M.E.F., n.d.

Çaycı, Abdurrahman. *La question tunisienne et la politique ottomane (1881–1913).* Ankara: Société Turque d'Histoire, 1992.

———. *Al-Sira' al-Turki-al-Faransi fi al-Sahara' al-Kubra.* Translated from Turkish to Arabic by Ali A'zazi. Tripoli: Markaz Dirasat Jihad al-Libiyyin Did al-Ghazw al-Itali, 1982.

Çelik, Zeynep. *Empire, Architecture, and the City: French-Ottoman Encounters, 1830–1914.* Seattle: University of Washington Press, 2008.

Çetinsaya, Gökhan. "The Ottoman View of British Presence in Iraq and the Gulf: The Era of Abdulhamid II." *Middle Eastern Studies* 39 (2003): 194–203.

al-Dajani, Ahmad Sidqi. *Al-Haraka al-Sanusiyya: Nash'atuha wa Numuwwuha fi al-Qarn al-Tasi' 'Ashar.* Cairo, 1967.

Davison, Roderic H. *Essays in Ottoman and Turkish History, 1775–1923: The Impact of the West.* Austin: University of Texas Press, 1999.

———. *Nineteenth Century Ottoman Diplomacy and Reforms.* Istanbul: ISIS, 1999.

"Death of Lord Kimberley." *New York Times,* April 9, 1902.

"Death of Rustem Pasha, the Turkish Ambassador to Britain for Ten Years." *New York Times,* November 20, 1895.

De Candole, E. A. V. *The Life and Times of King Idris of Libya.* Privately published by Mohamed Ben Ghalbon, 1990.

Deguilhem, Randi. "A Revolution in Learning? The Islamic Contribution to the Ottoman State Schools: Examples from the Syrian Provinces." In *Proceedings of the International Congress on Learning and Education in the Ottoman World,* edited by Ali Çaksu, 285–295. Istanbul: IRCICA, 2001.

Deringil, Selim. "The Invention of Tradition as Public Image in the Late Ottoman Empire, 1808–1908." *Comparative Studies in Society and History* 35 (1993): 3–29.

———. "The Ottoman Response to the Egyptian Crisis of 1881–82," *Middle Eastern Studies* 24 (1988): 3–24.

———. "'They Live in a State of Nomadism and Savagery': The Late Ottoman Empire and the Post-Colonial Debate." *Comparative Studies in Society and History* 45 (2003): 311–342.

———. *The Well-Protected Domains: Ideology and the Legitimation of Power in the Ottoman Empire, 1876–1909.* London: I. B. Tauris, 1998.

Diyaf, Najmi Rajab. *Madinat Ghat wa Tijarat al-Qawafil al-Sahrawiyya Khilal al-Qarn al-Tasi' 'Ashar al-Miladi.* Benghazi: Markaz Jihad al-Libiyin li-l-Dirasat al-Tarikhiyya, 1999.

Dundar, Fuat. *Crime of Numbers: The Role of Statistics in the Armenian Question (1878–1914).* New Brunswick, NJ: Transaction, 2010.

Dunn, John P. *Khedive Ismail's Army.* London: Routledge, 2005.

Duveyrier, Henri. *Exploration du Sahara.* 2 vols. Paris, 1864.

Dwyer, John. *To Wire the World: Perry M. Collins and the North Pacific Telegraph Expedition.* Westport, CT: Praeger, 2001.

Eich, Thomas. "Abu al-Huda al-Sayyadi—Still Such a Polarizing Figure." *Arabica* 55 (2008): 433–444.

Eldem, Edhem. *Pride and Privilege: A History of Ottoman Orders, Medals, and Decorations.* Istanbul: Osmanlı Bankası Arşiv ve Araştırma Merkezi, 2004.

Ellis, Matthew. "Between Empire and Nation: The Emergence of Egypt's Libyan Borderland, 1841–1911." PhD diss., Princeton University, 2011.

Emrence, Cem. "Imperial Paths, Big Comparisons: The Late Ottoman Empire." *Journal of Global History* 3 (2008): 289–311.

Evans-Pritchard, E. E. "The Distribution of the Sanusi Lodges." *Africa: Journal of the International African Institute* 15 (1945): 183–187.

———. "Italy and the Bedouin in Cyrenaica." *African Affairs* 45 (1946): 12–21.

———. "Italy and the Sanusiya Order in Cyrenaica." *Bulletin of the School of Oriental and African Studies* 11 (1946): 843–853.

———. *The Sanusi of Cyrenaica.* Oxford: Clarendon, 1949.

Fahmy, Khaled. *All the Pasha's Men: Mehmed Ali, His Army and the Making of Modern Egypt.* Cambridge: Cambridge University Press, 1997.

Farah, Caesar E. "Arab Supporters of Sultan Abdulamid II: Izzet al-Abid." *Archivum Ottomanicum* 15 (1997): 189–219.

———. *The Politics of Interventionism in Ottoman Lebanon, 1830–1862.* New York: I. B. Tauris, 2000.

———. *The Sultan's Yemen: Nineteenth-Century Challenges to Ottoman Rule.* London: I. B. Tauris, 2002.

Faroqhi, Suraiya. *Approaching Ottoman History: An Introduction to the Sources.* Cambridge: Cambridge University Press, 1999.

———. *Pilgrims and Sultans: The Hajj under the Ottomans.* London: I. B. Tauris, 1994.

Faroqhi, Suraiya, et al. *The Economic and Social History of the Ottoman Empire.* Vol. 2: *1600–1914.* New York: Cambridge University Press, 1994.

Fawaz, Leila Tarazi. *An Occasion for War: Civil Conflict in Lebanon and Damascus in 1860.* Berkeley: University of California Press, 1994.

Ferris, John. "'The Internationalism of Islam': The British Perception of a Muslim Menace, 1840–1951." *Intelligence and National Security* 24 (2009): 57–77.

Ferro, Marc. *Colonization: A Global History.* London: Routledge, 1997.

Findley, Carter. *Bureaucratic Reform in the Ottoman Empire: The Sublime Porte, 1789–1922.* Princeton, NJ: Princeton University Press, 1980.

———. *Ottoman Civil Officialdom: A Social History.* Princeton, NJ: Princeton University Press, 1989.

Finkel, Caroline. *Osman's Dream: The History of the Ottoman Empire.* New York: Basic Books, 2006.

Finlayson, Bill, and Samantha Denis. "Landscape, Archaeology and Heritage." *Levant* 34 (2002): 219–227.

Fitzpatrick, Peter. "Terminal Legality: Imperialism and the (de)Composition of Law." In *Law, History, Colonialism: The Reach of Empire*, edited by Catharine Coleborne and Diane Kirkby, 9–25. Manchester: Manchester University Press, 2001.

Fletcher, Robert S. G. *British Imperialism and "The Tribal Question": Desert Administration and Nomadic Societies in the Middle East, 1919–1936*. Oxford: Oxford University Press, 2015.

Fortna, Benjamin C. *Imperial Classroom: Islam, the State, and Education in the Late Ottoman Empire*. Oxford: Oxford University Press, 2002.

———. *Learning to Read in the Late Ottoman Empire and the Early Turkish Republic*. London: Palgrave Macmillan, 2011.

Foucault, Michel. "Governmentality." In *The Foucault Effect: Studies in Governmentality*, edited by Graham Burchell, Colin Gordon, and Peter Miller, 87–104. Chicago: University of Chicago Press, 1991.

Fremont-Barnes, Gregory. *The Wars of the Barbary Pirates: To the Shores of Tripoli: The Rise of the US Navy and Marines*. Oxford: Osprey, 2006.

Gallagher, John, and Ronald Robinson. *Africa and the Victorians: The Official Mind of Imperialism*. London: Macmillan, 1965.

Gavin, R. J. *Aden under British Rule: 1839–1967*. London: C. Hurst, 1975.

Gawrych, George Walter. *The Crescent and the Eagle: Ottoman Rule, Islam and the Albanians, 1874–1913*. London: I. B. Tauris, 2006.

Gazzini, Claudia Anna. "Jihad in Exile: Ahmad al-Sharif al-Sanusi, 1918–1933." Master's thesis, Princeton University, 2004.

Gelvin, James. *The Modern Middle East: A History*. 3rd ed. New York: Oxford University Press, 2011.

Genell, Aimee M. "Empire by Law: Ottoman Sovereignty and the British Occupation of Egypt." PhD diss., Columbia University, 2013.

Georgeon, François. *Abdulhamid II: Le sultan calife*. Paris: Librairie Arthème Fayard, 2003.

Ghazal, Amal. "An Ottoman Pasha and the End of Empire: Sulayman al-Baruni and the Networks of Islamic Reform." In *Global Muslims in the Age of Steam and Print*, edited by James Gelvin and Nile Green, 40–58. Berkeley: University of California Press, 2014.

———. "Transcending Area Studies: Piecing Together the Cross-Regional Networks of Ibadi Islam." *Comparative Studies of South Asia, Africa, and the Middle East* 34 (2014): 582–589.

Ghosh, Durba, and Dane Kennedy. "Introduction." In *Decentering Empire: Britain, India and the Transcolonial World*, edited by Durba Ghosh and Dane Kennedy, 1–8. Hyderabad, India: Orient Longman, 2006.

Gingeras, Ryan. *Sorrowful Shores: Violence, Ethnicity, and the End of the Ottoman Empire, 1912–1923*. Oxford: Oxford University Press, 2011.

Goffman, Daniel, and Christopher Stroop. "Empire as Composite: The Ottoman Polity and the Typology of Dominion." In *Imperialisms: Historical and Literary Investigations, 1500–1900*, edited by Balachandra Rajan and Elizabeth Sauer, 129–145. New York: Palgrave Macmillan, 2004.

Gollwitzer, Heinz. *Europe in the Age of Imperialism, 1881–1914*. Norwich, UK: Harcourt, Brace & World, 1969.

Gordon, John Steele. *A Thread across the Ocean: The Heroic Story of the Transatlantic Cable*. New York: Walker, 2002.

Göçek, Fatma Müge. "Ethnic Segmentation, Western Education, and Political Outcomes: Nineteenth-Century Ottoman Society." *Poetics Today* 14 (1993): 507–538.

Griset, Pascal, and Daniel R. Headrick. "Submarine Telegraph Cables: Business and Politics, 1838–1939." *Business History Review* 75 (2001): 543–578.

Gülsöy, Ufuk. *Hicaz Demiryolu*. Istanbul: Eren, 1994.

Hakim, Carol. *Origins of the Lebanese National Idea: 1840–1920*. Berkeley: University of California Press, 2013.

Hallam, William Keith. "The Chad Basin." *Nigeria Magazine* (1966): 261.

———. "An Introduction to the History of Bornu." *Nigerian Field* (1977): 147–164.

———. *The Life and Times of Rabih Fadl Allah*. Devon, UK: Arthur H. Stockwell, 1977.

Hämäläinen, Pekka, and Samuel Truett. "On Borderlands." *Journal of American History* 98 (2011): 338–360.

Hanioğlu, M. Şükrü. *A Brief History of the Late Ottoman Empire*. Princeton, NJ: Princeton University Press, 2008.

Hanssen, Jens. "Malhamé–Malfamé." *International Journal of Middle East Studies* 43 (2011): 25–48.

Harris, Christina. "The Persian Gulf Submarine Telegraph of 1864." *Geographical Journal* 135 (1969): 169–190.

Herzl, Theodor. *The Complete Diaries of Theodor Herzl*. Vol. 5. Edited by Raphael Patai, translated by Harry Zohn. New York: Herzl Press, 1960.

Herzog, Christopher. "Nineteenth Century Baghdad through Ottoman Eyes." In *The Empire in the City: Arab Provincial Capitals in the Late Ottoman Empire*, edited by Jens Hanssen, Thomas Philipp, and Stefan Weber, 311–328. Beirut: Ergon Verlag Würzburg in Kommission, 2002).

Hess, Andrew C. *The Forgotten Frontier: History of the Sixteenth-Century Ibero-African Frontier*. Chicago: University of Chicago Press, 1978.

al-Hindiri, Sa'id 'Abd al-Rahman. *Al-'Alaqat al-Libiyya al-Tchadiyya, 1843–1975*. Tripoli: Markaz Dirasat Jihad al-Libiyyin Did al-Ghazw al-Itali, 1983.

Hobsbawm, Eric. *The Age of Empire, 1875–1914*. New York: Pantheon, 1987.

Hogarth, David. *Hejaz before World War I: A Handbook*. 2nd ed. London: Falcon-Oleander, 1978.

Holt, P. M. *The Mahdist State in the Sudan, 1881–1898: A Study in Its Origins, Development and Overthrow*. Oxford: Clarendon, 1970.

Hopkins, A. G. "The Victorians and Africa: A Reconsideration of the Occupation of Egypt, 1882." *Journal of African History* 27 (1986): 363–391.

Hornik, M. P. "The Anglo-Belgian Agreement of 12 May 1894." *English Historical Review* 57 (1942): 227–243.

al-Hourier, A. S. "Social and Economic Transformations in the Libyan Hinterland during the Second Half of the Nineteenth Century: The Rule of the Sayyid Ahmad al-Sharif al-Sanusi." PhD diss., University of California, Los Angeles, 1981.

Houtsma, M. *First Encyclopedia of Islam*. Vol. 4. Leiden: Brill, 1913–1936.

Hull, Isabel V. *A Scrap of Paper: Breaking and Making International Law during the Great War*. Ithaca, NY: Cornell University Press, 2014.

Hume, L. J. "Preparations for Civil War in Tripoli in the 1820s: Ali Karamanli, Hassuna D'Ghies and Jeremy Bentham." *Journal of African History* 21 (1980): 311–322.

Imber, Colin. *The Ottoman Empire, 1300–1650: The Structure of Power*. London: Palgrave Macmillan, 2002.

İnalcık, Halil. "Decision Making in the Ottoman Empire." In *Decision Making and Change in the Ottoman Empire*, edited by Caesar E. Farah, 9–18. Kirksville, MO: Thomas Jefferson University Press, 1993.

İnalcık, Halil, and Mehmet Seyidanlıoğlu, eds. *Tanzimat: Değişm Sürecinde Osmnalı İmparatorluğu*. Ankara: Phoenix, 2006.

İrtem, Süleyman Kani. *Osmanlı Devleti'nin Mısır, Yemen, Hicaz Meselesi*. Edited by Osman Selim Kocahanoğlu. Istanbul: Temel Yayınları, 1999.

Jamieson, Alan G. *Lords of the Sea: A History of the Barbary Corsairs*. London: Reaktion, 2012.

al-Jarrah, Nuri, ed. *Rihlat al-Habasha: Min al-Istana ila Addis Ababa*. Beirut: Almu'asasa al-ʿArabiyya li-l-Dirasat wa-l-Nashr wa Dar al-Swaydi li-l-Nashr wa-l-Tawziʿ, 2002.

Kafadar, Cemal. *Between Two Worlds: The Construction of the Ottoman Empire*. Berkeley: University of California Press, 1995.

Kansu, Aykut. *The Revolution of 1908 in Turkey*. Leiden: Brill, 1997.

Kanya-Forstner, A. S. "French Expansion in Africa: The Mythical Theory." In *Studies in the Theory of Imperialism*, edited by Roger Owen and Bob Sutcliff, 277–294. London: Longman, 1972.

Kapteijns, Lidwien. "Mahdist Faith and the Legitimating of Popular Revolt in Western Sudan." *Africa: Journal of the International African Institute* 55 (1985): 390–399.

———. *Mahdist Faith and Sudanic Tradition: The History of the Masalit Sultanate, 1870–1930*. London: Kegan Paul, 1985.

Kapteijns, Lidwien, and Jay Spaulding. *After the Millennium: Diplomatic Correspondence from Wadai and Dar Fur on the Eve of the Colonial Conquest, 1885–1916*. East Lansing: Michigan State University Press, 1988.

Karpat, Kemal. "The Hijra from Russia and the Balkans: The Process of Self-Definition in the Late Ottoman State." In *Muslim Travellers: Pilgrimage, Migration, and the Religious Imagination*, edited by Dale Eickelman and James Piscatori, 131–152. Berkeley: University of California Press, 1990.

———. *Islam: Reconstructing Identity, State, Faith, and Community in the Late Ottoman State*. Oxford: Oxford University Press, 2001.

———. *The Politicization of Islam: Reconstructing Identity, State, Faith, and Community in the Late Ottoman State*. Oxford: Oxford University Press, 2001.

Kasaba, Reşat. *A Movable Empire: Ottoman Nomads, Migrants, and Refugees*. Seattle: University of Washington Press, 2009.

Kavas, Ahmet. *Geçmişten Günümüze Afrika*. Istanbul: Kitabevi, 2005.

———. *Osmanlı-Afrika İlişkileri*. Istanbul: Tasam Yayınları, 2006.

Kayalı, Hasan. *Arabs and Young Turks: Ottomanism, Arabism, and Islamism in the Ottoman Empire, 1908–1918*. Berkeley: University of California Press, 1997.

Kayaoğlu, Turan. *Legal Imperialism: Sovereignty and Extraterritoriality in Japan, the Ottoman Empire and China*. New York: Cambridge University Press, 2010.

Kazamias, Andreas M. *Education and the Quest for Modernity in Turkey*. Chicago: University of Chicago Press, 1966.

Keddi, Nikki R. "The Pan-Islamic Appeal: Afghani and Abdülhamid II." *Middle Eastern Studies* 3 (1966): 46–67.

Keith, Arthur Berriedale. *The Belgian Congo and the Act of Berlin*. Oxford: Oxford University Press, 1919.

Kennedy, P. M. "Imperial Cable Communication and Strategy, 1870–1914." *English Historical Review* 86 (1971): 728–752.

Khan, ʿAbd al-Hamid al-Thani. *Mudhakarati al-Siyasiyya (1891–1908)*. Unknown translator, Ottoman-Turkish to Arabic. Beirut: Muʾasasat al-Risala, 1979.

Khoury, Dina Rizk, and Dane Kennedy. "Comparing Empires: The Ottoman Domains and the British Raj in the Long Nineteenth Century." *Comparative Studies of South Asia, Africa, and the Middle East* 27 (2007): 233–244.

Khoury, Philip. *Urban Notables and Arab Nationalism: The Politics of Damascus, 1860–1920*. Cambridge: Cambridge University Press, 1983.

Klein, Janet. *Kurdish Militias in the Ottoman Tribal Zone*. Stanford, CA: Stanford University Press, 2011.

Knuesel, Ariane. "British Diplomacy and the Telegraph in Nineteenth-Century China." *Diplomacy and Statecraft* 18 (2007): 517–537.

Koliopoulos, John S., and Thanos M. Veremis. *Modern Greece: A History since 1821*. Chichester, UK: Wiley Blackwell, 2010.

Kostopoulou, Elektra. "Armed Negotiations: The Institutionalization of the Late Ottoman Locality." *Comparative Studies of South Asia, Africa, and the Middle East* 33 (2013): 295–309.

Kratochwil, Friedrich. "Of Systems, Boundaries, and Territoriality: An Inquiry into the Formation of the State System." *World Politics* 39 (1986): 27–52.

Kreiser, Klaus. "Public Monuments in Turkey and Egypt, 1840–1916." In *Muqarnas: An Annual on the Visual Culture of the Islamic World*, edited by Gülru Necipoğlu, 14:103–117. Leiden: Brill, 1997.

Kühn, Thomas. *Empire, Islam, and Politics of Difference: Ottoman Rule in Yemen, 1849–1919*. Leiden: Brill, 2011.

———. "An Imperial Borderland as Colony: Knowledge Production and the Elaboration of Difference in Ottoman Yemen, 1872–1918." *MIT Electronic Journal of Middle East Studies* 3 (2003). http://web.mit.edu/cis/www/mitejmes/. Accessed August 17, 2015.

———. "Ordering Urban Space in Ottoman Yemen 1872–1914." In *The Empire in the City: Arab Provincial Capitals in the Late Ottoman Empire*, edited by Jens Hanssen, Thomas Philipp, and Stefan Weber, 329–367. Beirut: Ergon Verlag Würzburg in Kommission, 2002.

———. "Shaping and Reshaping Colonial Ottomanism: Contesting Boundaries of Difference and Integration in Ottoman Yemen, 1872–1919." *Comparative Studies of South Asia, Africa and the Middle East* 27 (2007): 315–331.

Kürekli, Recep. "Hicaz Demiryolu'nun Akdeniz'e Açılası ile Yaşayan Sosyo-Ekonomik Dönüşüm: Hayfa Kazası Örneği." Special issue, *History Studies: International Journal of History* (2010): 245–269.

Kushner, David. "The Mutasarrıflık of Jerusalem at the End of the Hamidian Period." In *Eighth International Congress of the Economic and Social History of Turkey Papers*, edited by Nurcan Abacı, 121–125. Morrisville, NC: Lulu Press, 2006.

Lafi, Nora. *Une Ville du Maghreb Entre Ancien Régime et Réformes Ottomanes: Genèse des Institutions Municipales à Tripoli de Barbarie*. Paris: Harmattan, 2002.

Lambert, David, and Alan Lester, eds. *Colonial Lives across the British Empire: Imperial Careering in the Long Nineteenth Century*. Cambridge: Cambridge University Press, 2006.

———. "Imperial Spaces, Imperial Subjects." In *Colonial Lives across the British Empire: Imperial Careering in the Long Nineteenth Century*, edited by David Lambert and Alan Lester, 1–31. Cambridge: Cambridge University Press, 2006.

Landau, Jacob M. *The Hejaz Railway and the Muslim Pilgrimage: A Case of Ottoman Political Propaganda*. Detroit: Wayne State University Press, 1971.

Lea, David, and Annamarie Rowe, eds. *A Political Chronology of Africa*. London: Europa, 2001.

Le Gall, Dina. *A Culture of Sufism—Naqshbandis in the Ottoman World, 1450–1700*. Albany: State University of New York Press, 2005.

Le Gall, Michel. "The Ottoman Government and the Sanusiyya: A Reappraisal." *International Journal of Middle East Studies* 21 (1989): 91–106.

———. "Pashas, Bedouins and Notables: Ottoman Administration in Tripoli and Benghazi, 1881–1902." PhD diss., Princeton University, 1986.

Lenin, Vlademir. *Imperialism: The Highest Stage of Capitalism: A Popular Outline*. Rev. trans. London: Lawrence & Wishart, 1948.

Lewis, David Levering. *The Race to Fashoda: European Colonialism and African Resistance in the Scramble for Africa*. New York: Weidenfeld & Nicolson, 1987.

Lewis, Mary Dewhurst. *Divided Rule: Sovereignty and Empire in French Tunisia, 1881–1938*. Berkeley: University of California Press, 2013.

Lewis, Norman. *Nomads and Settlers in Syria and Jordan, 1800–1980*. Cambridge: Cambridge University Press, 1987.

"Libya'da Osmanlı Türbesine Saldırı." *NTVMSNBC*, November 28, 2013. http://NTVMS NBC.com/id/25482517. Accessed August 17, 2015.

Lloyd's Register of Ships, 1900–1. London: Ross, 1901.

London, Joshua. *Victory in Tripoli: How America's War with the Barbary Pirates Established the US Navy and Built a Nation*. Hoboken, NJ: Wiley, 2005.

Lorimer, James. *The Institutes of the Law of Nations*. London: Blackwood, 1883.

Low, Michael Christopher. "Empire and the Hajj: Pilgrims, Plagues, and Pan-Islam under British Surveillance, 1865–1908." *International Journal of Middle East Studies* 40 (2008): 269–290.

Lowe, John. *The Great Powers: Imperialism and the German Problem, 1865–1925*. New York: Routledge, 1994.

Ludden, David. "The Process of Empire: Frontiers and Borderlands." In *Tributary Empires in Global History*, edited by Peter Fibiger Bang and C. A. Bayly, 132–150. London: Palgrave Macmillan, 2011.

MacFie, A. L. *The Eastern Question: 1774–1923*. Rev. ed. Harlow, UK: Addison Wesley Longman, 1996.

MacKenzie, John M. *Law, History, Colonialism: The Reach of Empire*, edited by Catharine Coleborne and Diane Kirkby, vii–viii. Manchester: Manchester University Press, 2001.

al-Madani, ʿUmar. *Bunat al-Majd al-ʿArabi fi Ifriqya: Muhammad al-Khamis, Idris al-Sanusi, Al-Habib Burayqa, Jamal ʿAbd al-Nasser*. Amman: Dar al-Muttahida li-l-Nashr, 1997.

Makdisi, Ussama. *Artillery of Heaven: American Missionaries and the Failed Conversion of the Middle East*. Ithaca, NY: Cornell University Press, 2008.

———. *The Culture of Sectarianism: Community, History, and Violence in Nineteenth-Century Ottoman Lebanon*. Berkeley: University of California Press, 2000.

———. "Rethinking Ottoman Imperialism: Modernity, Violence and Cultural Logic of Ottoman Reform." In *The Empire in the City: Arab Provincial Capitals in the Late Ottoman Empire*, edited by J. Hanssen, T. Philipp, and S. Weber, 29–48. Beirut: Ergon Verlag Würzburg in Kommission, 2002.

Mamdani, Mahmoud. *Citizen and Subject: Contemporary Africa and the Legacy of Late Colonialism*. Princeton, NJ: Princeton University Press, 1997.

Mansour, Johnny. *Al-Khat al-Hadidi al-Hijazi: Tarikh wa Tatawor Qitar Darʿa–Haifa*. Jerusalem: Muʾasasat al-Dirasat al-Maqdisiyya, 2008.

Marcus, Harold G. *A History of Ethiopia*. Updated ed. Berkeley: University of California Press, 2002.

Martin, B. G. "Kanem, Bornu, and the Fazzan: Notes on the Political History of a Trade Route." *Journal of African History* 10 (1969): 15–27.

al-Marwani, Ahmad Raʾfat. "Al-Khat al-Hadidi al-Hijazi." PhD diss., University of Damascus, 1959.

Massey, Doreen. *For Space*. London: Sage, 2005.

McDougall, James. "Frontiers, Borderlands, and Saharan/World History." In *Saharan Frontiers: Space and Mobility in Northwest Africa*, edited by James McDougall and Judith Scheele, 73–91. Bloomington: Indiana University Press, 2012.

McLachlan, K. S. "Tripoli and Tripolitania: Conflict and Cohesion during the Period of the Barbary Corsairs (1551–1850)." *Transactions of the Institute of British Geographers* 3 (1978): 285–294.

Medlicott, W. N. *The Congress of Berlin: A Diplomatic History of the Near Eastern Settlement, 1878–1880*. London: Methuen, 1938.

Meining, Donald, ed. *The Interpretation of Ordinary Landscapes*. Oxford: Oxford University Press, 1979.

Merrifield, Andrew. "Place and Space: A Lefebvrian Reconciliation." *Transactions of the Institute of British Geographers*, n.s., 18 (1993): 516–531.

Metcalf, Thomas. *Imperial Connections: India in the Indian Ocean Arena, 1860–1920.* Berkeley: University of California Press, 2007.

Meyers, James. "Immigration, Return, and the Politics of Citizenship: Russian Muslims in the Ottoman Empire, 1860–1914." *International Journal of Middle East Studies* 39 (2007): 15–32.

Micara, Ludovico. "The Ottoman Tripoli: A Mediterranean Median." In *The City in the Islamic World*, edited by Salma Khadra Jayyusi, Renata Holod, Attilio Petruccioli, and Andre Raymond, 1:383–406. Leiden: Brill, 2008.

Minawi, Mostafa. "Beyond Rhetoric: Reassessing Bedouin-Ottoman Relations along the Route of the Hijaz Telegraph Line at the End of the Nineteenth Century." *Journal of Economic and Social History of the Orient* 58 (2015): 75–104.

———. "Techno-Imperialism, Telegraphs, and Territoriality in Ottoman Africa and Arabia during the Age of High Imperialism." *Journal of Balkan and Near Eastern Studies* 18 (2016).

Miran, Jonathan. "Mapping Space and Mobility in the Red Sea Region, c. 1500–1950." *History Compass* 12 (2014): 197–216.

———. *Red Sea Citizens: Cosmopolitan Society and Cultural Change in Massawa.* Bloomington: Indiana University Press, 2009.

Moalla, Asma. *The Regency of Tunis and the Ottoman Porte, 1777–1814: Army and Government of a North-African Ottoman Eyalet at the End of the Eighteenth Century.* London: RoutledgeCurzon, 2004.

Mohammed, Kyari. *Bornu in the Rabih Years, 1893–1901: The Rise and Crash of a Predatory State.* Maiduguri, Nigeria: University of Maidurguri, 2006.

Morsy, Magali. *North Africa 1800–1900: A Survey from the Nile Valley to the Atlantic.* London: Longman, 1984.

al-Muʾayyad al-ʿAzm, Sadiq, *Rihlat al-Habasha: Min al-Istana ila Addis Ababa.* Edited by Nuri al-Jarrah. Beirut: Almuʾasasa al-ʿArabiyya li-l-Dirasat wa-l-Nashr wa Dar al-Swaydi li-l-Nashr wa-l-Tawziʿ, 2002.

al-Muwaylihi, Ibrahim. *Spies, Scandals, and Sultans: Istanbul in the Twilight of the Ottoman Empire.* Translated from Arabic and introduced by Roger Allen. Lanham, MD: Rowman & Littlefield, 2008.

el-Müeyyed Azmzade, Sadık. *Afrika Sahra-yı Kebiri'nde Seyahat.* Istanbul: Ahmed İhsan ve Şürekası, 1899.

———. *Afrika Sahra-yı Kebiri'nde Seyahat, Bir Osmanlı Zabitinin Büyük Sahra'da Seyahati.* Translated from Ottoman-Turkish to Turkish and introduced by İdris Bostan. Istanbul: Çamlıca, 2008.

———. "Bir Osmanlı Zabitinin Afrika Sahra-yı Kebirinde Seyahati ve Şeyh Sunusi ile Mülakatı." *Servet-i Fünun* 354 (December 23, 1897): 252–253.

———. "Bir Osmanlı Zabitinin Afrika Sahra-yı Kebirinde Seyahati ve Şeyh Sunusi ile Mülakatı." *Servet-i Fünun* 362 (February 17, 1898): 372–374.

———. "Bir Osmanlı Zabitinin Afrika Sahra-i Kebirinde Seyahati ve Şeyh Sunusi ile Mülakatı." *Servet-i Fünun* 364 (March 3, 1898): 406–407.

Nachtigal, Gustav. *Sahara and Sudan.* Vol. 1: *Tripoli, Fezzan and Tibesti or Tu.* Translated by Allan and Humphrey Fisher. London: C. Hurst, 1971.

———. *Sahara and Sudan.* Vol. 4: *Wadai and Darfur.* Translated by Allan and Humphrey Fisher and Rex O'Fahey. Berkeley: University of California Press, 1971.

Nashwan, Jamil Omar. *Al-Taʿlim fi Filastin Munzu al-ʿAhd al-ʿUthmani wa Hatta al-Sulta al-Wataniyya al-Filastiniyya.* Amman: Dar al-Furqan, 2004.

Newbury, C. W., and A. S. Kanya-Forstner. "French Policy and the Origins of the Scramble for West Africa." *Journal of African History* 10 (1969): 253–276.

Northrop, Douglas. *An Imperial World: Empires and Colonies since 1750.* Upper Saddle River, NJ: Pearson, 2013.

Ochonu, Moses E. *Colonialism by Proxy: Hausa Imperial Agents and Middle Belt Consciousness in Nigeria.* Bloomington: Indiana University Press, 2014.

Ochsenwald, William. "The Financing of the Hijaz Railroad." *Die Welt des Islams* 14 (1973): 129–149.

———. *The Hijaz Railroad.* Charlottesville: University Press of Virginia, 1980.

———. "A Modern Waqf: The Hijaz Railroad, 1900–48." *Arabian Studies* 3 (1976): 1–12.

———. "Ottoman Subsidies to the Hijaz (1877–1886)." *International Journal of Middle East Studies* 6 (1975): 300–307.

———. *Religion, Society and the State in Arabia: The Hijaz under Ottoman Control, 1840–1908.* Columbus: Ohio State University Press, 1984.

Orhanlu, Cengiz. *Habeş Eyaleti, Osmanlı İmparatorluğu'nun Güney Siyaseti.* Istanbul: İstanbul Üniversitesi Edebiyat Fakültesi Yayınları, Edebiyat Fakültesi Matbaası, 1974.

Özbek, Nadir. "Policing the Countryside: Gendarmes of the Late 19th-Century Ottoman Empire (1876–1908)." *International Journal of Middle East Studies* 40 (2008): 47–67.

Özcan, Azmi. *Pan-Islamism: Indian Muslims, the Ottomans and Britain (1877–1924).* Leiden: Brill, 1997.

Özendes, Engin. *Photography in the Ottoman Empire, 1839–1923.* Istanbul: YEM Yayın, 2013.

Öztuna, Yılmaz. *Devletler ve Hanedanlar: Türkiye (1074–1990).* Vol. 2. Ankara: Kültür Bakanlığı Yayınları, 1989.

———. *Devletler ve Hanedanlar.* Vol. 3. Ankara: Kültür Bakanlığı, 2005.

Özyüksel, Murat. *Hicaz Demiryolu.* Istanbul: Tarih Vakfı Yurt Yayınları, 2000.

Pakenham, Thomas. *The Scramble for Africa.* London: Abacus, 1991.

Panzac, Daniel. *Barbary Corsairs: The End of a Legend, 1800–1820.* Leiden: Brill, 2005.

Peacock, A. C. S., ed. *The Frontiers of the Ottoman World.* Oxford: Oxford University Press, 2009.

Peters, Emrys L. *The Bedouin of Cyrenaica: Studies in Personal and Corporate Power.* Edited by Jack Goody and Emanuel Marx. New York: Cambridge University Press, 1990.

Peters, F. E. *The Hajj: The Muslim Pilgrimage to Mecca and the Holy Places.* Princeton, NJ: Princeton University Press, 1994.

Peters, Rudolph. *Jihad in Classical and Modern Islam: A Reader.* 2nd ed. Princeton, NJ: Markus Wiener, 2008.

——. What Does It Mean to Be an Official Madhhab? Hanafism and the Ottoman Empire." In *The Islamic School of Law: Evolution, Devolution, and Progress,* edited by Peri J. Bearman, Rudolph Peters, and Frank E. Vogel, 147–158. Cambridge, MA: Harvard University Press, 2005.

Pham, J. Peter. *Boko Haram's Evolving Threat.* Washington, DC: Africa Center for Strategic Studies, 2012.

Philliou, Christine. *Biography of an Empire: Governing Ottomans in the Age of Revolution.* Berkeley: University of California Press, 2011.

Pike, Robert M., and Dwayne R. Winseck. *Communication and Empire: Media, Markets, and Globalization, 1860–1930.* Durham, NC: Duke University Press, 2007.

Prado, Fabricio. "The Fringes of Empires: Recent Scholarship on Colonial Frontiers and Borderlands in Latin America." *History Compass* 10 (2012): 318–333.

"Protocol between Italy and Colombia for the Arbitration of the Cerruti Claim." In "Official Documents," supplement, *American Journal of International Law* 6 (1912): 240–242.

Quataert, Donald. "Ottoman Reform and Agriculture in Anatolia, 1876–1908." PhD diss., University of California, Los Angeles, 1973.

Rabasi, Muftah Yunus. *Al-ʿAlaqat Bayna Bilad al-Maghreb wa Dawlat al-Kanem wa-l-Borno (7–10 AH/13–16 AD).* Benghazi: Seventh of October University, 2008.

Rafeq, Abdul-Karim. "New Light on the Transportation of Damascene Pilgrimage during the Ottoman Period." In *Islamic and Middle Eastern Societies,* edited by R. Olson, 127–136. Brattleboro, VT: Amana, 1987.

Redhouse, James W. *Redhouse Turkish and English Lexicon.* Istanbul: Çağrı Yayınları, 1890.

Redhouse Sözlüğü Türkçe/Osmalıca-İngilizce. 7th ed. Istanbul: SEV Matbaacılık ve Yayınlılık A.Ş., 1999.

Reinkowski, Maurus. "Hapless Imperialists and Resentful Nationalists: Trajectories of Radicalization in the Late Ottoman Empire." In *Helpless Imperialists: Imperial Failure, Fear and Radicalization,* edited by Maurus Reinkowski and Gregor Thum, 47–67. Göttingen: Vandenhoeck & Ruprecht, 2014.

Republic of Turkey, Ministry of Foreign Affairs, Turkish Embassy in London. *Mission History.* http://london.emb.mfa.gov.tr/MissionChiefHistory.aspx. Accessed August 17, 2015.

Rinn, Louis. *Marabouts et Khouan: Étude sur l'Islam en Algerie.* Algiers, 1884.

Robinson, Ronald. "The Case for Economic Aid." In *Developing the Third World: The Experience of the Nineteen-Sixties,* edited by Ronald Robinson, 259–268. London: Cambridge University Press, 1971.

Rogan, Eugene L. "The Aşiret Mektebi: Abdülhamid II's School for Tribes (1892–1907)." *International Journal of Middle East Studies* 28 (1996): 83–107.

——. *Frontiers of the State in the Late Ottoman Empire: Transjordan, 1850–1921.* New York: Columbia University Press, 1999.

——. "Incorporating the Peripheries: The Ottoman Extension of Direct Rule over Southeast Syria (Transjordan), 1867–1914." PhD diss., Harvard University, 1992.

——. "Instant Communication: The Impact of the Telegraph in Ottoman Syria." In *The Syrian Land: Processes of Integration and Fragmentation: Bilad al-Sham from the 18th to the 20th Century*, edited by Thomas Philipp and Birgit Schaebler, 113–128. Stuttgart: Franz Steiner, 1998.

Royal Geographical Society. "Delimitation of British and French Spheres in Central Africa." *Geographical Journal* 13 (1899): 524–528.

Rumford, Chris. "Theorizing Borders." *European Journal of Social Theory* 9 (2006): 155–169.

Said, Edward. *Orientalism*. New York: Random House, 1978.

Sajdi, Dana. "Decline, Its Discontent and Ottoman Cultural History: By Way of Introduction." In *Ottoman Tulips, Ottoman Coffee: Leisure and Lifestyle in the Eighteenth Century*, edited by Dana Sajdi, 1–40. London: I. B. Tauris, 2007.

al-Sallabi, ʿAli Muhammad Muhammad. *Tarikh al-Haraka al-Sanusiyya fi Ifriqya, al-Qism al-Awwal: al-Imam Muhammad Bin ʿAli al-Sanusi wa Nahjoh fi al-Taʾsis al-Taʿlimi wa-l-Haraki wa-l-Tarbawi wa-l-Daʿawi wa-l-Siyasi*. Beirut: Dar al-Maʿrifa li-l-Tabʿ wa-l-Nashr, 2005.

——. *Al-Thimar al-Dhakiyya li-l-Haraka al-Sanusiyya fi Libya: Sirat al-Zaʿimayn Muhammad al-Mahdi al-Sanusi wa Ahmad al-Sharif*. Pt. 2. Cairo: Dar al-Tawziʿ wa-l-Nashr al-Islamiyya, 2005.

Salt, Jeremy. "Britain, the Armenian Question, and the Cause of Ottoman Reform: 1894–96." *Middle Eastern Studies* 26 (1900): 308–328.

Salzmann, Ariel. "Citizens in Search of a State: The Limits of Political Participation in the Late Ottoman Empire." In *Extending Citizenship, Reconfiguring States*, edited by Michael Hanagan and Charles Tilly, 37–66. Lanham, MD: Rowman & Littlefield, 1999.

al-Sawwaf, Faʾiq Bakr. *Al-ʿAlaqat Bayn al-Dawla al-ʿUthmaniyya wa Iqlim al-Hijaz fi Fatrat ma Bayn 1293–1334 H (1876–1915 M)*. Mecca: Abdul Aziz University, 1978.

Schatkowski-Schilcher, Linda. *Families in Politics: Damascene Factions and Estates of the 18th and 19th Centuries*. Stuttgart: Franz Steiner, 1985.

——. "Railways in the Political Economy of Southern Syria 1890–1925." In *The Syrian Land: Processes of Integration and Fragmentation: Bilad al-Sham from the 18th to the 20th Century*, edited by Thomas Philipp and Birgit Schaebler, 97–112. Stuttgart: Franz Steiner, 1998.

Schölch, Alexander. *Egypt for the Egyptians! The Socio-Political Crisis in Egypt, 1878–1882*. Oxford: Oxford University Press, 1981.

——. "Jerusalem in the 19th Century." In *Jerusalem in History*, edited by K. J. Asali, 228–248. Brooklyn: Olive Branch, 2000.

Schreuder, D. M. *The Scramble for Africa, 1877–1895: The Politics of Partition Reappraised*. Cambridge: Cambridge University Press, 1980.

Sessions, Jennifer E. *By Sword and Plow: France and the Conquest of Algeria*. Ithaca, NY: Cornell University Press, 2011.

Shahvar, Soli. "Concession Hunting in the Age of Reform: British Companies and the Search for Government Guarantees; Telegraph Concessions through Ottoman Territories, 1855–58." *Middle Eastern Studies* 38 (2002): 169–193.

———. "Tribes and Telegraphs in Lower Iraq: The Muntafiq and the Baghdad–Basrah Telegraph Line of 1863–65." *Middle Eastern Studies* 39 (2003): 89–116.

Sharma, Surya. *Territorial Acquisition, Disputes, and International Law.* The Hague: Kluwer Law International, 1997.

Shaw, Ezel Kural. "Integrity and Integration: Assumptions and Expectations behind Nineteenth Century Decision Making." In *Decision Making and Change in the Ottoman Empire,* edited by Caesar E. Farah, 39–52. Kirksville, MO: Thomas Jefferson University Press, 1993.

Shaw, Stanford, and Ezel Shaw. *History of the Ottoman Empire and Modern Turkey.* Vol. 2: *Reform, Revolution, and Republic: The Rise of Modern Turkey, 1808–1975.* Cambridge: Cambridge University Press, 1977.

Shepperson, George. "The Centennial of the West African Conference of Berlin, 1884–1885." *Phylon* 46 (1985): 37–48.

Silverman, Kenneth. *Lightning Man: The Accursed Life of Samuel F. B. Morse.* New York: Knopf, 2003.

Sluglett, Peter, and M. Hakan Yavuz, eds. *War and Diplomacy: The Russo-Turkish War of 1877–78 and the Treaty of Berlin.* Salt Lake City: University of Utah Press, 2011.

Somel, Selçuk Akşin. *The Modernization of Public Education in the Ottoman Empire, 1839–1908: Islamization, Autocracy, and Discipline.* Leiden: Brill, 2001.

Spaulding, Jay, and Lidwien Kapteijns. *An Islamic Alliance: ʿAli Dinar and the Sanusiyya, 1906–1916.* Evanston, IL: Northwestern University Press, 1994.

Standage, Tom. *The Victorian Internet: The Remarkable Story of the Telegraph and the Nineteenth Century On-Line Pioneers.* New York: Walker, 1998.

Stone, Jeffrey C. "Imperialism, Colonialism, and Cartography." *Transactions of the Institute of British Geographers,* n.s., 13 (1988): 57–64.

Strohmeier, Martin. "Muslim Education in the Vilayet of Beirut, 1880–1918." In *Decision Making and Change in the Ottoman Empire,* edited by Caesar E. Farah, 215–241. Kirksville, MO: Thomas Jefferson University Press, 1993.

Şehbenderzade, Ahmed Hilmi. *Asr-ı Hamidî'de Alem-i İslam ve Senusiler.* Istanbul: İkdam Matbaası, 1907.

———. *Senusiler ve Sultan Abdülhamid.* Edited and translated from Ottoman-Turkish to Turkish by İsmail Cömert. Istanbul: SES Yayınları, 1992.

Şenışık, Pınar. *The Transformation of Ottoman Crete: Revolts, Politics and Identity in the Late Nineteenth Century.* London: I. B. Tauris, 2011.

Talhami, Ghada H. *Suakin and Massawa under Egyptian Rule, 1865–1885.* Washington, DC: University Press of America, 1979.

Tandoğan, Muhammed. *Afrika'da Sömürgecilik ve Osmanlı Siyaseti (1800–1922).* Ankara: Türk Tarih Kurumu Yayınları, 2013.

Telgraf Rehebleri. Istanbul: Posta ve Telgraf ve Telefon Nezareti, 1912.

Triaud, Jean-Louis, ed. *La légende noire de la Sanusiyya: Une confrérie musulmane saharienne sous le regard français, 1840–1930.* 2 vols. Paris: Éditions de la Maison de Science de l'Homme; Aix-en-Provence: Institut de Recherches et d'Études sur le Monde Arabe et Musulmane, 1995.

Troutt Powell, Eve. *A Different Shade of Colonialism: Egypt, Great Britain, and the Mastery of the Sudan.* Berkeley: University of California Press, 2003.

Trumbull, George, IV. *An Empire of Facts: Colonial Power, Cultural Knowledge and Islam in Algeria, 1870–1914.* Cambridge: Cambridge University Press, 2009.

Türk Dil Kurumu, Büyük Türkçe Sözlük. http://www.tdk.gov.tr. Accessed August 17, 2015.

Uzoigwe, Godfrey N. "The Scramble for Territory." *UNESCO Courier (1984).* http://bi.galegroup.com.proxy.library.cornell.edu/essentials/article/GALE%7CA3247483?u=nysl_sc_cornl. Accessed August 17, 2015.

———. "Spheres of Influence, Effective Occupation and the Doctrine of Hinterland in the Partition of Africa." *Journal of African Studies* 3 (1976): 183–203.

Vikør, Kunt S. "Mystics in the Desert." In *The Middle East: Unity and Diversity: Papers from the Second Nordic Conference on Middle Eastern Studies,* edited by K. Vikør and H. Palva, 133–145. Copenhagen: Nordic Institute of Asian Studies Press, 1993.

———. *Sufi and Scholar on the Desert Edge: Muhammad b. Ali al-Sanusi and His Brotherhood.* London: Hurst, 1995.

Voll, John. "The Sudanese Mahdi: Frontier Fundamentalist." *International Journal of Middle East Studies* 10 (1979): 145–166.

Walker, Andrew. *What Is Boko Haram?* Washington, DC: US Institute of Peace, 2012.

Wang, Xiuyu. *China's Last Imperial Frontier: Late Qing Expansion in Sichuan's Tibetan Borderlands.* Plymouth, UK: Lexington, 2011.

Watt, W. M. *Islamic Creeds: A Selection.* Edinburgh: Edinburgh University Press, 1994.

Weber, Stefan. *Damascus: Ottoman Modernity and Urban Transformation, 1808–1918.* Vol. 1 of *Proceedings of the Danish Institute in Damascus V.* Aarhus: Aarhus University Press, 2009.

Wesseling, Henk L. *Divide and Rule: The Partition of Africa 1880–1914.* Westport, CT: Praeger, 1996.

———. *The European Colonial Empires, 1815–1919.* Translated by Diane Webb. Harlow, UK: Pearson, 2004.

Whipple, A. B. C. *To the Shores of Tripoli: The Birth of the US Navy and Marines.* Annapolis, MD: Naval Institute Press, 2001.

Who's Who, 1906. London: A & C Black, 1906.

Who's Who, 1918. London: A & C Black, 1918.

Who's Who, 1925. London: A & C Black, 1925.

Willis, John. *Unmaking North and South: Cartographies of the Yemen Past, 1857–1934.* New York: Columbia University Press, 2012.

Wright, James. *The Trans-Saharan Slave Trade.* London: Routledge, 2007.

Wright, John. *A History of Libya.* New York: Columbia University Press, 2010.

———. *Libya, Chad and the Central Sahara.* Totowa, NJ: Barnes & Noble Books, 1989.

Wright, William. *A Tidy Little War: The British Invasion of Egypt, 1882.* Stroud, UK: Spellmount, 2009.

Yasamee, F. A. K. *Ottoman Diplomacy: Abdulhamid II and the Great Powers, 1878–1888.* Istanbul: ISIS, 1996.

al-Zaʾidi, Muhammad Rajeb. *Qbaʾil al-ʿArab fi Libya.* Pt. 1. Benghazi: Dar al-Kitab al-Libi, 1968.

al-Zawi, al-Tahir Ahmad. *Wulat Tarablus min Bidayat al-Fath al-ʿArabi ila Nihayat al-ʿAhd al-Turki.* Beirut: Dar al-Fath li-l-Tibaʿa wa-l-Nashr, 1970.

Zeltner, Jean-Claude. *Histoire des Arabes sur les rives du lac Tchad.* Paris: Karthala, 2002.

———. *Pages d'histoire du Kanem: Pays tchadien.* Paris: Harmattan, 1980.

———. *Les pays du Tchad dans la tourmente, 1880–1903.* Paris: Harmattan, 1985.

Ziadeh, Nicola A. *Barqat al-Dawla al-ʿArabiyya al-Thamina.* Beirut: Dar al-ʿIlm li-l-Malayin, 1950.

———. *Sanusiyah: A Study of a Revivalist Movement in Islam.* Leiden: Brill, 1968.

Zürcher, Erik Jan. *Turkey: A Modern History.* 2nd ed. London: I. B. Tauris, 2004.

INDEX

Printed in the USA
CPSIA information can be obtained
at www.ICGtesting.com
CBHW030731051124
16923CB00074B/476

9 780804 799270